the Unofficial Guide to Beating Debt

Greg Pahl

W9-ATK-740

IDG Books Worldwide, Inc.
An International Data Group Company
Foster City, CA • Chicago, IL •
Indianapolis, IN • New York, NY

IDG Books Worldwide, Inc.
An International Data Group Company
919 E. Hillsdale Boulevard
Suite 400
Foster City, CA 94404

For general information on IDG Books Worldwide's books in the U.S., please call our Consumer Customer Service department at 800-762-2974. For reseller information, including discounts and previous sales, please call our Reseller Customer Service department at 800-434-3422.

ISBN: 0-02863337-7

Manufactured in the United States of America

10 9 8 7 6 5 4 3 2 1
First edition

To my parents. And to Ron Rood, my uncle, who for many, many years tirelessly encouraged, motivated, and inspired me to follow in his worthy footsteps as a writer.

Acknowledgments

Aproject like this is always a team effort. There are many people who deserve credit for helping to bring this book to a successful conclusion.

Some of the individuals who graciously shared their knowledge, time, and expertise include Ken Perine, president of the National Bank of Middlebury; Caroline Carpenter, electronic services manager, and Jan Smith, loan officer, National Bank of Middlebury; Mark Wetmiller, executive vice president at the Howard Bank; William O'Brien, senior vice president at Banknorth Group; and Kerry York, director of operations at Consumer Credit Counseling Service of Vermont–New Hampshire. I'd also like to thank Jonathan Adkins, media representative, Mike Kidwell, vice president, and Gerri Detweiler, education advisor, Debt Counselors of America; Norm Magnuson, vice president for public affairs of the Associated Credit Bureaus, Inc.; and Linda Sherry, spokesperson, Consumer Action, in San Francisco.

I am also deeply indebted (if you'll pardon the expression) to Jef and Lorraine Murray of Georgia, as well as Jim and Jennifer of Vermont, Melanie from South Carolina, and Peg from Montana, all of whom graciously agreed to share their personal experiences concerning their struggles with debt. It is my hope (and theirs as well) that their stories will offer inspiration and encouragement to others who find themselves in a similar situation.

I also want to thank William Laberge of Laberge Insurance, David Belcher of Tax Team, Tom Walsh of Coldwell Banker Bill Beck Real Estate, Paul Hood, Peggy Kadima-Mazela, Penny Yunuba, Jim Carroll, and a large group of local friends whose suggestions, advice, and encouragement helped to keep me heading in the right direction throughout the course of this project.

In addition, I want to thank Nancy Dunnan, Warren Ladenheim, and Steve Rhode, the technical experts, who put every page of the book through their rigorous examination process to make sure that everything was accurate.

I also want to thank Amy Langston, and Randy Ladenheim-Gil, my editors at Macmillan, who encouraged and aided me in many ways throughout the process.

Last, but by no means least, I want to thank my wife, Joy, for her invaluable assistance in many different aspects of this project, including, but not limited to, patiently reading every single word, locating useful resource material, chasing down obscure statistics, and offering constructive criticism throughout the entire process.

Greg Pahl
Middlebury, Vermont
June 1999

Contents

The *Unofficial Guide* Reader's Bill of Rights

We Give You More Than the Official Line

Welcome to the *Unofficial Guide* series of Lifestyles titles—books that deliver critical, unbiased information that other books can't or won't reveal—*the inside scoop*. Our goal is to provide you with the *most accessible, useful* information and advice possible. The recommendations we offer in these pages are not influenced by the corporate line of any organization or industry; we give you the hard facts, whether those institutions like them or not. If something is ill-advised or will cause a loss of time and/or money, we'll give you ample warning. And if it is a worthwhile option, we'll let you know that, too.

Armed and Ready

Our hand-picked authors confidently and critically report on a wide range of topics that matter to smart readers like you. Our authors are passionate about their subjects, but they have distanced themselves enough to help you be armed and protected, and to help you make educated decisions as you go through your process. It is our intent that, after having read this book, you will avoid the pitfalls everyone else falls into and you'll get it right the first time.

Don't be fooled by cheap imitations; this is the *genuine article Unofficial Guide* series from IDG Books Worldwide, Inc. You may be familiar with our proven track record of the travel *Unofficial Guides*, which have more than two million copies in print. Each year thousands of travelers—new and old—are armed with a brand new, fully updated edition of the flagship *Unofficial Guide to Walt Disney World*, by Bob Sehlinger. It is our intention here to provide you with the same level of objective authority that Mr. Sehlinger does in his brainchild.

The Unofficial Panel of Experts

Every work in the Lifestyle *Unofficial Guides* is intensively inspected by a team of three top professionals in their fields. These experts review the manuscript for factual accuracy, comprehensiveness, and an insider's determination as to whether the manuscript fulfills the credo in this Reader's Bill of Rights. In other words, our panel ensures that you are, in fact, getting "the inside scoop."

Our Pledge

The authors, the editorial staff, and the Unofficial Panel of Experts assembled for *Unofficial Guides* are determined to lay out the most valuable alternatives available for our readers. This dictum means that our writers must be explicit, prescriptive, and, above all, direct. We strive to be thorough and complete, but our goal is not necessarily to have the "most" or "all" of the information on a topic; this is not, after all, an encyclopedia. Our objective is to help you narrow down your options to the best of what is available, unbiased by affiliation with any industry or organization.

In each *Unofficial Guide* we give you:

- Comprehensive coverage of necessary and vital information
- Authoritative, rigidly fact-checked data
- The most up-to-date insights into trends
- Savvy, sophisticated writing that's also readable
- Sensible, applicable facts and secrets that only an insider knows

Special Features

Every book in our series offers the following six special sidebars in the margins that were devised to help you get things done cheaply, efficiently, and smartly.

1. "Timesaver"—tips and shortcuts that save you time.
2. "Moneysaver"—tips and shortcuts that save you money.
3. "Watch Out!"—more serious cautions and warnings.
4. "Bright Idea"—general tips and shortcuts to help you find an easier or smarter way to do something.
5. "Quote"—statements from real people that are intended to be prescriptive and valuable to you.
6. "Unofficially…"—an insider's fact or anecdote.

We also recognize your need to have quick information at your fingertips, and we have thus provided the following comprehensive sections at the back of the book:

1. **Glossary:** Definitions of complicated terminology and jargon.

2. **Resource Guide:** Lists of relevant agencies, associations, institutions, Web sites, etc.

3. **Recommended Reading List:** Suggested titles that can help you get more in-depth information on related topics.

4. **Important Documents:** "Official" pieces of information you need to refer to, such as government forms.

5. **Important Statistics:** Facts and numbers presented at-a-glance for easy reference.

6. **Index.**

Letters, Comments, and Questions from Readers

We strive to continually improve the *Unofficial* series, and input from our readers is a valuable way for us to do that. Many of those who have used the *Unofficial Guide* travel books write to the authors to ask questions, make comments, or share their own discoveries and lessons. For Lifestyle *Unofficial Guides*, we would also appreciate all such correspondence, both positive and critical, and we will make our best efforts to incorporate appropriate readers' feedback and comments in revised editions of this work.

How to write to us:

Unofficial Guides

Lifestyle Guides

IDG Books

1633 Broadway

New York, NY 10019

Attention: Reader's Comments

About the Author

Greg Pahl, a former Military Intelligence officer in the U.S. Army, has been involved in a variety of small-business ventures since the 1970s, including a 150-acre purebred sheep farm in Vermont. Now a full-time freelance journalist and feature writer, he has written extensively about business, finance, and consumer issues for a number of publications, including the *Vermont Times, The Champlain Business Journal,* and others. Following his own best financial advice, Greg has managed to stay out of the hands of bill collectors.

The *Unofficial Guide* Panel of Experts

The *Unofficial* editorial team recognizes that you've purchased this book with the expectation of getting the most authoritative, carefully inspected information currently available. Toward that end, for each and every title in this series, we have selected a minimum of three "official" experts who constitute the "Unofficial Panel." These experts painstakingly review the manuscripts to ensure: factual accuracy of all data; inclusion of the most up-to-date and relevant information; and insights drawn from an insider's perspective so that you are armed with all the necessary facts you need—but the institutions don't want you to know.

For *The Unofficial Guide to Beating Debt,* we are proud to introduce the following panel of experts:

Nancy Dunnan. Nancy Dunnan is a columnist, author, and financial analyst, based in New York City. She is the author of a number of nonfiction books, including the annual bible in the field of personal finance, *The Dun & Bradstreet Guide to Your Investments,* as well as *How to Invest $50 to $5,000* (8th edition), and *Your First*

Financial Steps. Since 1989, Ms. Dunnan has been the financial advisor to WNYC Public Radio in New York City and appears regularly there on a live call-in show. She is also a contributor to Business News Network Radio every Friday.

Warren Ladenheim. Warren Ladenheim is a director at Peak Search, Inc., an executive recruitment firm in New York City that specializes in accounting and financial recruitment. Mr. Ladenheim has been in executive recruitment for 11 years. He is a Certified Public Accountant and began his career after attending graduate school at Baruch College, City University of New York, in National and Big-5 CPA firms. He has also been a controller specializing in the real estate and financial service industries. He lives on Long Island with his wife and two children.

Steve Rhode. Steve Rhode is the president and cofounder of Debt Counselors of America®, the first Internet-based nonprofit financial counseling agency. Mr. Rhode, with DCA® cofounder Michael Kidwell, cohosts a weekly two-hour radio talk show, "Get Out of Debt—the Radio Show," and he is the coauthor of *Get Out of Debt: Smart Solutions to Your Money Problems.* He has also spoken on consumer money matters for programs on CNN, PBS, and ABC.

Introduction

W e are the wealthiest nation on Earth. Yet, millions of Americans are drowning in debt. How can this be? Encouraged by the second-longest economic expansion in history (the longest was in the 1960s), Americans are spending more and saving less than ever before. Much of that spending has been fueled by the easy availability of credit. Through the 1990s, U.S. households have been taking on debt at record levels. Credit card debt alone has increased from $247 billion in 1991 to a staggering $555 billion in 1999, according to a recent Federal Reserve report. And that trend has continued. The report goes on to say that the growth in the number of households that have access to a card accounts for only 17 percent of that increase, while 77 percent of the growth is due to a higher rate of utilization. It seems that Americans are charging more and more on their cards than ever before. But it's not just credit cards. Overall consumer credit is growing 13.5 percent annually according to the Federal Reserve Board. At the end of January 1999, American consumers were $1.315 *trillion* in debt, exclusive of home mortgages.

It gets worse. U.S. families with at least one credit card carried an average revolving debt of between $7,000 to $8,000 in late 1997, up from $6,000 to $7,000 the previous year, according to the Consumer Federation of America. That's the average. Some are struggling with a lot more. Carrying debt at even the average level costs these families about $1,000 in interest payments and fees annually. Is your family one of them? Do you owe more? Regardless of the actual amount of debt you're carrying on your credit accounts, the money you're currently spending on improving the bottom line of some bank could be earning you compound interest on a solid retirement investment. Sound interesting? Read on. *The Unofficial Guide™ to Beating Debt* can help you.

If you think that debt is a problem only for poor, unsophisticated folks, who simply don't know how to handle their money, think again. Significantly, the largest increases in debt have not been at the bottom of the economic scale among low-income families, but among those earning $50,000 to $100,000 a year, according to Juliet Schor in her excellent book, *The Overspent American.* "Overall, half the population of the richest country in the world say they cannot afford everything they really need. And it's not just the poorer half," she says. Yesterday's luxuries have become today's necessities in an ever-increasing upward spiral of desire fueled by our hyper-consumptive economy, where greed has increasingly replaced actual need. We'll be looking at this phenomenon, and I'll offer practical suggestions on how you can identify the causes of bad spending habits and how to change them—whether you make $20,000 or $200,000.

Okay, so why do so many Americans, regardless of their income level, have so much trouble with debt? Well, aside from compulsive overspending, we also have one of the lowest savings rates for any country on the planet. The average Japanese household saves about 13 percent of its after-tax income. The figure for American households, which has been declining for years, moved into negative territory in 1999 and is expected to be around *minus* 1 percent at year's end. That's just plain scary. This lack of savings leaves little room for maneuvering in the event of unexpected financial difficulty, like a serious illness or loss of employment—or a major downturn in the economy.

Crisis? What crisis?

All of these depressing statistics are bad enough. We're spending too much and saving too little. Assuming that these trends continue, we're almost certainly heading for disaster. Yet, when you listen to the radio or watch television or read the morning paper, it seems as if things couldn't be better. There is a bizarre detachment from reality involved here that I find extremely disturbing. We are a nation in denial.

Sometimes I get the uneasy feeling that we are like the passengers aboard the ill-fated *Titanic.* It's a splendid ship and represents the height of technological sophistication. Inside, everybody feels good. Not everyone is in first class, of course; a lot of folks are down in steerage. But, overall, everyone is enjoying the ride. Outside it's dark and cold. Up on the bridge, the captain has been warned about the presence of icebergs. Yet, the ship is steaming full-speed ahead through the North Atlantic. But it's okay. The *Titanic* is unsinkable. And the band plays on.

Like those reports of drifting icebergs back in 1912, recent economic events around the globe should be giving us plenty of early warnings about the dangers involved with our heedless rush to spend ourselves into oblivion. Much of this spending spree is aided and abetted by various forms of easy credit— especially credit cards. Still, the message in the media remains the same: Buy! Buy! Buy! And if you've run out of options to pay for it all, why, just mortgage your house too! When was the last time you saw an ad on TV suggesting that, perhaps, you might want to consider spending a little less money on stuff that you really don't need and really can't afford and instead put that money in the bank? Never seen such an ad, you say. I haven't either.

The collapse of the former Asian Tiger economies, followed by Russia and, more recently, by Brazil, are striking—and cautionary—examples of just how fragile our increasingly interdependent global economy can be. Yet many Wall Street experts babble on about the "new economy" and "new paradigms" and keep on insisting that "the old rules no longer apply." Rubbish. One old rule hasn't changed a bit. "What goes up must come down." Eventually. Another old saying also comes to mind. "Those who do not learn from the lessons of history are doomed to repeat it."

Recent studies show that somewhere between 25 and 30 percent of U.S. households live paycheck to paycheck. With the margin of error so razor-thin, it's no wonder that personal bankruptcies are at record levels. If you are carrying a heavy debt load— especially on your credit cards—you are in even more danger because your options are very limited. When, not if, the current record economic expansion finally comes to an end, Americans who have been enjoying the Good Times Cruise on our luxury liner—particularly those who charged their trip on plastic—are all going to rush up on deck only to find that, even after all these years, there still aren't enough lifeboats for everyone.

If ever we needed some practical, down-to-earth advice about getting our collective financial house in order, now is the time. *The Unofficial Guide*™ *to Beating Debt* can be your ticket to one of those limited seats in the lifeboats.

Help for the credit-impaired

You don't have to wait for the economy to hit an iceberg before you decide to get your financial act together. In fact, if you're reading this right now, you've probably already been thinking that you need to do something about your debt situation. Good. Realizing you have a problem is your first step to recovery. Even if you are just slightly credit-impaired, there is no time like the present to give yourself, and your finances, a helping hand.

Why choose this book, rather than the dozens of others that line the shelves of most bookstores? There are lots of reasons. First, as you can already see from its design and format, this is a guidebook. It's designed to help you navigate quickly through the crucial information that you need to get a handle on credit and debt. It's hard to deal with one without fully understanding the other. I'll cover both. If you're an absolute beginner who is applying for your first loan, I'll offer suggestions in Chapter 1 on how to increase your chances of getting your application approved on the first try. On the other hand, if you've been a bit too successful in obtaining credit in the past and are now facing the unhappy task of trying to crawl out from under a mountain of debt, I'll walk you through your various options in Chapter 12, and also in many other places in this book.

But that's not all. In between I'll show you how to find the cheapest credit cards with the best features. You'll learn about the differences between green cards and gold cards and the new platinum and titanium cards as well. No doubt you've heard about the wonderful features of the new debit cards promoted by most banks these days. I'm sure they've told you how fast and hassle-free these cards are and how simple they are to use. Swipe the card, and the amount of your purchase is immediately deducted from your checking account. No muss, no fuss. Why, you even get a receipt for easy record-keeping with every transaction and a detailed statement at the end of the month! I bet they didn't tell you how dangerous a debit card can be in the wrong hands, though. Under certain circumstances, a crook can clean out your bank accounts, even your investment accounts at your broker's. At least you'll get a printed record of the transactions on your statement at the end of the month. By then, of course, your thief will be long gone. And so will your money. We'll cover this, and much, much more in Chapter 2.

A crook stealing your money isn't the only thing you need to be careful about these days. Trying to deal with problems that you have created for yourself by your own imprudent spending habits is bad enough. Trying to extricate yourself from the financial and legal morass created for you by someone else—especially someone that you don't even know—is worse. I'll tell you how to protect yourself from losses due to credit card theft and other types of credit fraud, including the bizarre and frightening world of identity theft and the havoc it can wreak on you, your family, and your credit. Chapter 3 has the eye-opening details.

While we're talking about fraud and debt, let's not forget the Internet. The Information Superhighway has certainly opened up wonderful new possibilities for tapping vast resources of information, to say nothing of the rapidly expanding world of e-commerce. Unfortunately, it's also opened up a whole new Pandora's box of criminal activity that law enforcement agencies in this country are just beginning to grapple with.

It wasn't until early 1999 that the Federal Trade Commission pulled some of its existing resources together to form its new Computer Fraud Team. They already have their hands full. And the FTC isn't the only government agency that is busy. The Federal Bureau of Investigation and the Securities and Exchange Commission are among the many other government agencies scrambling to deal with the flood of new perils spewing out of the Internet. Such headlines as "SEC Chief Concerned by Internet Trading" are becoming increasingly common these days. With a few keystrokes and the click of a mouse, you can spend—and lose—hundreds, perhaps thousands, of dollars. Instantly. Check out Chapter 4 for more on the wild new world of cyberdebt. If just one suggestion in this book helps you avoid a peril that is lurking out there, waiting to sink your financial ship, you will easily recover the money that you spent on this guide. You'll probably save a lot more.

Taking back control

Still not convinced? Okay, have you ever looked at your credit report? You should. Did you really understand it? You can. Do you know how to fix it if it's broken? I'll tell you how. Your credit report is the key to understanding much about your financial situation. If you don't know what it means or how to use it, you are at a decided disadvantage. Unfortunately, what you don't know can hurt you. *The Unofficial Guide™ to Beating Debt* will give you the information you need to actually use your credit report as an effective tool to get the credit you need, when you need it.

Are you already in financial trouble? *The Unofficial Guide™ to Beating Debt* is just what you need. If you have gotten yourself deeply in debt, you are probably feeling as if things are out of control. They probably are at the moment. Do angry creditors constantly besiege you on the phone? Are you being pursued by collection agencies. Have they threatened to take your car? Are they making your life completely miserable? Although things may be bad, they can get worse. You can lose your home, your self-respect, your marriage, and maybe your family.

Life doesn't have to be like this. How would you like to regain a measure of control over your life and resolve your debt problems at the same time? You can do it. I'll tell you how to stop the bill collectors in their tracks, end the harassing phone calls, and work out a negotiated settlement that can save you hundreds, maybe thousands, of dollars. While I hasten to add that money problems don't have a quick fix, there are numerous well-tested steps that you can take to eventually put your finances back in order. I'll even show you a way to improve your finances in the future.

Some people can conquer debt by themselves. However, if you are not one of those people and are feeling overwhelmed, you don't have to struggle alone. I'll tell you where to go for assistance—most help is free or almost free. A huge network of non-profit debt counseling agencies exists out there, waiting to help you. Perhaps even more important, I'll give you the lowdown on where not to go for help. The explosion of debt in this country has encouraged the rapid growth of the for-profit debt repair industry. You have probably seen their ads on TV or the Internet, or received unsolicited junk mail promising to "fix" your credit instantly and end your financial worries forever. Far from fixing your problems, these companies may put you deeper in debt if you're not careful. At the very least, you may end up spending much more money than you need to. Of course, not everyone in the business is a crook, but these are shark-infested waters, and I'll help you navigate safely through them.

In some cases, the financial quicksand you have waded into is so deep that the only way to save yourself is to grasp at anything that is available—like bankruptcy. Although bankruptcy isn't the end of the world, it's not a strategy that you should use lightly. The implications of its use will haunt your credit history for many years (up to 10 in some cases) and may cause you a good deal of inconvenience. This is particularly annoying if you really have cleaned up your act and are ready to live a normal life again. I'll tell you what you need to know in order to decide whether you should consider this last resort. Chapter 13 describes the process, and Chapter 14 will help you decide which method to use and how to use it.

Throughout this book, I've done most of the time-consuming legwork for you. I've pored over tons of statistics, books, studies, government reports, Web sites, bank brochures, newspaper and magazine articles, case histories, credit card offers, and other sources of information too numerous to mention, and gleaned what I felt was the most useful and immediately helpful for people like you.

It's important to remember that backing up my efforts is a professional team of credit and debt experts who have carefully labored over every sentence to ensure that the information in this book will be readable, helpful, and accurate. No incomprehensible financial jargon here. Just plain, straight talk.

In the interests of giving you the most critical information on a wide range of subjects, I've had to be somewhat selective about what I've covered. So, if you want to learn more about something, I've included a wealth of additional sources—phone numbers, mailing addresses, contact people, Web sites, and so on—to help you find it fast.

Is there life after debt?

You've managed to crawl out of debt hell and make your way through the long dark tunnel of recovery toward the beckoning light of financial redemption. How do you get firmly back on your feet at the end of the tunnel? I'll offer sound advice about how to rebuild your tattered credit rating and regain the use of credit cards (if you decide you want to use them again), and I'll caution you about pitfalls to watch out for as you learn to walk tall again.

I'll also offer lots of suggestions on how to avoid future credit and debt problems, develop new financial goals, and establish new, healthier habits that should improve the quality of your life in many ways. Instead of worrying about which creditor is going to call next, you'll be able to think about more pleasant things. Like the possibility of paying off your mortgage years ahead of schedule and saving thousands of dollars in the process. Sound impossible? It's not.

However, I'm not going to drop you there and say, "Have a nice life. Stay out of debt." I'll take you one step further. Anyone who's gone through a near-death experience like heavy debt invariably emerges with some keen insights about what's important—and what's not. I'll help you explore those insights and share some that have been gleaned by others who have struggled through the same process.

Building on the many suggestions about how to save money in earlier sections of *The Unofficial Guide™ to Beating Debt,* I'll look at additional ways to save money, consume less, and live better—all at the same time. The same basic strategies that will work for you can also work for our society as a whole. Chapter 17 will introduce you to increasingly popular concepts like downshifting and voluntary simplicity, and to people and organizations who have intriguing ideas about building a new, sustainable economy and, by extension, a sustainable world. That's encouraging news for our children and grandchildren. Best of all, these ideas are customizable in almost any combination to create a new lifestyle on the ashes of your old one, a lifestyle that suits your individual needs and goals. You can take it or leave it, as you wish.

And that's the whole philosophy behind *The Unofficial Guide™ to Beating Debt.* It's a guide. A roadmap for individual improvement and development, not a set of strict rules to follow. And there's no hidden agenda. No expensive seminars to sign up for. No Great Secrets to instant wealth. Because there aren't any. Just down-to-earth suggestions and tips that should help you manage your debts more intelligently and effectively. And if the ideas you glean here help improve the rest of your life too, that's great. I hope they do.

Easy Money

Credit Basics

Chapter 1

We can't talk about debt without first discussing credit. Credit is the driving force of our economy. It essentially finances the American Dream—our homes, our automobiles, our vacations—and helps us pay for things like big appliances and even bigger college bills. In short, for many people, credit is the Good Life. Like most things, credit is neither inherently good nor evil. It just depends on how you use it.

Credit not only greases the wheels of commerce but also allows you to carry less cash, avoid long lines at the ATM machine, and check into a hotel or rent a car without a lot of hassles. Credit is almost the only way to buy airline tickets or to purchase items online. In an emergency, it can even help you pay for unexpected medical bills.

The flip side is that the misuse of credit can ruin your financial health and destroy your self-esteem, your marriage, perhaps your entire life. Fortunately, many credit problems are avoidable. According to the National Foundation for Consumer Credit in Silver Spring, Maryland, 52 percent of its clients are having financial problems because of poor money management. Another 23 percent are in trouble because of reduced income or unemployment, and only 10 percent list divorce or separation as the cause of their financial woes. Surprisingly, medical bills are near the bottom of their list at only 7 percent. So what's going on here?

Clearly, we are dealing with a largely preventable problem. So how do you avoid stumbling into the money pit? Part of the secret is to know what your options are. And Americans, as a whole, are abysmally ignorant about their personal finances—and their options. Remarkably, some students in this country can graduate from college with advanced degrees yet not be able to manage their own charge accounts. That basic skill is just one of the many important things you will learn as we navigate the often troubled waters of debt management. In this chapter, I'll cover the ins and outs of credit for first-time borrowers, women, and even children. By the end of the chapter, you will have begun laying the foundation for beating your debts.

Credit 101

Basically, *credit* is promising to pay for something in the future that you have received in the present. It's instant gratification. Because so many different types of credit are being offered these days, it's important to know what's out there before you try to match your needs to what's available. The tips and hints in the following sections will help you get off to a good start if you're a first-time borrower, and will help more experienced borrowers tighten up their acts—especially if they've managed to get themselves into financial difficulty. It's never too late to become more savvy about credit and debt.

How much is it going to cost?

Most creditors are quite happy to lend you money, but they aren't doing this because they think you are a nice person. They're giving you the money (or product or service) in order to make money. And the main thing you need to focus on, as a savvy borrower, is how much you are actually going to have to pay. The difference between the original amount of the loan and the total amount you pay back, including interest and other fees, is the cost of the loan. This cost of borrowing can vary widely, so it's important to know what the actual costs are.

If you understand two terms—the finance charge and the annual percentage rate—you can compare credit costs offered by different lenders without getting lost in reams of fine print. The *finance charge* is the total amount in dollars that you pay the lender to use the lender's credit. It includes interest costs and other fees, such as service charges and sometimes credit-related insurance premiums.

For example, if you borrow $1,000 for a year, the loan might cost you $100 in interest. If there is a service charge of, say $10, the total finance charge would come to $110.

The *annual percentage rate* (APR), on the other hand, is the percentage cost of credit determined on a yearly basis. For example, if you borrowed that $1,000 and paid it back in a year, at the end of that time, including a finance charge of $100, your APR is 10 percent.

It gets a little more complicated with monthly payments, but it's still the same general idea. The main thing to remember is that regardless of the details of a particular loan, APR simply is the amount of interest you will pay on a yearly basis. APR is your key to comparing credit costs, regardless of the amount of credit or the length of the repayment period.

Truth in lending

Fortunately for borrowers, the federal Truth in Lending Act (also known as Regulation Z) requires virtually all creditors to give you access to important information about the costs of credit. Truth in Lending was launched by the Consumer Credit Protection Act of 1968. Since then, credit protections have multiplied to cover a wide range of issues. We'll take a closer look at the Consumer Credit Protection Act in Chapter 3. Although the law does not set interest rates or other charges, it does mandate their disclosure so that you can compare credit costs and make an informed decision.

If you're applying for open-end credit (bank and department store credit cards, gasoline company cards, home equity credit lines, and so on), Truth in Lending requires that creditors tell you what the terms of the credit plan are, including when finance charges are applied to your account, so you know how much time you have to pay your bill before the finance charge is added.

The following chart is a typical summary of terms for a credit card. It's normally referred to as the Schumer Box, after Congressman Charles Schumer of New York who introduced a bill in 1988 requiring credit companies to use it.

The law says that you must be shown the finance charge and the annual percentage rate in writing before you are asked to sign a credit contract or before you receive a credit card for the first time.

SUMMARY OF TERMS FOR A CREDIT CARD

Annual Percentage Rate (APR)	2.99% introductory rate for first six months, a 17.99% fixed rate thereafter
Grace Period for Repayment of Balances for Purchases	Not less than 25 days (no grace period for balance transfers)
Annual Fee	None
Minimum Finance Charge	$.50 (if a finance charge is imposed)
Method of Computing Balance for Purchases	Average Daily Balance (including new purchases)
Miscellaneous Fees	Cash advance fee: 2.5% of amount of the cash advance, but not less than $2.50
	Late payment fee: $25
	Over-the-credit-limit fee: $25

Can you afford it?

Before you decide to take out a loan, you need to be sure you can afford it. Although this rule applies to all types of loans, including credit card purchases, we'll examine a fixed loan first. This isn't rocket science, but there are a few things you need to look at. You should consider the amount of the loan, the rate of interest, and the length of time you will need to pay it back. The longer the term of the loan, the more affordable the amount of the monthly payments. However, the longer you take to pay back the loan, the greater your ultimate cost of credit will be.

For example, if you borrowed $10,000 at 10 percent interest for one year (assuming no other fees), your monthly payments would be $879.20. The same loan amount paid back over two years would have monthly payments of $461.50. However, the one-year loan would cost you only $550.40 for interest charges ($879.20 × 12 = $10,550.40), but the two-year loan would ultimately cost you $1,076 ($461.50 × 24 = $11,076.00). Obviously, the more quickly you

Watch Out!
If you're not sure what some of the information in the fine print on a credit agreement means, don't hesitate to ask the lender. Ignorance is no excuse. Many people who neglect to ask questions end up regretting it later on. If the lender does not give you an answer you understand, ask to take the documents to someone who can explain the agreement to you. Never sign a legal contract you do not understand.

pay off a loan, the less it costs. But that has to be balanced against your ability to afford the monthly payments.

Shop around

It's a good idea to compare the credit costs of all types of loans, and it's especially important when you're shopping for an open-ended loan. The APR that the creditor tells you about is only one part of the picture. A number of potentially expensive zingers like annual membership fees, transaction charges, cash advance charges, late fees, over-limit fees, and other charges are listed separately and are not included in the APR. Be sure to compare all the costs involved, not simply the APR, because these other charges can make a huge difference in the ultimate cost of credit.

You should also be aware of the many different methods that creditors use to figure the balance on which you will pay the finance charge. This is where the fine print is not just difficult to read—it's also downright hard to understand. There's the average daily balance method (the most common), the adjusted balance method, the previous balance method, the two-cycle average daily balance method, and so on. Depending on the plan, new purchases may or may not be included. The worst deal from a consumer standpoint is the two-cycle average daily balance method. If you fail to pay off your balance in one of two successive months, you basically are charged two month's worth of interest. It's legal. But it stinks.

Even some bankers I've talked to have trouble explaining the differences between these methods, so the main point to be aware of is that the amount of the finance charge may vary depending on which method is used, even for the same general pattern of purchases and payments. In the end, however, comparing the APR is still your best guide to what you'll be paying.

Consumer leasing

Leasing is an increasingly popular strategy these days for everything from cars to computers. Truth in Lending credit disclosure rules also apply to consumer leasing plans. This information can help you compare the cost and terms of one lease over another, and help you decide whether leasing is a good idea or not. The law applies to items you lease for more than four months for personal, family, or household use. Such things as long-term rentals of cars, furniture, and appliances are covered.

Before you sign a lease, the leasing company is required to give you a written statement of costs, including the amount of monthly payments and, if applicable, such things as security deposits, licensing, registration, taxes, and maintenance. The statement also must cover such items as insurance, guarantees, who is responsible for service work, and whether you have the option to buy the leased property.

Consumer leases usually come in two flavors: closed-end and open-end agreements. The distinctions between them can get a little complicated, but the two main points to remember are that closed-end leases normally have higher monthly payments than open-end leases and there is no extra, so-called "balloon payment" at the end of a closed-end lease. As a rule, the balloon payment is usually limited to no more than three times the average monthly payment. The relative advantages and disadvantages of these different kinds of leases largely depend on the situation. Ask your lender to explain the pros and

Bright Idea
The annual percentage rate (APR) is the most effective tool for comparing the costs of credit among different lenders.

cons of your lease options before you sign on the dotted line.

Types of credit

Now it's time to look at your many credit options. Which one is right for your particular needs? That depends on a number of factors. How much credit do you need? What do you need it for, and how soon do you expect to be able to pay it back? The answers to these and other questions will become apparent as we go through the options. This brief overview will be followed by a more detailed exploration of each option in Chapter 2. Here are your main choices:

■ **Credit cards.** Credit cards come in four main types: bank cards, retail cards, travel and entertainment cards, and affinity/hybrids. There are also a number of variants, such as the secured credit card and other cards that are linked to home equity loans or lines of credit. These cards and their differences, benefits, and limitations are explained more fully in Chapter 2.

Credit cards offer some key benefits. One big advantage of using credit cards is the wide array of free stuff offered by many card issuers as an inducement to get you to use their card. These can range from cash rebates, to free merchandise, to frequent-flyer miles, and much more. In order to make such perks useful, however, you have to pay your account balance in full every month; otherwise, the interest charges will quickly eat up any possible benefit of the freebies.

The use of credit cards also provides you with a good record of where you spent your money (handy at tax time); allows you to travel with less cash (almost always a good idea); gives you stop-payment rights and extended warranty, theft, and damage protection; improves your credit rating (as long as your payments are current); and, perhaps best of all, allows you to play with the float (the time between your purchase and when you actually have to pay the bill). Although credit cards can be used to buy almost anything these days, they are most suitable for purchases that you can pay for in a fairly short time.

Moneysaver
Be smart: Pay off your credit card account in full every month. If you do, it doesn't matter what your interest rate is or what method is used to calculate your balance; there won't be one.

- **Charge accounts.** These open-end charge or revolving-credit accounts permit you to make repeated purchases until you reach your pre-arranged credit limit. You generally have the option of paying the balance in full or in a series of installments, but you need to be aware that a finance charge is levied on the unpaid balance. Minimum payments are usually based on a percentage of the remaining balance. It's not a good idea to leave large, unpaid balances in these accounts for very long because of the interest charges. These accounts include such things as credit cards, various lines of credit, and retail charge accounts.

- **Installment loans.** Also referred to as a closed-end credit plan, this class of loan involves a predetermined number of monthly payments for a set amount of money. Interest is charged from the day the loan is made. An installment loan is typically used to finance cars, boats, furniture, and similar items, which serve as collateral for the loan. Although it's cheaper to pay cash, most people don't or can't, so an installment loan is the next best alternative.

- **Mortgages.** A mortgage is another type of closed-end credit plan that is often used to finance the single largest investment most people make—their home. A mortgage allows you to make a very large purchase that you otherwise would not be able to pay for up front. The down side is that in order to do that, you have to put the house up as collateral for the loan. If you ever default on the payments, the lender may foreclose on the property in order to recover the amount of the loan. The mortgage lending process includes two basic documents, a note and a mortgage. The note details the terms of the agreement, and the mortgage contains a legal description that also pledges the property as security for the loan. The term "mortgage," however, is commonly used to describe both documents. Unless you're lucky enough to be independently wealthy, you'll probably need a mortgage. (Note: Some states use a deed of trust, rather than a mortgage.)

- **Home equity loans.** Home equity loans are currently all the rage. These generally open-ended plans allow you to borrow money against the equity you have accumulated in your home, up to a predetermined limit. You usually have the choice of making use of that amount right away or having it available for future needs. Just because home equity loans are popular doesn't mean they're always a good idea (more on this in Chapter 2).

- **Secured loans.** Secured loans describe a class of loan that requires some sort of collateral (security) to back the loan. Many installment loans fall into this category. The lender keeps a security interest in the item pledged and will repossess the item in the event of a default. Secured loans are generally appropriate for big-ticket items like cars, especially if the old clunker you're driving dies unexpectedly, and you're not financially prepared for the unhappy event.

■ **Unsecured loans.** Unsecured personal loans do not require the use of security or collateral to obtain the loan. They are generally based upon your income and ability to repay the lender. Personal lines of credit and personal installment (so-called signature) loans are examples of this type of plan. These are often the most expensive loans, since the lender does not have collateral that can be repossessed if you do not pay as agreed.

Getting credit

Applying for credit can seem like a daunting task, especially considering the fact that millions of people are turned down for loans and credit cards every year. But you don't have to be among them. There are a few basic steps that will help you get through the process with a minimum of pain and will improve your chances of being successful with your initial application.

Borrowing for the first time

Being a first-time borrower can be a frustrating experience. It's a classic Catch-22 situation. You can't get credit without a credit history. How can you develop a credit history if no one will give you credit? The secret is to start small and work your way up gradually as you begin to build a positive credit history. Gasoline credit cards are generally much

66

As far as I was concerned, credit was the ultimate luxury. It wasn't what Thoreau had in mind, but more than anything else I'd ever experienced, it made life simple.
—Lia Matera,
Prior Convictions

99

easier to get than premium bank cards. Unfortunately, gasoline cards rarely report to credit bureaus—unless you are delinquent. In addition, gas and store cards will do the least to build your credit. If you can't qualify for an unsecured major credit card, try to obtain a secured credit card (see "Secured Credit Cards" in Chapter 15).

It might help to first open a small checking or savings account at the bank where you are going to apply for a loan or credit card. Or try applying for a card with a very low credit limit. The more restrained your initial credit request is, the greater the chance of your success. Once you have obtained a credit card, use it and scrupulously pay at least the minimum due every month. Pay the balance off in four to six months. That's good advice for anyone, but it's especially important for first-time borrowers who are trying to build a good credit history. Creditors are looking for people who will make steady payments on time rather than for people who pay their balance off in full every month. You can use your first credit card as a stepping stone to obtain more credit, or perhaps a loan.

First-time borrowers can avoid potential pitfalls in the loan application process (and wasted time) by following the suggestion of an acquaintance of mine who's an officer of a large local bank. "My advice would be to thoroughly understand the process before you embark on it," he says. "That means sitting down with a good lender and having them walk you through the steps before you even get involved in the application process." That's good advice. Not only will this strategy give you a better idea about what's involved, it also will give you advance warning if there is something about your present financial situation that might cause your application to be rejected. A word of caution. Bank employees are not financial advisors. They are often compensated by commissions; they may be directed to max you out on loans and to sell you credit life insurance you probably don't need. Nevertheless, talking to your local banker to get a better understanding of the process can be helpful in many situations.

Credit application tips

Whether you are a first-time borrower or already have a long credit history, try to find out what your potential creditor's criteria are for giving a loan. And the best way to find out is to ask. Some lenders may require you to have a savings or checking account (or both) with them. There may be minimum balance requirements or other restrictions as well. Whatever the requirements are, make sure you meet them before you attempt to apply for credit. You will save yourself, and the lending institution, a lot of unnecessary trouble.

Another advantage of checking the loan criteria beforehand is that if you don't meet a particular requirement, you may be able to take the steps necessary to meet it. Then you can submit an application that has a better chance of succeeding on the first try. Yet another advantage of checking first with various lenders is that you can make comparisons between them. You may find a better deal in the process. At the very least, you should be able to locate the right credit product for your specific needs.

If you have had past difficulties with your credit, it is a good idea to check with the lender to find out whether your application will even be considered. Be sure to carefully explain what your problems were. This is important because every application

Watch Out!
Be careful about applying for too many loans in a short period of time. Every application adds another inquiry to your credit report. Five or more inquiries within a six-month period can actually result in your being turned down for a loan.

for credit generates another inquiry on your credit file. The depression of being turned down repeatedly is reason enough to avoid this scenario, but there is another reason. When lenders see too many inquiries in a short time span listed on your credit report, they get nervous and may perceive you as too great a credit risk.

Make sure you fill out credit applications as completely and accurately as possible. Although this step seems obvious, disregarding it may have adverse effects. Many applications are routinely turned down because they are incomplete—especially those that do not disclose all debts. Even if you simply forget to include something, the lender may assume that you are deliberately trying to hide it. This will not improve your chances of getting your application approved.

If there isn't enough room on the application to fully respond to a question, don't be afraid to add a typewritten attachment. Just make a notation regarding the attachment in the appropriate place on the form.

Be sure that your responses to questions on a credit application present you and your financial situation in the best possible light. Don't lie. There are potentially serious legal repercussions if you do. But why not make the best of what you've got? List all of your assets, whether they are held individually or jointly. Don't overlook such items as valuable jewelry, antiques, and stocks or bonds. Also, be sure to include current market value rather than original purchase price if the asset has increased in value since you bought it. This is particularly relevant for real estate. List your gross income (before deductions) unless you are specifically asked for taxable income. And don't forget part-time income, rental income, regular overtime, and pensions or other government benefits.

When you list your credit obligations, you can list your most favorable ones first, but be sure to list them all. Also, you'll want to estimate your current remaining balances, rather than the original amount of credit extended. For example, if you took out a $16,000 car loan two years ago and have one year left on the loan, list today's balance rather than the original amount.

If you have any additional information that might help the institution make a favorable decision, you should include it. For example, if you have had a mortgage in the past or have had previous favorable accounts that do not appear on your current credit report, list them. If your name or address has changed, providing this data may be helpful—as long as it leads to positive information.

Keep copies of all credit applications that you submit. Having the basic information (account numbers, balances, etc.) handy will make future applications that much easier to fill out. It will also ensure consistency between applications, something lenders look for. Finally, you may need to refer to your application if you pursue an appeal.

What if you're turned down?

Nobody likes to be rejected, and being turned down for credit is no exception. However, in this case "no" isn't necessarily the final word. Under the federal Equal Credit Opportunity Act, a lender has to tell you within 30 days whether your application has been approved or not. If it is not approved, the lender must tell you in writing why your application has been rejected, or at least inform you of your right to ask for an explanation. The rejection letter must also include the name and address of the credit bureau that supplied the credit report, if one was used in making the decision. Note, however, that the lender, not the credit bureau, ultimately makes the lending decision.

If the reasons for your rejection are not clearly spelled out in the letter, be sure to contact the creditor promptly. The law gives you 60 days to ask for an explanation. If the reason for your rejection was based in whole or in part on your credit report, you should contact the credit bureau (see "Credit Bureaus" in Appendix B for contact information). If you do so within 60 days, you are entitled to a free copy of your credit report.

Once you receive the report, check it carefully. If there are mistakes, you can correct them (see "Correcting Mistakes" in Chapter 6). It's even possible that the rejection may have been based on faulty or misleading information in your credit report. If this is the case, you should also obtain your report from the other two major credit bureaus to see if the same information is listed in their reports. Obtaining just one report may not be sufficient to correct inaccurate information. After making a careful evaluation, if you feel that your rejection was unjustified, you have the right to appeal the decision.

Contact the credit grantor and explain why you should be given the credit you applied for. It's best to do this in writing. In your letter, be sure to address the specific reasons why you were rejected. Give the creditor as many valid reasons as you can why they should reconsider the decision. The very fact that you are not giving up easily demonstrates

Bright Idea
If your application for credit was rejected due to information in your credit report, contact the appropriate credit bureau within 60 days for a free copy of your report. Always take advantage of this option.

your confidence in your ability to repay the obligation. This may help.

If you believe that your rejection violates your rights under the Equal Credit Opportunity Act (denial due to age, gender, marital status, religion, race, color, national origin, etc.), you should let the creditor know that you are aware of the law and your rights under it. Try to resolve the problem with the lender first, but if that doesn't work, you can contact the appropriate federal agency. (see "How to Enforce Your Rights" in Chapter 3 and the sample consumer complaint letter in Appendix D.)

Your credit worthiness

Assuming that a loan officer has your credit application sitting on their desk, how does the officer decide whether to approve it or not? Although the process may seem capricious—especially if you're turned down—it generally isn't. There are two main ways of determining your credit worthiness. The first, the "Three C's" (character, capacity, and collateral) is the traditional method. The second, "credit scoring," is an increasingly popular alternative. In either case, creditors are trying to evaluate what the odds are that you will repay the debt. Here's what they look for:

■ **Character—Will you repay the debt?** Creditors will look at your credit history to determine how much you owe, how frequently you borrow, and whether you pay your bills on time. They are also interested in evidence of stability: how long you have lived at your current address, how long you have worked for your present employer, and whether you rent or own your residence.

- **Capacity—Can you repay the debt?** Capacity indicates your ability to pay back your obligation. Creditors will ask how much you earn and what type of work you do. They'll also want to know about your expenses, including how many dependents you have and what your other obligations are.

- **Collateral—Is the creditor protected?** Collateral represents security for the lender if you are unable to pay back the loan. Sometimes the lender will require that you put up as collateral the item you are buying with the loan, a new car for example.

Using the Three C's method represents a judgmental process that is fairly labor intensive. Each application is evaluated on an individual basis by a real person. Today, however, with the millions of applications that are made annually to banks and other lending institutions (which may not even be located in your home state), most credit applications are decided on the basis of credit scoring—by computers.

The lenders are still looking for the same basic information contained in the Three C's, but they get it through the use of complex mathematical formulas instead of through personal evaluation. Credit scoring is an incredibly complicated field, using many different methods, but the basic idea is straightforward. Stated simply, creditors assign different values to such things as your income, the number of credit accounts you have, late payments, length of residence at your current address, and so on. All of these different values will be tallied and you will be given what amounts to a grade. If your total exceeds the minimum passing score, you likely will receive credit. If not, your application will probably be rejected.

One thing to remember about credit scoring is that because it's basically a statistical exercise, the more your score looks like that of all the other applicants who pay their bills on time, the more likely you are to receive the credit you've applied for. Because the scoring system has so many variations, however, it's not always possible to predict what the outcome will be.

The main advantage of credit scoring is that it can eliminate discrimination from the process, since it's all done by the numbers, rather than by the color of your eyes or the length of your hair. On the other hand, credit scoring's greatest strength is also its main weakness. It eliminates the human factor. Those extenuating circumstances that perhaps caused you to miss making some payments a few years ago just don't get figured in. If you feel that you've fallen through the statistical cracks, you may want to appeal a computer-based rejection.

Credit issues for women

Not so long ago, a married woman who had paid her credit accounts faithfully for years could suddenly find herself without a credit history—and without credit—either upon the death of her husband or after a divorce. The feudal attitude that encouraged this scenario on the part of the credit industry fortunately has changed with the passage of the Consumer Credit Protection Act (CCPA) in 1968 and the half-dozen related acts that have followed since then. Although these laws contain provisions designed to eliminate discrimination based on race, religion, national origin, and other factors, the protections afforded to women are

Unofficially...
Credit scoring systems have become so complicated that it's frequently difficult to figure out why some people are turned down. It's possible to be approved by one lender and rejected by another even though you used the same information on the two applications.

substantial—in direct proportion to the previous bias. I'm not suggesting that women don't continue to have problems with credit discrimination, many do, but the laws on the books at least help level the playing field. It's up to you to know what those laws are and how to use them (see Chapter 3 for more information).

Discrimination against women

The Equal Credit Opportunity Act contains the same prohibitions against discrimination as the CCPA. What's more, it specifically says that creditors may not ask about your sex or your marital status (unless you live in a community property state: Arizona, California, Idaho, Louisiana, Nevada, New Mexico, Texas, Washington, and Wisconsin). They cannot ask you to choose a title such as Miss, Mrs., or Ms.; nor can they ask for information about your husband or ex-husband (unless, again, you live in a community property state, and your income comes from alimony or his support, or he will use your account). In addition, the Act prohibits requiring you to have a cosigner or to get your husband's signature, and exempts you from having to reapply for credit if your marital status changes. (We'll get to divorce and separation issues in a moment.)

Develop your own credit history

Regardless of your gender, it's important for you to develop a strong, independent credit identity. There simply is no excuse for a woman to play second fiddle to her husband when it comes to credit. And the perils of doing so are considerable in a society where credit is the key—or obstacle—to seemingly everything. I am constantly amazed by the number of generally older (but not always) women who appear content to drift along with the traditional way of handling family finances—even if they're the ones who actually write the checks! I don't get it. And neither do they.

Having a strong, separate financial identity not only offers you an insurance policy of sorts should your marriage end up on the rocks but also offers a good marriage the advantage of greater independence—and flexibility—in managing day-to-day financial matters. If this idea is viewed less than enthusiastically by your spouse, maybe you should be on the lookout for those rocks.

If you are a woman who has never had credit in your own name, right now is the time to get started. If you've been using credit cards (even with your name on them) that were originally issued for your husband's accounts (an "authorized user" card), try contacting the card issuer and ask for an application to become a joint applicant. You can move on from there to gradually add more accounts and build an independent credit history. If you don't even have an authorized user card to start with, you'll need to follow the same credit application strategies mentioned earlier in this chapter for first-time borrowers. Also, be sure to use your own name and Social Security number and list your own financial resources. It's okay to include joint assets that you and your husband may share, but don't include those that are just his. Once your own credit has been established, use it, and be sure to pay your accounts on time. If you do, you'll be well on your way to greater independence and security.

Joint obligations and assets

If you and your husband have joint credit obligations, make sure that they are listed on both of your credit reports, not just his. Since you are both

Bright Idea
If you have been or currently are married, it's vital that you develop a separate financial identity from your spouse. This identity is crucial in the event of divorce, death, or incapacity.

equally responsible for the repayment of these debts, both of you should get the recognition for doing so. The same strategy applies when you apply for new joint credit. It doesn't matter who is going to use the account most often. A joint account is a joint account. Period. Both of your names should be on it.

The Equal Credit Opportunity Act entitles you to have existing joint accounts that you use (opened after June 1, 1977) listed on both your credit reports and your husband's. If there are accounts like this that are not listed on your credit report, you can ask to have them listed. And you don't need your husband's permission to do so. Just send a letter asking your joint account creditors to make certain that both of your names appear on bills and are used when they send information to credit agencies. Don't forget to include your Social Security number. For joint accounts opened before June 1, 1977, the law does not require dual reporting, but you can politely request that your creditors do so anyway. You may be asked to verify some information, and you may be charged a small fee.

In the case of joint assets, be sure that they are actually held not only in your spouse's name but in yours as well. This goes for your home or farm, your automobiles, your investments, whatever. Also, be sure that you have a right to survivorship. You can never be too careful.

Divorce or separation

One of the main reasons you need to be careful is that, even with the best of intentions, you may suddenly find yourself among the approximately 1 million Americans annually who face the unhappy prospect of divorce or separation. When it comes to divorce and credit—and debt—things can get very messy very quickly. Going through divorce is bad enough, but to end up being cut off from your credit lifeline because you didn't plan ahead makes a bad situation even worse.

One of your first actions in the case of a divorce is to try to remove your name from any joint accounts you may share. Unfortunately, this will be very difficult if any of those accounts still have a balance due. Your creditor may not let you out of the joint obligation. You need to understand that a divorce does not end your responsibility to pay back joint debts incurred while you were married, regardless of who actually ran up the debts. Verbal agreements made prior to a divorce about debt have a tendency to evaporate like the morning mist. Even after a divorce, more debt problems can develop if you're not careful. Closing out those joint accounts should protect you from having your ex make more charges on them. It's best to contact your creditors in writing, so you will have a record of your requests and their responses.

It's in the best interests of both of you to pay off these prior joint obligations so that your respective credit ratings are protected. In some cases that's enough incentive. Unfortunately, that's not always the case. If your ex has already defaulted on joint loans or is deliberately making things hard for you, the problem is more serious. Try to settle with your creditors for a reduced amount of the balance in order to get your name off the account. In situations like this, however, you should get the advice of a good attorney—and also a tax advisor, since settling debts can result in additional income tax due to the IRS.

Watch Out!
If you are getting divorced, immediately close all of your joint accounts. If you don't, you may be left holding the bag.

Taking responsibility for other people's credit

Dealing with our own credit issues is challenging enough for most of us, but in certain circumstances you may be asked to help others deal with theirs. Perhaps it's someone in your family, or a boyfriend or a girlfriend, who is having trouble getting a loan because of credit problems. Maybe it's your own son or daughter. Regardless of who it is, the temptation (and pressures) to help out can be enormous. Resist the temptation.

Cosigning a loan

For years I'd heard bad things about cosigning loans—from my parents, from teachers, from business associates, from financial advisors. This is a case where they were all right. If you're considering cosigning a loan for someone, think again. If you agree to cosign, you are signing a legal document agreeing to pay back the entire debt if the other person doesn't, including late fees and collection costs. Late payments or other failures to perform on the part of the so-called "primary borrower" may appear on your credit report for up to seven years. In many states, if the primary borrower misses even one payment, the creditor can immediately come to you for repayment. And they probably will.

Before you cosign, you should seriously consider all the consequences. You need to assess the other person's ability to repay the loan. Also, will you be able to recover the losses from the other person if that person defaults? This gets especially sticky when a close family member is involved. Even more to the point, can you really afford to pay in the event of a default? If you can't, you may be sued by the creditor and possibly have your wages garnished or your property taken to satisfy a judgment. While this can't happen without court proceedings, the fact that it can happen at all is important to understand. Yet another down side is that your liability for the cosigned debt may keep future lenders from giving you credit because they may view you as financially overextended.

Cosigning is a risky activity at best. It can even be bad news for the primary borrower if the person really can't afford the loan and your involvement encourages unhealthy financial habits. If you still are absolutely determined to be helpful, you might be better off taking out the loan yourself and having the other person cosign.

Children and credit

There is one final subject I want to touch on briefly: children and credit. I'm not talking about your adult children who need a little helping hand. I mean your underage kids. I'm well aware that this can be a controversial subject for some. What's more, this issue touches both on taking responsibility for someone else's credit and on cosigning. Double trouble. Let's take a look anyway.

In 1989, a bank in Denver caused quite a stir when it offered kiddie MasterCards, with an initial credit limit of $100, to anyone twelve and older who could get a parent to cosign. Now this admittedly sounds like a pretty crude attempt to hook young spenders before they know what they're getting into. Maybe it is. If used carefully, though, these cards with training wheels could also help to educate your kids on the wise use of plastic. Many adults could use a little help in this department. And part of the adult problem is that they didn't learn these skills when they were younger.

Bright Idea
Cosigning a loan for someone is generally not a good idea. If you still want to help, consider taking out the loan yourself and let the other person cosign— and give you the money to repay the loan. That way, at least the bills come to you and you can keep a watchful eye on things.

So, perhaps it's a good idea to consider a credit card for your kids, especially if you make sure that they actually earn the money to pay for their purchases. It could be an excellent vehicle for talking about money in general, and credit in particular. And besides, a hundred-dollar mistake in high school sure beats a thousand-dollar disaster in college. Many college kids are notoriously undisciplined when it comes to being away from the watchful eyes of mom and dad for the first time. Armed with a credit card and no experience, they can be downright dangerous. Think about it.

Just the facts

- Borrowing can be expensive. Compare total costs carefully.

- Selecting the right type of loan to match your needs is important.

- Borrowing for the first time doesn't have to be a hassle.

- Married women should establish their own credit history—it can be invaluable.

- Carefully weighing the advantages and risks before you cosign that loan is critical.

GET THE SCOOP ON...
The main types of loans available ▪ How to pick
the right credit cards for your needs ▪
What they don't tell you about debit cards ▪
Other places you can get money ▪ Avoiding
questionable loans

Money, Money Everywhere

F olk wisdom says that money doesn't grow on trees. Some of the apple growers I know up in northern New England might not agree, but picking the right sources of money is not unlike harvesting a good crop of apples. It requires the right tools, some basic knowledge of how to go about it, and the patience to pick carefully. And like apples, your available sources of credit come in many different varieties, each with a flavor (and often a specific purpose) of its own.

In this chapter, you'll learn more about the main types of credit and what things you should look for when you're picking a loan. We'll give the money tree a shake and see where your credit dollars can come from. Read on and you'll also learn how to handle some ubiquitous but potentially hazardous items—credit cards and debit cards. Finally, I'll tell you what kinds of loans to be wary of. There's only one thing worse than biting into a fresh-looking apple and finding a worm: It's finding half a worm.

Similarly, some loans may look good on the outside, but beware of what's lurking in the fine print.

Common types of loans

You don't have to look very far in this country for sources of credit. Banks, savings and loan associations (S&Ls), and credit unions immediately come to mind. It's also possible to borrow money from retirement plans, life insurance policies, even your employer. Depending on your particular circumstances, one or more of these options will probably meet your needs. Remember, it pays to shop around. Every year people spend millions of dollars more on finance charges than they need to because they didn't take the time to thoroughly check out their loan options. It's possible to get a loan for almost anything, though most loans fall into four main types: home mortgages, home equity loans, auto loans, and student loans. We'll briefly explore the big four and offer some suggestions that should help you get a better deal.

Home mortgage

Unofficially...
According to the Federal Reserve, in 1998, Americans had an outstanding mortgage debt of $5.7 trillion in the United States.

Entire books have been written on the subject of home mortgages (*The Unofficial Guide*™ *to Buying a Home* is a good place to start), so I'm going to hit only a few key points here. Typically, you can qualify for a mortgage loan of two to two and one-half times your household's annual income. For example, if your family earns $40,000 a year, you can usually qualify for a mortgage of $80,000 to $100,000. Lenders will want to know about your employment and credit history, including your current job and income and how well you have handled your past debts. The Fair Credit Reporting Act includes guidelines on how this information may be used. The Equal Credit Opportunity Act prohibits discrimination in lending based on sex, marital status, race, national origin, religion, or age, or because you receive public assistance (such as veteran's benefits, welfare, or Social Security), or because you have exercised your rights under the federal credit laws.

Probably the single most important thing to look for when you're shopping for a home mortgage is the *annual percentage rate*. The APR includes all of the costs of credit, including such things as interest, *points* (fees that allow you to "buy down" the rate of the mortgage in advance), and mortgage insurance. Points, incidentally, are completely tax deductible in the year of the closing. There are two major types of mortgages—fixed-rate and variable-rate. Since there are many variations, you need to shop carefully for a mortgage that best meets your particular needs. In addition, the lender generally expects you to make a down payment of between 10 and 20 percent of the house's price and to pay the so-called closing costs, generally around 3 to 6 percent of the total loan amount. You may be required to pay for mortgage insurance as well, especially if your down-payment is less than 20 percent. Under the federal Real Estate Settlement Procedures Act, the lender must provide you with information on all known and estimated closing costs. Details of your particular mortgage loan may vary. Be sure you understand all the provisions before you sign on the dotted line.

Home equity loan

Home equity loans are increasingly popular. If you listen to the promotions, they sound like deals made in heaven, but it's reality-check time. Should you fail to make your payments, you could actually lose your home to the lender. Some people do every year. Just keep that in mind.

Moneysaver
Most lenders require you to pay a fee when you file a loan application. This fee varies but can range from $100 to $300. Before you apply, ask the lender if there is an application fee, how much it is, and if it is refundable.

There are two main ways to tap your home's equity: a second mortgage or a home-equity line of credit. A *second mortgage* is an installment loan for a fixed amount, which you pay back in monthly payments. With a *home-equity line of credit,* however, you get approval for a certain amount up to your "credit limit." With the line-of-credit there are no monthly payments until you actually make use of it. As with standard home mortgages, it's very important to compare the APR on home equity loans to find the best rates. One key thing to remember, however, is that the advertised APR for home equity credit lines is based on interest alone. To make a true comparison of credit costs, be sure to compare other charges, such as closing costs and points, which increase the total cost of your home equity loan. This is especially important if you are comparing a home equity credit line with a regular installment mortgage, where the APR includes the total costs.

Home equity loans have some real tax advantages, especially if you are trying to consolidate your debts. We'll cover that in more detail in Chapter 12. The main thing to remember at this point is that home equity loans, despite their popularity, have one overriding risk: You're putting your house on the line in order to get that line of credit.

Auto loan

After your home, a new car is probably the second largest purchase you are going to make. The average price of a new car as of June 1998 was $23,480, according to the National Automobile Dealers Association. It's not hard to see why making a smart deal can pay off handsomely. Unfortunately, unlike your home, which will probably appreciate in value over the years, your shiny new automobile begins to

Unofficially...
The average amount financed on a new car loan in 1999 was $19,304.

depreciate in value the moment you drive it off the lot. So, you don't want to spend too much money on a long-term auto loan.

As with any loan, it's a good idea to do some research first to decide what you really need for a vehicle. Particularly when you are going to finance most of your purchase, keeping your initial price within reasonable bounds will save you a lot of interest expense over the life of the loan. Many auto buyers don't realize that they can often get a better financing deal from a lender other than the car dealer. Shop around and compare. For auto loans, credit unions typically offer some of the best rates, ranging from one or more percentage points less than commercial banks and S&Ls. The better your credit, the less likely it is that your auto dealer will be the one to offer you the best deal. And by the way, don't ever tell a car dealer how much you can afford to pay per month. That's an invitation to be taken for a ride. For more on auto loans, check out *The Unofficial Guide™ to Buying or Leasing a Car.*

Student loan

The subject of student loans, like most government programs, fills whole bookshelves and takes up gigabytes of hard-drive storage space as well. Your choices include Stafford loans, PLUS loans, consolidation loans, Federal Perkins loans, and a whole slew of grants and work-study options. Loans must eventually be paid back with interest. The grants are financial aid that you don't have to pay back, which is great, if you can get them. Work-study, as the name implies, lets you work and earn money while you study. Undergraduates may be eligible to receive all three kinds of aid. Graduate students may receive the loans and work-study but not the federal

Watch Out!
When you negotiate on the financing of a car, be wary of focusing only on the size of the monthly payment. The total amount you will actually pay depends on the price of your car, the APR, and the length of your loan.

grants, which are mainly intended for undergraduates (though there are many private grants available for grad students). Aid from most of these programs is awarded based on need. A Free Application for Federal Student Aid (FAFSA) can be made in a variety of ways, but the most convenient is through a U.S. Department of Education Web site located at: www.fafsa.ed.gov. Additional information is contained in a comprehensive student guide available at: www.ed.gov/prog_info/SFA/StudentGuide or by calling (800) 433-3243.

Unofficially...
You cannot qualify for a deferment on a student loan if your loan is already in default. So, don't wait to apply for a deferment if you think you are going to have trouble making your payments.

Student loans typically offer a six-month grace period from the time you graduate or leave school to the due date of the first payment. Under certain circumstances, it's possible to receive a deferment or forbearance on your loan if you are in financial difficulty. If your loan is deferred, you don't have to make any payments during the deferment period (up to three years in some situations) and no interest will accrue during that time. In the case of a forbearance, your payments are decreased or even postponed for a limited and specified period until you get back on your financial feet. Interest, however, continues to accrue during a forbearance. In certain cases, it's even possible for your loan to be discharged (cancelled) altogether. Check with the U.S. Department of Education for additional details.

There are thousands of other, nonfederal student loan possibilities as well, far too numerous to cover in detail here. A good place to go for further information is The Smart Student Guide to Financial Aid located at www.finaid.org. The site describes a wide array of loans and scholarships and offers a good selection of useful tools to guide you through the process.

Sources of money

Now that you've looked at the main reasons people apply for loans, it's time to figure out the best places to go for them. This is an area where taking the time to explore your options can pay off handsomely in lower-cost loans. Looking up into the money tree, I see a number of main branches overhead. Let's climb up and check them out.

Banks and savings and loan associations

There's no lack of banks and savings and loan associations (S&Ls) to choose from in this country. As of the first quarter of 1999, the United States had 8,721 FDIC-insured commercial banks and 1,669 S&Ls, according to the FDIC. And all those vaults have a lot of money stashed in them (or at least on their computers): $5.4 trillion for the banks and about $1.1 trillion for the S&Ls as of the first quarter of 1999. Okay, they've got the money, but should you go to a bank for a loan? It depends. Banks and S&Ls tend to charge more for loans than credit unions (info on them in a moment). On the other hand, banks and S&Ls generally offer a broader array of borrowing options. In many cases, they also offer attractive price breaks for their more-established customers. You should try to be one of them.

Probably one of the smartest things you can do is to establish a good, long-term relationship with a smaller local bank, or at least the local branch of a larger bank. This is admittedly getting more and more difficult as the current trend of bank mergers and consolidations continues, but do the best you can. The main idea is to get to know the local people in the bank so that you can take advantage of the trend toward preferred rates on loans and savings to people that the bank knows. Local branch managers are almost always allowed to recommend loans for special handling or special pricing. Getting a bank loan to pay for something like furniture or a vacation is probably a better alternative than charging the items on your credit card (more on plastic in a moment), but be sure to compare interest rates first. Of course, paying cash for these things is better still. We'll discuss the benefits of cash in Chapter 16, "Avoiding Future Problems."

Credit unions

Despite the fact that over 11,000 credit unions exist in the U.S. today, they remain an underutilized financial resource. They're a great choice for savings, with returns consistently better than banks and S&Ls, and credit unions offer loans at rates that are uniformly lower. For example, in early 1999, rates for car loans from banks averaged around 9.6 percent, while the rate at credit unions averaged around 8.5 percent. What's more, credit unions typically allow you to apply for a small loan—possibly as low as $50 to $100—something most banks don't want to be bothered with unless it's at least $2,000. In addition, credit unions are not allowed to charge prepayment penalties. All of these advantages are hard to ignore.

So what is a credit union? Basically, it's a not-for-profit financial service cooperative owned and operated by its members. Many of the larger ones offer the same basic services that banks and S&Ls do, such as savings accounts, checking accounts (known as "share draft" accounts), credit cards, direct deposits, and so on. On the other hand, some of the smaller ones offer only a few basics and will not be able to meet all of your other banking needs. Nevertheless, a recent Gallop poll revealed that for

Unofficially...
In 1752, Benjamin Franklin and some of his neighbors organized the Philadelphia Contributionship for the Insurance of Houses from Loss, the oldest fire insurance company and oldest operating cooperative in the country.

the eleventh consecutive year, credit union members are more satisfied with their institution than bank customers are.

Credit unions do tend to be somewhat more selective than banks about their membership. This so-called field of membership, however, is not as exclusive as many people assume. In fact, with a little investigation, you can probably find a credit union that you can join. One good place to start looking is the Credit Union National Association Web site: www.cuna.org.

Retirement plans

Banks and credit unions aren't the only sources of money. Retirement plans are one of the more neglected borrowing options in the country. Many companies allow such loans from their 401(k) and 403 plans. A wide range of other organizations, as well as state, county, municipal, and even federal entities permit similar borrowing from their plans. This kind of loan is useful for debt consolidation, home improvements, and vehicle purchases, among other things. There are a number of advantages:

- Low rates
- Little paperwork
- No credit check
- Quick access to the money
- Simple repayment via payroll deduction
  Naturally, there are some disadvantages:
- You may miss out on major increases in the financial markets (and growth in your retirement plan) while your money is tied up in a loan to yourself.
- The repayment term is short, five years or less in most cases.

- If you leave your employer, you'll probably have to repay the loan immediately (depending on your employer). If you are unable to do so, there may be taxes and penalties involved.

Life insurance

Life insurance, a rather obscure branch of the money tree, is overlooked by many consumers—but not by life insurance salespeople. They love to tout the many benefits of borrowing against your life insurance policy. Actually, there's some merit to the idea. Once your policy has been in place for a few years, you have an enforced savings plan that you can tap whenever you wish. With this type of loan, you are borrowing against the cash value of the policy. The portion of your policy that you borrow against, however, will grow more slowly because of the outstanding loan. You need to consider this in your calculations of the actual cost of the loan. Since the cost may be based on the prime rate (the interest rate banks charge their most creditworthy customers) plus about 1 percent, life insurance loans can be a good deal. This strategy works with universal life, whole life, and variable life policies. It cannot be used with term insurance policies, however. The advantages are similar to those previously mentioned for borrowing against retirement plans. The disadvantages are a little different:

- You may be tempted not to repay the loan.

- There may not be much to borrow against in the early years.

- Generally, outstanding loans become taxable withdrawals if you cash in your policy. Check with your insurance agent to be sure.

IRAs

I mention the IRA option with some trepidation. Technically, you can't borrow from your IRA. However, there is a way to make temporary use of the money stashed in your plan on an emergency basis, once a year. If you roll the money from an existing IRA into another IRA, you have 60 days in which to complete the transaction. So, in a pinch, you could make a temporary bridge loan to yourself for a month or so. This strategy works only if you request that the previous IRA issuer send you a check for the rollover. If you ask the financial institution to send the rollover amount directly to the new institution, you won't have access to the money. The price is right, but this quick and dirty strategy is potentially very, very dangerous. If you don't replace the money in time, you'll end up paying income tax on the whole amount, plus a 10 percent penalty. Is it worth the risk? I don't think so. But in rare circumstances, it might be a useful strategy.

Credit cards: plastic explosives!

Now we're going to look at one of the biggest branches in the money tree. I don't know about you, but I've lost track of the number of exciting invitations to sign up for a new credit card that I received in the mail this week. It's no wonder. With an estimated 3.5 billion credit-card offers flooding our collective mailboxes every year, we can be forgiven if we begin to feel just a bit shell-shocked. With special introductory interest rate offers as low as 3.9 percent and all sorts of other attractive features offered as bait, it's hard to resist them. But credit cards, which have been aptly described as plastic explosives, need to be handled with care. If not, the debt

Watch Out!
The amount you borrow against the value of a life insurance policy is always subtracted from the death benefit. If you borrow $20,000 from a $100,000 policy and then die, your heirs will collect only $80,000.

they can produce may explode and demolish your credit rating, and possibly much more.

Don't get me wrong. When used wisely, credit cards can be extremely useful tools that save you both time and money. They can make travel, especially overseas, much more convenient. And many cards these days offer some neat perks, like rebates on gasoline purchases, or frequent flyer miles, or even free merchandise. Credit cards can now be used to buy almost anything almost anywhere. Cards are now accepted at fast food outlets, movie theaters, hospitals, supermarkets—even by the IRS!

Americans probably misuse credit cards more frequently than any other form of credit. And that misuse, which has grown to epidemic proportions, is causing untold misery for millions of our fellow citizens every day. Most credit card issuers assume (correctly, I'm afraid) that many consumers will not use their cards to their best advantage. This less-than-flattering but accurate appraisal has led to enormous profits in the credit card sector in the past. However, recent years have seen declining profit margins caused in part by intense competition and increased defaults by cardholders. As a result, card issuers have been backpedaling on their freebies and jacking up all sorts of miscellaneous fees to try to regain their previous financial advantage. In fact, the average credit card APR climbed to about 19 percent in 1998, up from 16 percent just five years ago, according to Ram Research, a credit card research firm. Nevertheless, the number of credit cards and the amount of indebtedness on them continue to spiral upward. It's no accident that one of the basic rituals in almost any credit counseling office is the deliberate destruction of the client's credit cards (more on that in Chapter 9).

Moneysaver
If you're a good credit card customer, don't be afraid to call customer service if you occasionally have a problem. Did your last payment arrive a day or two late due to slow mail? Ask to have the late fee waived. Is the interest rate too high? Even that is sometimes negotiable. It never hurts to ask.

Having said that, it's time to choose your plastic weapon—carefully. Picking one from the plethora of cards available can be a daunting experience. MBNA America Bank, one of the largest so-called monoline card issuers in the country (because they focus solely on credit cards), offers over 4,700 different kinds of affinity cards (more on affinity cards in a moment). And MBNA isn't the only one. This staggering profusion of cards gives the United States the dubious distinction of being undisputed world champion of the credit card sweepstakes. At last count, the nation's 151 million credit card holders owned an average of nine cards each, according to The Nilson Report. Some countries, like Australia, have more sheep than people. The United States has more credit cards than citizens. Many more. The current ratio is about five to one in favor of plastic.

With so many choices, it seems almost impossible to sort through them all in a single lifetime. The Internet offers savvy Web surfers some great shortcuts to finding the best deals on credit cards. Try www.bankrate.com and check out their Credit Card Search Engine (you may have to tunnel down through several layers of Web pages, but it's worth the effort). You'll be asked to answer some brief questions:

1. Your primary objective

2. The type of card you are looking for

3. The class of card—Gold, Platinum, etc.

4. The number of cards to be displayed

And voilà!, you'll have a list of anywhere from ten to fifty cards arranged in order of attractive features. You can also customize the search by state, though that tends to limit your choices. There are lots of other card sites, but this is one of the best. It also offers a wealth of other related data and information. See "Credit Card Information" in the Resource Guide, Appendix B.

Before we look at the different types of credit cards, you need to understand a few basics. If you don't pay off your balance every month, you should find a card with the lowest rate that you can get. On the other hand, if you are using your card mainly as a convenience and will be paying your balance in full regularly, then you should look for a card with no annual fee. Also, credit cards offer either fixed or variable rates on the interest they charge. If interest rates are headed up, you might want to lock into a fixed-rate card. However, if rates are headed down, a variable-rate card might make more sense. You need to be aware, though, that even "fixed-rate" cards can have their rates changed with as little as 15 days notice. Practically speaking, there isn't much difference between the two rate structures.

Bright Idea
The best deals on most credit cards are offered on cards with variable rates. Most fixed-rate cards, on the other hand, tend to have higher interest rates.

One important item to look for when card shopping is the annual fee. Credit card issuers charge anywhere from nothing to $300 a year for the use of their cards. Because of the intense competition in the credit card arena, many cards have dropped their annual fees, but not all of them. Some cards that offer the lowest finance charges come with annual fees (often in the $40 to $75 range), so look at the terms carefully.

As I mentioned in Chapter 1, regardless of the annual fee or even the interest rate, there are many different (and confusing) ways that card issuers calculate their finance charges. Because of the many variables, it's hard to anticipate every possible combination, but your best bet is to get a card that makes its calculation based on the adjusted balance in the most recent cycle and that excludes new purchases. And the worst deal, as I've mentioned previously, is the two-cycle average daily balance method. If you fail to pay off your balance in one of two successive months, you basically get charged two month's worth of interest.

You also need to check the grace period (or float—the time between your purchase and when you actually have to pay the bill). There are still a few Neanderthal card issuers who don't allow any grace period at all. Avoid them. You get charged interest from the instant your purchase transaction is posted to your account. The standard grace period these days is still 25 days, although that is beginning to drop to 20 days in some cases because of retrenchment in the industry. Savvy use of the float can be a debt management tool. If you keep careful track of the closing date for your billing cycle (which appears on your account bill) and then make a purchase with your card the next day, the transaction won't show up until your next billing cycle—giving you almost two months to pay the bill.

Finally, you need to realize that while a low minimum monthly payment may look attractive compared to a higher minimum, it also means that you will be in debt for a longer period of time if you only make minimum payments. A low rate card can actually be more expensive than a high rate card because of a low minimum monthly payment.

Enough basics. Now let's look at the many different flavors of credit cards that you can get, and explore their relative advantages and disadvantages. Which card is best? That depends entirely on your needs and personal preferences. But for most folks, a bank card is probably the first choice.

Bankcards

Bankcards are the most popular and useful credit cards. Visa and MasterCard, the two big names in bankcards, don't actually issue the cards—the banks do. The main advantage of bankcards is their wide acceptance. Many bankcards are now offered with no annual fee. You can charge almost anything with a bankcard and then take advantage of the float. Look for a grace period of at least 25 days—anything less isn't a very good deal. A bankcard can be especially useful if you make a lot of purchases because you can then pay with one check and get a fully itemized bill at the same time. The bill becomes a convenient record and can be handy at tax time.

There are three key disadvantages associated with bankcards:

- Some banks still charge an annual fee.
- They are so convenient that many people are tempted to overuse them and can quickly get themselves into credit trouble (more on that in Chapter 7).
- Bankcard interest rates and other fees tend to be high.

Of course, if you pay off your card account in full every month, the interest rate is not a key factor in deciding which type of card to select.

Store cards

Retail or store cards are issued by many retailers like Sears, Neiman Marcus, and JCPenney, as well as gasoline companies and numerous other businesses. Studies have shown that people who have credit cards with retailers tend to buy more from those retailers. And these businesses have been paying attention. Retail cards have a couple of advantages: they're fairly easy to obtain (especially gasoline company cards), and they will sometimes smooth the way for preferred treatment or will help you resolve problems or complaints about merchandise. On the down side, retail cards tend to carry very high interest rates, often even higher than bankcards, and gasoline cards usually force you to pay the gas balance in full each month.

Travel and entertainment cards

American Express, Carte Blanche, and Diners Club are the big three travel and entertainment (T&E) cards. These cards are somewhat different from their plastic peers in that they offer only very short-term credit and do not charge you direct interest. You usually have from one to two months to pay your bill in full. The T&E companies make up for the lack of interest income by charging you hefty annual fees, from $55 and up. They also charge merchants a large percentage of the purchases made with the card—up to 10 percent—which is why these cards traditionally have not been popular with many merchants.

The advantages of T&E cards include generally quick resolution of billing problems, a variety of special services, no preset spending limit, and, finally, prestige. I'm not sure about the value of the last point, but the others might actually be useful. The disadvantages of T&E cards start with the sizable annual fee. In an emergency, it's hard to arrange for extended payments. The limited number of places where you can use these cards and the difficulty (sometimes impossibility) of getting a cash advance are other drawbacks. However, some people actually

Moneysaver

If you are look-
ing for a low-
interest-rate
credit card, con-
sider joining a
credit union.
These organiza-
tions frequently
charge around 13
percent or less
on fixed-rate
cards.

prefer to use T&E cards because they have to pay them off in full every month. They like the enforced self-discipline. If that appeals to you, then by all means get yourself a T&E card.

Affinity/hybrid cards

Affinity cards include a wide—and sometimes bizarre—number of ways to personalize your credit purchases. Are you a Boston Celtics fan? There's a Platinum MasterCard for you. Or perhaps an environmental organization is more to your liking; there are numerous environmentally friendly choices. And there's more. Ducks Unlimited? *Sports Illustrated?* The NFL and NHL? They're all available. There's even one for Star Trek fans. Beam me up, Scottie—and charge it. A wide variety of labor unions and professional associations have also jumped on the bandwagon. Every major airline offers an affinity card that earns frequent flyer miles. The interest rates of some affinity cards tend to be a bit lower than for other cards, but their annual fees traditionally are higher, though many have now dropped the annual fees. Some affinity cards such as L.L. Bean's for example, offer free shipping. This can be a good deal if you order merchandise from them on a regular basis. But some other affinity cards offer little besides a clever marketing ploy based on a theme. Comparison-shop carefully, and then decide whether these unique cards are worth it.

Another recent trend has been the growing number of store/bank cards. These hybrids have become increasingly popular with lenders because, unlike straight store cards, the hybrids are not subject to the consumer protection laws of the state in which the store is located, but rather to the laws of the state in which the bank is located. You don't have to be a genius to figure out why so many of these banks are located in states like Delaware and South Dakota, where banking laws are more favorable—for the banks.

Online cards

Online cards are the latest trend in the credit card business. Like just about everything else, credit cards are going where the money is (or, perhaps more accurately, where they hope the money is going to be)—the Internet. We'll cover the brave new world of online cards in greater detail in Chapter 4, "Credit, Debt, and the Internet." For the moment, suffice it to say that there are already 297 different online card offers from 59 issuers, according to a recent survey. And the number is growing exponentially as you read this.

Before we end our discussion of plastic, a few comments about Gold, Platinum, and Titanium cards.

Question: "What is the difference between a Green Card and a Gold Card?"

Answer: "The difference is that the Green Card is green and the Gold Card is gold, and if you don't understand that, then you don't understand this company."

This pithy observation, attributed to Aldo Papone, chairman of American Express Travel-Related Services Division, speaks volumes on the subject of heavy metal cards—Gold, Platinum, Titanium, etc. Although these cards may offer some unique services and may have credit lines of up to $100,000, these features come at a price: with annual fees ranging anywhere from $50 to $300. Generally speaking, you should judge a credit card

by its interest rate, fees, and services, rather than by
its color.

Finally, regardless of which type of credit card
you choose, the key point to remember is that the
individual issuers are the ones who set the terms for
the cards, and those terms vary widely. Comparison-
shop carefully. All Visa and MasterCards are not created equal!

Debit cards

Whether you know it or not, you're probably carrying a debit card around with you right now. And I
suspect you use it all the time. That's right, it's your
ATM card. Originally designed to be used only at
the issuing bank's ATM machines, these cards have
become increasingly powerful financial tools at
home and abroad. While not all ATM cards work
everywhere, I have been repeatedly amazed (and
impressed) that my own ATM card issued by the tiny
National Bank of Middlebury (Vermont) has caused
ATM machines in such diverse places as Canada,
Germany, Greece, and Slovakia to spew out fistfuls
of dollars, *deutsche marks, drachmas,* and *korunas,*
respectively. And at very attractive exchange rates, I
might add. Chances are yours will work the same
magic, too. Debit cards are becoming increasingly
popular. By the year 2000, it is estimated that two-
thirds of American households will have a debit
card.

Unfortunately, many people who already use
debit cards are not particularly well informed about
them. According to a National Consumers League
survey, more than a third of the consumers who
use debit cards don't fully understand their rights
and responsibilities. "We were concerned to learn
that people are using a card without knowing their

WORKSHEET FOR COMPARING CREDIT CARD BENEFITS

Card Company Name and Telephone Number				
Annual Percentage Rate (APR)				
Grace Period				
Annual Fee				
Minimum Finance Charge				
Method of Computing Balance				
Cash Advance Fee				
Overlimit Fee				
Late Fee				
Bounced Check Fee				

liability and how they are protected," Linda Golodner, NCL president, said in a New Orleans *Times-Picayune* article about the survey. About 50 percent of those surveyed incorrectly believed that their debit card has the same purchase protections that a credit card has (see Chapter 3 for credit card protections).

Here's what you should know about debit cards. Increasingly, older-style ATM cards are being upgraded by their issuers to have full debit card features. Still other debit cards look like a regular credit card because they carry a Visa or MasterCard logo but definitely are not. The main way you can tell the difference is by the things they do to your bank account. A debit card, as the name implies, subtracts money from your bank account either immediately (a so-called on-line debit card—not to be confused with the new online *credit* cards used on the Internet) or within a few days (an "off-line" debit card). To confuse the issue, some debit cards combine these two features on the same card. To muddy the waters still further, some debit cards are referred to as "electronic checks." They're all essentially the same beast.

On-line debit cards work in combination with a personal identification number (PIN), just like your ATM card. Swipe the card, enter your PIN, and the system checks to see if you have enough money in your account to cover the transaction. If so, zap, the money vanishes from your account. In the off-line scenario, the card is read by the system and a debit is generated against your account. You sign a receipt, as you would in a regular credit card transaction. The debit against your account is processed in a day or so.

There are advantages to debit cards:

- It's usually easier to obtain a debit card than a credit card.

- You don't need to carry much cash or bring your checkbook.

- You don't need to carry traveler's checks.

- Debit cards are accepted at more places than personal checks. Ever tried to cash an out-of-town personal check in New York City? I have. Forget it.

Debit cards have very real disadvantages, however:

- Since you "pay now," you lose the grace period that comes with a credit card. And if the store would accept a check, you lose that grace period too.

- You lose some of the legal protections that come with a credit card or even a check. Since the transaction is instantaneous, you can't stop payment afterward. The protections against fraudulent use are significantly fewer than with a credit card.

- Since no credit is involved, the use of a debit card will not improve your credit rating.

- Many banks charge fees for using the debit feature of an ATM card. They may charge as much as $2.00 per transaction.

- If your debit card is ever lost or stolen, a thief could conceivably clean out your bank accounts. In an extreme case, if your debit card is tied to your broker's cash management account, those funds could disappear in a nanosecond. Unlikely, but possible. Do you want to take the chance?

If your debit card is lost or stolen, be sure to notify the issuer immediately, or at least within two days. Federal regulations limit your liability to $50 if you do so. If you notify the bank within 2 to 60 days, your liability increases to $500. Not so good. If you notify your issuer more than 60 days after the date you received a statement, you could lose everything in your checking and overdraft account. That's scary. Also, be sure to keep receipts from your debit card transactions. A thief could obtain your name and debit card number from a receipt and order merchandise over the phone or by mail. You won't know about it until you get your next statement. With a credit card you have considerable legal protections in the event you have a problem. With a debit card you're pretty much left to fend for yourself. Still want a debit card?

How many cards are enough?

With all these choices, it's tempting to fill your wallet with lots of colorful plastic. You never know when one of these cards might come in handy, right? Resist the temptation. While it's nice to have several choices of bankcards—one for business expenses and one for personal charges, for example—carrying too many cards can be a problem. The logistics of trying to notify a dozen or more issuers that you've managed to lose their cards is daunting enough, but there is another reason why you should limit your collection of plastic. Too many cards can have a negative affect on your credit rating. The upper threshold is around four or five bankcards. Beyond that number, you may start having trouble getting additional credit. Some people with otherwise good credit histories have actually been turned down because they held too many cards. Two bankcards really should be enough.

Watch Out!
If you have a pin number that you use with a debit card, never write it on the card or keep it with the card. When you are using the terminal, don't let people see the number you punch in.

Sometimes this situation can happen to you even though you routinely carry only a few cards. The culprit(s)? Those old credit card accounts you stopped using years ago but neglected to officially close out. Many of the issuers continue to keep the accounts open in the hope that you might decide to use them again. My advice is to close any revolving credit account that you do not plan to use again. Federal law now requires lenders to notify credit bureaus when you close an account, but some older accounts may still be floating around on your credit history and may come back to haunt you. One of the best ways to find out what's still out there is to get a consolidated credit report. This includes information from all three major credit bureaus, and is available from www.credit.com at a cost of $29.95 (see "credit report consolidators" under "credit bureaus" in the Resource Guide, Appendix B for additional contact information).

Bright Idea
If you do not plan to use a credit card again, be sure to officially close the account with the issuer and request that they report your action to the credit bureaus as "account closed at consumer's request." Ask for written verification that this has been done.

Other sources of money

We've explored most of the sound parts of the money tree. There are still a few smaller branches up there that we need to look at. Not all of these sources of money are necessarily bad, but you do need to check them out carefully and know what you're getting into before resorting to them.

Finance companies

One of the main differences between finance companies and banks is that the former typically lend money to individuals or institutions but don't take in deposits like the latter. As a rule, finance companies do part of their business with people who are having, shall we say, "some difficulties" with their credit rating. You've heard the sales pitch: "Bad credit? No problem!" And it's generally true. You've got to have really, really serious problems—like a string of repossessions, a recent bankruptcy, and a slew of late payments—before you'll be turned down for a loan. Of course, there's a price to pay for the easy money. Higher interest rates for starters. And high late-payment fees too. Not surprisingly, late fees represent a major source of income for these lenders. Ironically, the people who feel they have to resort to a finance company are just the ones who really can't afford the higher costs in the first place. It's a vicious circle. In some poorer neighborhoods where banks have pulled out altogether, finance companies may be one of the few alternatives that are left.

There is, perhaps, one reason why someone with a good credit rating might actually want to borrow from a finance company—it's fast. If you're in a big hurry to make a payment on something, coming up with the money doesn't get much quicker or easier—sometimes you'll have the money in just an hour or so. The trade-offs include higher interest; worse yet, using the finance company will likely hurt your credit rating. People who regularly deal with finance companies are often higher risks, so you may be considered a higher risk simply by association—even if you aren't.

Other second-mortgage lenders

We've already covered standard home equity loans at the beginning of this chapter. This section mainly refers to the second-mortgage lenders (not your local banks) who advertise heavily, especially on TV, and increasingly on the Internet. They may promise you low rates on home equity money, but by the time the special promotional introductory rates expire and all the other points and fees are added in, the bloom starts to fade from many of these offers. If your credit is good, your local bank or credit union can usually beat the rates these folks offer. Of course, if you have good credit, you probably aren't giving these offers any serious consideration in the first place. And remember, a home equity loan of any type puts your house at risk if you fail to repay.

Loans in the mail

This one's easy. Unless the loan offer is from your local bank, any loan solicitation that arrives through the mail should be shredded and then tossed in the circular file (or the recycling bin, if you live in an enlightened part of the country). Even if the offer comes from your bank, you'll want to scrutinize the fine print thoroughly to see exactly what they're trying to promote.

Loans from phone solicitations

This is one area where I admittedly get a little hot under the collar. There I am, about to put a forkful of hot dinner into my mouth—and the phone rings. Nine times out of ten, I can bet it's not a friend on the other end of the line. Now, if the unfortunate individual who has just interrupted my meal happens to work for a loan-hawking company, they're in even more trouble than if they were soliciting for some Worthy Cause. Not only do I decline the honor of taking advantage of their wonderful offer, but I specifically request—no, demand—that they permanently remove my name from their call list. And you should do the same when this happens to you. The Telephone Consumer Protection Act of 1991 requires these companies to remove your name from their call lists if you specifically ask. If they call you again, you should hang up and report them to your state Attorney General. You can even take them to small-claims court if they persist. Be polite but firm. Don't, under any circumstances, ever give out any personal information like your Social Security or bank account numbers to these jokers (the Federal Trade Commission has a lot of additional information about telemarketing sales rules). Never, never, never agree to any phone solicitation for a loan. Never. We all need to do our part to make these obnoxious intrusions into our privacy nonproductive.

Just the facts

- Using your home to obtain low-interest money can be a useful, but somewhat risky, strategy.
- Credit cards, like any powerful tool, need to be handled with care.
- Debit cards are convenient—and potentially very dangerous.
- If someone offers you an unsolicited loan, be extremely careful.

Chapter 3

GET THE SCOOP ON...
Maintaining good credit ▪ How federal credit
laws can help you ▪ Billing disputes and how to
resolve them ▪ The many types of fraud and
theft ▪ How to protect yourself

Protecting Yourself and Your Credit

"There's a sucker born every minute."
This quote was falsely attributed to P.T.
Barnum by a show business rival in a
newspaper interview. But Barnum, ever the savvy
promoter, did nothing to dispel the free publicity.
Regardless of who actually said it, the comment is as
relevant today as it was in the nineteenth century.
Maybe even more so. You have to be constantly on
your guard to protect your credit rating, your financial rights, your credit accounts, even your good
name and reputation, from a host of perils.

But now that your wallet is equipped with a shiny
new credit card or two, you're probably itching to
venture out into the marketplace and flex some of
your newfound purchasing muscle. Okay, but before
you do, I urge you to read the next two chapters.
Even if you are a relatively seasoned financial veteran, I think you will learn some new tips that could
potentially save you hundreds—maybe thousands—
of dollars. Establishing credit for the first time may

be a short-term hassle for the beginner, but protecting it (and yourself) can be a full-time, ongoing job for everyone. Don't believe me? You soon will.

In the next few pages, we'll start by looking at some commonsense ways to help you keep your credit rating safe. Then we'll explore the maze of federal consumer credit laws in greater detail and look at how they can protect your interests in a variety of different situations. I'll tell you the best ways to resolve your billing problems and explain what your creditors are required to do under the law. And if they don't, I'll tell you about your options. Finally, I'll offer tips on how to protect yourself against the many forms of fraud and theft that are lurking in the shadows, just waiting to take your money—and even your identity. It can happen. Don't be a sucker.

Stay current with your debts

The single best protection for your credit and your credit rating is to pay your bills and other obligations on time. This may seem obvious; nevertheless, the credit industry rakes in millions of dollars in late fees every year, often from people who thought they had paid their bills on time. This is particularly true of the credit card industry. Gone are the balmy days when you could have your payment postmarked on the due date and the card company would consider it paid on time. "If the bill says it's due on the 18th, that means it's due in their paws on the 18th," notes Catherine Williams, president of Consumer Credit Counseling Service of Greater Chicago in a recent bankrate.com article.

She's right. Credit card companies have recently been tightening up their rules and jacking up their fees, so it's easier than ever to get hit with a late fee—frequently $25 or more. Ouch! And this may not help your credit rating much either, although a late payment made before the next bill is due probably won't get reported. Some credit card companies even require payments by 9 a.m. on the due date to be considered on time—meaning that it's really due the day before. To avoid the late fees, be sure to send your check well before the due date. Although the U.S. Postal Service maintains that most first class letters will reach their destinations within three days, we all know that this is over-optimistic. Stuff happens. To be safe, give your payment a week for transit. If you're sending a very important payment, perhaps on a mortgage or major loan, you might want to send it "certified mail—return receipt requested" to make sure it reaches its intended destination.

Follow the instructions

Follow the instructions for how and where to make your payments. This may seem basic, but please bear with me on this. Write your account number on your check, include the pay stub, and be sure the correct address shows through the window of the envelope. Even if you send your payment on time, it won't do you much good if it goes astray because you weren't paying attention to detail. Use the envelope supplied with your statement. This is extremely important. Here's why. Although the Fair Credit Billing Act requires issuers to credit your payment the day it is received, each issuer is allowed to set their own guidelines. If any of the guidelines are not met (such as the wrong envelope), the creditor can take as many as five days to credit your account. Five days. And guess what? You may have just earned yourself another late-fee. That's a valuable little envelope. Don't lose it.

Bright Idea
If you have a consistent problem meeting the due date on a particular credit account because it falls at an inconvenient time of the month, call the issuer and ask them to move it to a more convenient date. They may accommodate you.

Check your statement promptly

Check your statements promptly when they arrive to ensure that your payments have been properly credited and that all charges are correct. An ounce of prevention now may help to avoid tons of hassles later on. If there are problems with your account, you need to contact your creditor immediately. More on that a little later in this chapter. If you haven't got a clue about what your credit account statements should be this month, or generally just don't pay much attention to them, you need to carefully read the rest of this chapter and all of Chapter 4. You are risking a host of potential problems if you do not closely examine your statements every single month.

Set up a system

Another important strategy to help you protect your credit is to have an organized system in place for paying your bills. It doesn't really matter whether your bills go into a neat file folder, a cigar box, or cookie jar (minus the cookies), or whether you stash them on a shelf or in a drawer. The main point is to establish a regular system that works for you and gets your bills paid on time. Once a month. Twice a month. It really doesn't matter. The only wrong system is the one that doesn't get your bills paid when they should be. There's simply no excuse for losing or misplacing your bills, or forgetting about them. If you do, you run the risk of damaging your credit rating. So get organized.

The easiest way to remember to pay your bills on time, of course, is to write the checks and mail them upon receipt. You won't forget, and that will give you the greatest amount of time for them to arrive so you've got the best chance of avoiding late fees and unnecessary interest charges.

Setting your priorities

Admittedly there are times when even the best-laid plans go astray, and you may find yourself temporarily facing a pile of bills that is a bit larger than the pile of cash available to pay them. When this happens, prioritize your bills. Your mortgage payment (if you have one) comes first. Always. Then sort through your other bills and try to pay those with the highest late payment charges or over-the-limit fees. Especially in the case where you are being charged an over-the-limit fee, you need to get your balance back down below your credit limit as quickly as possible. It might be helpful to find out what the trigger mechanism is for the fee (you may have to ask the creditor). Is it a single penny over the limit or perhaps a percentage like 10 percent? Armed with that information, you may be able to send a payment that just covers the amount. This may save you a $20 or $30 fee. Also, while paying off your credit cards in full every month is always the best strategy, if you come up short now and then, all you officially need to pay is the minimum balance to keep your credit rating squeaky clean. But don't let it become a habit. That usually leads down the slippery slope to serious debt. See Chapter 7, "The Credit Crunch," for the warning signs.

Help from the Consumer Credit Protection Act

It's a sad fact that many adults get themselves into financial difficulty because they were never taught how to effectively handle their money when they were young. Combine that with a general lack of knowledge about their consumer legal rights, then shower them with zillions of credit card offers, besiege them daily with an unbelievable array of attractive-sounding opportunities for getting into debt, and you have a recipe for disaster. Many businesses, unfortunately, have made vast fortunes on this situation. I have nothing against making an honest buck. It's the dishonest (or questionable) dollars made by taking advantage of people's ignorance that concern me. Luckily for consumers, there is a safety net that protects you from the worst abuses and offers a variety of tools to help you get your financial house in order: the Consumer Credit Protection Act of 1968.

Unofficially...
In 1900 it was difficult or impossible for a working person to get a conventional loan. The first personal loan department at a commercial bank was not established until 1924.

As I mentioned in Chapter 1, this act was the primary legislation that paved the way for the group of consumer protection laws that followed, each designed to deal with a different problem area. The Truth in Lending Act, 1969 (see Chapter 1); the Fair Credit Reporting Act, 1971 (see Chapter 6); the Fair Credit Billing Act, 1975; the Equal Credit Opportunity Act, 1975; and the Fair Debt Collection Practices Act, 1978 (see Chapter 10), are the main ones we will look at. We'll also explore some of the provisions of the Electronic Fund Transfer Act, 1979 (see Chapter 4), and the Bankruptcy Reform Act, 1978 (see Chapter 13). All of these laws have been amended numerous times in response to pressures exerted by the credit and banking industry as well as by consumer advocacy groups. It's an ongoing tug-of-war whose outcome is never entirely clear.

Nevertheless, since 1968 the protections for consumers offered by these laws have multiplied like dandelions on a sunny spring day. The concepts of "fair" and "equal" credit have been included in these laws. In addition, the laws prohibit unfair discrimination in credit transactions; require that consumers be told why credit has been denied; give borrowers access to their credit records; and provide a method of settling billing disputes. Taken together, these laws set a national standard for how individuals should be treated in their financial dealings. Here are a few examples of what the laws say:

- You cannot be turned down for a credit card because you're a single woman.

- Your risk is limited to $50 if your credit card is lost or stolen.

- You can straighten out errors in your monthly bill without damage to your credit rating.

- Credit cannot be denied just because you've reached age 65.

These laws offer considerable protection, but they're worthless if you don't know about them or don't know how to use them. The responsibility for that rests squarely with you. Most businesses don't go out of their way to tell you about all of your protections under the law. In fact, some have been known to—um—forget, and they need to be reminded now and then. There are a number of places where you can learn more about your many protections under these laws. The Federal Reserve System Web site at www.ny.frb.org is a good place to go for additional help. Check out their extensive catalog of public information materials. The Federal Trade Commission also offers lots of information about consumer legal rights and protections. You'll find their Web site at www.ftc.gov. Also see the Resource Guide in Appendix B.

Leveling the playing field with the Equal Credit Opportunity Act

It wasn't that long ago in this country when people were routinely turned down for credit because of the color of their skin, their national origin, or any number of other arbitrary and unfair reasons. No longer. The Equal Credit Opportunity Act (ECOA) has created a generally level playing field for virtually every American who applies for credit, and the decision is now supposed to be based on a person's financial qualifications. Period. As mentioned in Chapter 1, creditors can look at the "Three C's" (character, capacity, and collateral) when they try to decide whether to give you a loan or not. But remember, ECOA does not guarantee that you will receive a loan. It just helps to ensure that the process will be as fair as possible. Each creditor sets their own lending guidelines. One lender may turn you down, while another may offer you credit, based on the same information. Regardless of their decision, the lender may not discriminate against you because of your age, gender, marital status, race, color, religion, or national origin, or because you receive public assistance or you have exercised your rights under the federal credit laws. Furthermore, according to the law, a creditor may not use any of those grounds to:

- Discourage you from applying for a loan.

- Refuse to give you a loan if you qualify.

- Lend you money on terms different from those given to another person with similar income, expenses, credit history, and collateral.

The ECOA also contains some special rules that deal with specific issues such as age. In the past, many older people complained that they were denied credit because of their age. This was undoubtedly true in many cases. The law is very specific about these issues. A creditor may not:

- Turn you down or offer you less credit because of your age.

- Ignore your retirement income in rating your application.

- Close your account or require you to reapply because you reach a certain age or retire.

- Deny you credit or close your account because credit life insurance or other related insurance is not available for people your age.

The ECOA also covers your application for a home mortgage or home improvement loan. It bans discrimination for the same reasons previously mentioned, but in addition the race or national origin of the people in the neighborhood where you live or want to purchase your home may not be considered. If race is used as a factor in an appraisal of the property being considered, the creditor is prohibited from using that appraisal.

ECOA also includes numerous provisions for women. You may not be denied credit just because you are a woman or because you are married, single, widowed, divorced, or separated. In addition, creditors may not ask you about your birth control practices or if you plan to have children. What's more, you don't have to disclose child support or alimony payments; but if you do, your creditor must count them as part of your income. Finally, the law says that creditors may not consider whether you have a telephone listing in your name, since this would discriminate against many married women. See

Bright Idea
If you paid for an appraisal as part of a credit application, you are entitled to receive a copy of the appraisal report. Just send a written request to the lender.

"Credit Issues for Women" in Chapter 1 for additional provisions.

Know your rights under the Fair Credit Billing Act

You've probably heard about people who've been billed for products they never bought or for services they've never received. Maybe it's happened to you. *Kiplinger's Personal Finance Magazine* relates the story of Marvin Peters, of San Antonio, who wrestled with a major Chicago bank for more than 18 months over two mysterious charges for airline tickets on his credit card bill. Peters disputed the charges within the 60 days specified by the Fair Credit Billing Act, and he received a credit to his account. Subsequently, the bank asked Peters to sign a statement that the charges were unauthorized. The bank later claimed it never received the statement and again posted the charges. But the bank had failed to notify Peters in writing that it had determined the charges were valid, something required by the FCBA. In the end, the bank was reminded that the burden of proof lay with the airline, not Peters, and the charges were again removed.

This is a good example of the sort of Byzantine situation you can suddenly find yourself in with a billing error, and of the protections offered under the FCBA to help you resolve it. It's always a good idea to try to straighten out the problem with the creditor first, but if that doesn't work the law is an effective tool that helps equalize the odds between the individual consumer and some very large and powerful entities.

The FCBA allows you to withhold payments on defective goods, and it sets up procedures that require creditors to correct billing mistakes and credit your payments promptly. If they don't, they may be subject to substantial penalties. The law defines a billing error as any of the following:

- Your statement lists something you did not buy or a purchase made by someone not authorized to use your account.

- Your statement shows an amount that is different from the actual purchase price or an incorrect date.

- Your statement lists something that you did not accept on delivery or was not delivered as agreed.

- Your statement shows an error in arithmetic.

- A credit for returned merchandise or payment to your account is not reflected on your statement.

- Your statement was not delivered to your current address, as long as you gave the creditor 20 days advance notice before the end of the billing cycle.

- Your statement contains questionable items or something for which you need more information.

Although mentioned in Chapter 2, I want to be absolutely certain that you understand that the legal protections we've been discussing here relate to credit card purchases—but *not* to debit card purchases. Debit cards may look like a credit card, but they definitely are not.

How to resolve billing errors and disputes

Okay, your latest credit card statement shows a $129.95 bill for a flock of pink flamingo plastic yard

Unofficially... Your legal protections under the Fair Credit Billing Act for correcting billing mistakes on your credit accounts or withholding payment on defective goods apply only to credit card purchases. If you paid for something with cash, check, or debit card, you're out of luck.

ornaments that you never bought. How do you get the charge for the phantom birds reversed? You are allowed by law to withhold payment on the charge in question and ask the creditor to investigate the matter for you. But the FCBA is very specific about how to go about it. Don't complain about a billing problem on the phone. It's usually a waste of time, especially since your protections under the law don't kick in when you telephone. "A phone call—even numerous phone calls—may not be sufficient," warns the Federal Deposit Insurance Corporation's Lisa Kimball in an FDIC *Consumer News* article. "I've seen several cases where people ended up responsible for fraudulent charges because they only notified the card issuer over the telephone."

Write to your creditor

Always explain your problem in writing. Your letter of complaint must arrive at your creditor's location not more than 60 days from the time the original disputed bill was mailed to you. According to the law, your letter should contain:

- Your name and account number.
- A statement that you believe the bill contains an error and why you believe it is incorrect.
- The date and amount of the error or the item you want to have explained.

I strongly recommend that you specifically use the words "billing error" somewhere in your description of the problem. This will eliminate any possible ambiguity or opportunity to misinterpret your complaint and will require the creditor to investigate the problem. Also, be sure to mention that you are exercising your rights under the Fair Credit Billing Act. This puts them on notice that you are aware of the law—and are prepared to use it if necessary. Send your letter by "certified mail—return receipt requested." This costs a bit more than a regular first class stamp and requires a trip to the post office, but it's good insurance against the creditor "losing" your complaint. If you are already embroiled in an ongoing dispute, you should definitely adopt this strategy. Always keep a copy of your letter(s) and the bill(s) in question. You may need them. It's quite possible that even after a disputed claim has been settled, the charge may return, zombie-like, to haunt you again. See Appendix D for a sample dispute letter.

Pay the part of the bill not in dispute

Under the provisions of the FCBA, you do not have to pay the charges you are disputing or the related finance charges. But this is where things get tricky, especially if you do not normally pay off the entire amount of your bill. Trying to sort out which part of the interest charge is which can give even an experienced accountant a headache. So it's probably simplest to pay only the part of your bill that is not in dispute, or the minimum payment. Things get even more interesting if only part of a questionable charge is incorrect. For example, if you discover that your husband did, in fact, order a $19.95 pink flamingo, but not the whole flock listed on your statement, the disputed amount would be reduced to $110. You can go ahead and pay the $19.95 undisputed amount, or you can correctly claim that the entire $129.95 figure is in dispute and pay nothing until the matter is sorted out. Either approach is okay. Be aware, however, that any amount in dispute can, and probably will, be deducted from your available credit limit.

Watch Out!
Never send a billing dispute complaint letter along with your check in the bill payment envelope. It probably will go astray because bill processing departments don't deal with administrative issues, and you may end up losing your protections under the law. Instead, send your letter to the address listed on your statement for "billing inquiries" or "billing errors."

What your creditor must do

Assuming that you have followed directions and have sent a letter disputing the billing error for the pink flamingos, what comes next? At this point, the responsibility shifts to the card issuer. The creditor must respond to your letter of dispute within 30 days of receipt. If they don't, technically they can never collect on the disputed amount up to $50. Ever. Even if you were wrong. A few companies may actually ignore your letter in the hope that you will give up. But most will promptly send a written reply in order to avoid losing their protections under the law.

According to the FCBA, the creditor must now conduct a reasonable investigation to find out if the charge is correct or not. It's important to understand that it is not your responsibility to prove that there is an error. The creditor must prove that the charge is correct. This is an important distinction. So don't be discouraged from protesting a charge if you are reasonably certain that there has been a mistake on your bill, even if you don't have a lot of evidence to support your claim. The creditor now has 90 days or two billing cycles (whichever is less) to resolve your billing problem from the date your original letter of complaint was received by them. Until your complaint is answered, the creditor may not take any action to collect the amount in dispute.

Once the investigation is complete, the creditor has several courses of action to choose from. They can post a credit or other correction to your account for the amount in dispute. Or, they can send you a letter that says the charge is correct, including an explanation of why they think that's the case. If the dispute is settled in your favor, the creditor cannot charge you interest on the disputed amount.

Still not satisfied? don't give up

Let's say the Skinflint National Bank is playing hard-ball with you and your pink flamingo problem. "We're right. You're wrong. Pay up!," they declare. So what do you do at this point? There's quite a few things you can do, actually. First, notify the bank in writing that the $110 for the nonexistent birds is still disputed. The law says you must do this "promptly" but offers no additional guidance. I think a week to 10 days is reasonably prompt and should suffice. Sending this letter gains you several important advantages:

- If the bank reports you as delinquent to any credit bureau, it must also report that the amount is in dispute.

- It must inform the credit bureau that you say you do not owe the disputed amount.

- The bank must provide you with the name and address of anyone or any credit bureau it tells about your alleged debt.

When the matter is eventually settled, the creditor must report the outcome to each person or bureau that has received reports on your supposed debt. You also have the option of presenting your side of the dispute on your credit record (see Chapter 6). If the matter remains unresolved, you may decide to file a complaint with the appropriate state or federal agency, or possibly resort to suing the creditor, or simply refuse to pay. Be aware, how-ever, that at this point the creditor may also try to collect the amount owed on your account. But if you are in the right, don't give up.

Bright Idea
If you are having trouble settling a credit card billing problem with your bank, try contacting the customer service department at MasterCard or Visa directly. It's in their best interests to have happy customers. They may be able to help you resolve the problem.

How to stop payment on your credit card

There is one more powerful tool available to you if a billing dispute concerns a credit card charge. And you may not have heard of it before. It's called a stop payment. While this may sound like a stop payment on a check, it's much better. It's quick and cheap, and it applies to all kinds of credit cards (but, alas, not to debit cards). Under the FCBA, you may withhold payment on any damaged or poor-quality goods or services purchased with a credit card as long as you have first made an attempt to resolve the problem with the merchant. This applies to virtually any purchase. Note that the main difference between this strategy and the others we've looked at is that in this case there has to be a problem with the product or service, rather than a billing error.

Naturally, there are some restrictions. The purchase must have been for more than $50, and it must have taken place in your home state, or within 100 miles of your home address. Telephone orders made from your home phone to mail-order businesses, regardless of their actual physical location, may be considered home-state purchases as well, although this is a matter of interpretation. That goes for mail-in orders as well. Basically, all you have to do is send your credit card issuer a written notice (to the address listed on your statement for "problems or disputes") that you have made a good faith effort to settle the problem with the merchant and that the matter has not been resolved to your satisfaction. Your good faith effort is all you need to trigger a stop payment. Technically, you don't even have to send a written notice to your card issuer, but I strongly suggest that you do.

And best of all, there is essentially no time limit placed on when you can demand a stop payment. Once you have officially complained to the merchant or the credit card company (or both) before you pay the bill, you have the right to exercise a stop payment at a later time, even if you subsequently pay all or part of the bill. The credit card company, not the merchant, is ultimately responsible for ensuring that your good-faith stop-payment rights are protected. In most cases, the card company will dump the problem back in the lap of the merchant with what is called a "charge-back"—the card company simply deducts the amount of the disputed transaction from the merchant's bank account. Now, this pits you against the merchant again, but at least you've got your money back. If you follow the proper good-faith procedure mentioned above, you have an absolute right to demand a stop payment under the law. Don't let a credit card company try to convince you otherwise.

How to enforce your rights

For the sake of discussion, let's say that the Pink Flamingo Caper still has not been resolved. Realistically speaking, a dispute of $110 probably would have been settled long before this, but let's say it hasn't. Perhaps by this time the money doesn't really matter anymore—it's the principle of the thing that is driving you on. Whatever the reason, you're left with a number of options. Ultimately, you may end up filing a complaint with a compliance agency or bringing suit in court. However, before you do, a few unofficial facts-of-life about compliance agencies are in order.

First the bad news. Even though these federal agencies are supposed to be looking out for our

collective interests, the fact remains that the banking and credit industry brings a lot of pressure to
bear on them to protect the industry's interests
instead of the consumer's. The dual role that some
of the agencies have of regulating these industries
while simultaneously making sure they remain
sound and profitable could be viewed as a contra-
diction. It's also no great secret that money talks
inside The Beltway. And the basso profundo of big
money tends to drown out the squeaky little voices
of individual consumers. The bottom line is that you
should not hold your breath expecting a lightning-
fast response or bold, decisive action to resolve your
little problem. I am not saying that these agencies
won't help you. They probably will, but don't expect
too much and you won't be disappointed. You also
need to be aware of the fact that some complaints to
agencies such as the Federal Trade Commission will
not result in direct action on your individual problem. But the FTC may use your case to identify patterns which they may act upon.

Now the good news. The *threat* of filing a complaint is often a more powerful incentive to settling
a billing dispute or other credit-related problem
than actually following through with the threat.
Most creditors will make a serious effort to work
things out with you if they believe you are about to
go to the Feds. There are at least seven federal
agencies to choose from (they don't make it easy),
depending on what the problem is and what kind of
creditor you are dealing with. There are also 50
state agencies who are supposed to be watching out
for your financial interests, as well. You might also
want to consider contacting your state or county
consumer protection offices for assistance. See the
Resource Guide in Appendix B for a complete list

of appropriate federal agencies and for the agency to contact for your particular problem. The same general guidelines apply for enforcing your legal rights under virtually all of the consumer credit laws.

Trying to deal with the federal bureaucracy can be a daunting prospect. There is one shortcut, however, that you may want to try. If your problem is related to a bank and concerns any of the federal credit laws, you can get help and advice from the Federal Reserve. Submit your complaint in writing to the Division of Consumer and Community Affairs, Board of Governors of the Federal Reserve System, Washington, D.C. 20551, or to the Federal Reserve Bank nearest you (see the Resource Guide in Appendix B). Be sure to describe the problem you are complaining about and give the name and address of the bank involved. You should receive a reply within 15 days.

If you want to read the actual federal statutes try www.law.cornell.edu/topics/consumer_credit.html. You'll find a brief overview of consumer credit as well as a menu of sources of federal and state material as well as other useful references. Be forewarned, however, that the federal statutes are heavy reading.

If all else fails, and you decide to take legal action against a merchant or bank, consider taking them to small claims court. In many cases, this may be just the added incentive needed to effect a settlement. Most banks and merchants don't want to deal with the time and expense of going to court, especially if there is a reasonable chance that you might win. Check out *Everybody's Guide to Small Claims Court*, by Nolo Press (see the Resource Guide), for additional information.

Unofficially...
If you're not sure which federal agency to send a formal complaint to, don't despair. If you mistakenly send your letter to the wrong agency, they are required to forward it to the right one.

Protecting yourself against fraud

Protecting yourself against billing errors or other unfair or discriminatory credit practices is one thing. Defending against outright fraud is another matter altogether. This is one area where you cannot be too careful. And there's a lot to be wary of. Every kind of credit card fraud imaginable (and some that you can barely imagine) competes with a seemingly endless parade of telemarketing scams to take advantage of an apparently inexhaustible supply of unfortunate victims. You've probably seen or heard some of these scams yourself. "You've just won $30,000!" Or a car, or boat, or whatever. "There's just this little service fee you need to pay before you can pick up your prize." Or maybe it's "Earn big money with vending machines!" or some other similar small business venture. Often, by the time you realize what has happened, your new business is going absolutely nowhere, while the promoters of the scheme have definitely left town—with your money. The list goes on and on. Travel scams, gemstone investments, fake charitable solicitations, advance fee loans, credit repair. Especially credit repair. Credit repair is definitely a growth industry. But I'm getting ahead of myself. Let's start with credit cards.

Credit card theft and fraud

Credit fraud is a multimillion dollar business and it shows no signs of going away. Quite the contrary, it's growing by leaps and bounds. Card fraud comes in many varieties. If you're unfortunate enough to lose your credit cards, chances are some Good Samaritan will not happen along and return them. In fact, the chances are good that you'll need to cancel all of them immediately.

Then, there's good old-fashioned theft, where someone steals your card and runs up a big bill before they can be stopped. In more-sophisticated variations of this scenario, your card is stolen, perhaps from the mail, and then used by well-organized gangs in conjunction with a portfolio of false identification papers to run up huge balances in a very short period of time. Lost and stolen cards account for about $270 million in annual losses to the industry. Let's not forget "account takeover" fraud, where a thief diverts your account to another address and uses it like crazy until either you or the card company finally blows the whistle. The industry estimates that account takeover fraud amounted to around $120 million last year. Add to that another $220 million for application fraud, and another $190 million for cards issued but not received, and the figures really begin to add up. But that's not all.

Last but not least, there are counterfeit cards. This is the fastest-growing type of bankcard fraud in both frequency and severity. The latest developments in technology have made it much easier for criminals to produce exact replicas of Visa and MasterCards from scratch. Right down to the magnetic strips and holograms used to supposedly safeguard against fraud. Most of the supplies for the manufacture of counterfeits are smuggled into the United States from the Far East, so it should come as no great surprise that this problem is particularly severe on the West Coast. But no region of the country is safe. CardData, an industry information source, says counterfeiters cost the card industry about $140 million in 1998. While credit card fraud of all types exceeded $1 billion last year, that figure represents only about .9 of 1 percent of the total amount charged by Americans during the same time period. Still, we're hardly talking about pocket change.

So what can you do about credit card fraud? For starters, always sign your card in the signature panel when you receive a new card. Keep a record of all your credit card numbers and where to call if they are lost or stolen. Virtually all cards come with a form containing this information when they are mailed to you. Protect your cards as if they were cash. Never leave them lying around anywhere, especially in public places. Here's some additional tips:

- Make sure you get your card back after every purchase.

- Never give out your card number over the phone, unless you are dealing with a company that you know.

- Never sign a blank imprinted credit-card sales slip.

- Always check the figures on the slip and draw a line through any blank spaces where additional amounts could be added later.

- If the salesperson makes a mistake on the sales slip and has to do another one, make sure the first slip is destroyed in your presence.

- Don't volunteer personal information when you use a credit card, other than an ID document.

- Never disclose your PIN to anyone. No one but you should know your PIN—not even the police or merchants.

If you believe you are the subject of credit card theft or fraud, contact your card issuer immediately using their toll-free number. This should be followed

Bright Idea
When you travel, carry the smallest number of credit cards possible. This will minimize your problems in replacing them and reduce your total potential liability if they are lost or stolen. Keep contact information for the credit card customer service in a location separate from your credit cards so that if they are stolen, you can contact customer service immediately for assistance.

up with a written notification as well. Include your name, card number, and the exact time, date, and location (if you know) of the loss or theft. Truth in Lending limits your loss for unauthorized use of your card to $50, regardless of how much is actually charged. If you notify the card issuer before any unauthorized charges are made, you owe nothing.

If your card(s) has been lost or stolen, examine your monthly statements carefully. If you spot any unauthorized charges, follow the same procedure outlined earlier in this chapter for settling billing errors. But there's another reason why it's important to check your statement regularly. If someone steals your statement out of the mail, they can use the information contained in it, combined with other personal data to make fraudulent charges on your account. If you don't receive your monthly statement, you should be on high alert. You may be in for some unpleasant surprises. I strongly recommend that you call your card issuer and find out what happened to your statement. A missing statement is considered a billing error, which gives you all of the protections under the FCBA for straightening things out.

Other fraud and theft

As I've already mentioned, consumer credit fraud comes in endless guises. And many of them are riding on the leading edge of today's major trends and technologies (more on that in Chapter 4). Yet, under their thin veneer of contemporary credibility, these scams are remarkably old-fashioned. In the case of fraudulent solicitations for charitable donations, they appeal to people's higher qualities, but usually they appeal to the timeless desire to get something for nothing—or almost nothing. Free gifts, cheap vacations, super-discount vitamins, vast profits in real estate—you name it—and somebody has probably been conned to buy or invest in it.

Unfortunately, many of the victims tend to be older citizens. They are viewed by the con artists as being easy pickings because many seniors were taught when they were young to be polite to people on the phone. "He sounded like such a nice young man," is a classic response from a senior who has just been fleeced. In fact, research has shown that around 57 percent of all telephone fraud victims are over age 50. Many seniors are also easily led astray by slick-looking offers they receive in the mail or hear on TV. Some of these promotions require you to initiate the phone call, rather than the other way around, adding yet another layer of credibility to the con.

In Chapter 2, I warned you about solicitations for loan offers over the phone, but there is an even more outrageous rip-off that you should be aware of: the "recovery scam." This one pushes the limits of credibility for me; obviously somebody is biting, though, or it wouldn't be so popular with the crooks. Here's how it works. Consumers who have lost money through prize promotions, merchandise sales, and so on are put on so-called sucker lists that are bought and sold by sleazy promoters who are betting that people who have been deceived once are prone to repeat their mistake.

When you are contacted, these slick talkers falsely promise that, for a fee or donation to a specific charity, they will recover your lost money, prize, or product. Variations on this basic theme abound, but in the end they will take your money and leave you empty-handed—once again. Basically they

Watch Out!
Beware of scam "Gold Cards." They're usually promoted through the mail to people with credit problems. Often tied to membership in some kind of exclusive buyer's club, they feature exorbitant fees and major restrictions. And they won't help you with your credit problems either.

aren't offering you anything that you couldn't do for yourself with a little help from a consumer protection agency or other nonprofit group.

Credit repair is another scam you need to watch out for. These operators offer to remove damaging information from your credit report—for a fee, naturally. The truth is that if you have credit errors on your report, you can fix them yourself without paying a fee (except possibly $8 for your credit report). We'll cover credit repair in detail in Chapter 6. But you can't remove damaging information from your report if it's accurate. No one can.

Here's another variation on this credit repair theme. Until fairly recently, a very active group of con artists around the country were selling instructions on how to clear up damaged credit records, often for as much as $399 a pop. These pricey "legal secrets" offered tips on how to switch Social Security numbers and otherwise cover your financial tracks. The strategy was, and is, a felony. "These scams target very vulnerable consumers," said Jodie Bernstein, director of the FTC's Bureau of Consumer Protection, in a recent *Los Angeles Times* article. "They prey on people… who may be desperate to develop a clean credit history so they can get a loan, get a job, or buy a car." The FTC and the attorneys general from 14 states filed civil actions aimed at crippling the scams. U.S. Treasury officials were also involved in the big bust. The unwitting clients were not prosecuted.

Identity theft

There is one more dark corner we need to explore: identity theft. And it's a very dark, rat-infested corner indeed. Unlike credit card theft or fraud, where thieves steal your card to rack up quick profits, identity thieves use your private personal information to take over your bank and/or credit card accounts, or open new ones. Then they make huge illegal purchases that sometimes continue for months, or even years, before they are discovered.

Endless variations exist on this basic theme. Identity theft is never a friendly act, but sometimes it can get downright nasty. In 1998, a widely publicized case in Vermont involved identity theft. A woman named Laura Burawa assumed the identity of a Burlington woman named Laurie Church. Burawa then proceeded to turn her victim's life upside down. With the aid of a duplicate birth certificate and marriage license, Burawa emptied Church's bank accounts, filed a restraining order against Church's husband, and even filed for a divorce between the couple, according to WCAX TV news accounts of the incident. Burawa was later found to be mentally incompetent to stand trial for her multiple felony counts. However, she was certainly competent enough to create chaos for her victims and make their lives completely miserable.

Horror stories like this, and worse, can be found all across the country. Some innocent victims have had their lives utterly ruined by this scourge. A few have even been jailed for crimes they didn't commit. And unlike the victim in the Burlington incident, most folks don't even know the perpetrator(s). Consumer advocates say that criminals assume the identities of about 350,000 people a year. Some authorities worry that the widespread availability of personal information, especially on the Internet (see Chapter 4), from data services, private companies, and government agencies could cause an epidemic of identity theft. Their concern is fully justified. Identity theft is one of the fastest-growing types of credit-related crime in the nation.

"This has become the path of least resistance for criminals," said Jim Bauer, deputy assistant director of the U.S. Secret Service, in a *Baltimore Sun* article. "At first, sophisticated rings were into it. Now, it is becoming commonplace." The Secret Service is responsible for monitoring identity theft, and in 1997 it arrested 9,455 people on charges of committing financial crimes while using someone else's identity.

Fortunately, there is a new federal law, the Identity Theft and Assumption Deterrence Act of 1998, that finally makes it a federal crime to steal someone's identity. Those convicted of identity theft can now be imprisoned for up to 15 years and fined $250,000. Before the passage of the law, it was extremely difficult for identity theft victims to make their case in court (or anywhere else, for that matter) because only the credit grantors who suffered monetary losses were considered victims. This absurd situation has now been remedied after years of tireless efforts on the part of identity theft victims and consumer right's groups. But just because there's a federal law on the books doesn't mean you can relax. Many states have yet to enact similar protections.

Even with the weight of the law on your side, dealing with the chaos of an identity theft attack can be a horrendous hassle. "The credit bureau says contact the creditor, the creditor says contact the credit bureau, and the consumer just gets ping-ponged back and forth," said Ed Mierzwinski, consumer program director for the U.S. Public Interest Research Group in Washington, D.C. in a *U.S. News & World Report* article. At least one Colorado victim

Unofficially...
Losses to victims and institutions in cases of identity theft were $745 million in 1997, up from $442 million in 1995, according to the Secret Service.

spent eight years trying to resolve his credit problems and eventually had to sue his creditors and the
credit bureaus. Scary? You bet.

So what can you do to prevent identity theft?
Frankly, there are so many possible ways for you to
become a victim of identity theft that there is no
sure-fire way to protect yourself. However, the following precautions will help you minimize the
likelihood:

- Don't carry your social security card in your
  wallet.

- Resist giving out your Social Security number
  as a means of identification, and don't have it
  printed on your checks.

- Shred or burn documents containing Social
  Security numbers and credit card numbers
  before you toss them in the trash.

- Don't use maiden names, birth dates, or
  anniversary dates as passwords on your
  accounts.

- Maintain the smallest number of open credit
  card accounts possible.

- Check your credit reports regularly—at least
  once a year.

- Ask credit bureaus to note in your file that no
  account in your name is to be opened unless
  the credit grantor calls you and gets your
  approval.

- Tell the credit bureaus that you do not want
  your file accessed for prescreened credit offers
  (see "prescreening" in Chapter 5).

- Have your name removed from promotional
  mailing lists. (You can remove yourself from

most national mailing lists by contacting the Direct Marketing Association's (DMA) Mail Preference Service, P.O. Box 9008, Farmingdale, NY 11735-9008.)

▪ Be careful when you fill out product registration forms. Many companies are primarily fishing for your personal information that they can use or sell to others.

If you have been the victim of identity theft, immediately call all the credit bureaus (see "Credit Bureaus" in Appendix B, Resource Guide) and have them put a fraud watch on your account. Then send the request in writing and ask that a fraud statement be added to your report. Also file a police report. You'll need it when you dispute charges with your creditors. Then settle down and start writing letters to have the fraudulent charges removed from your credit report. See "Identity Theft" in the Resource Guide for more help. And good luck. You're going to need it.

Bright Idea
If you have been victimized by identity theft, you are entitled to a free copy of your credit report from the credit bureaus. Be sure to ask for it.

Just the facts

▪ Paying your bills on time helps to maintain your credit rating and protects you from extra charges and fees.

▪ Checking your billing statements can catch problems before they become serious.

▪ Always notify your creditor of a billing error or dispute in writing.

▪ Taking steps to prevent fraud and theft is always the best strategy.

▪ Guard your personal information carefully.

GET THE SCOOP ON...
Electronic money ▪ Online credit cards ▪
Correcting errors ▪ Online invasion of privacy ▪
Scams, scams, and more scams

Credit, Debt, and the Internet

Chapter 4

N ot very long ago, the Internet was considered the realm of propeller-heads and university professors. Even as recently as a few years ago, conventional wisdom sneered at the very thought of people actually buying anything online. Conventional wisdom, of course, was wrong. Most of the members of the upper echelons of the business and financial community just didn't get it. Now they do; and banks, businesses, and all the rest of us are falling over each other to get in on the action. No wonder. According to IDC Research, global e-commerce grew to nearly $29 billion in 1998, up from about $11 billion in 1997 and $2 billion in 1996.

The rapidness of developments on the Internet makes getting a handle on it hard. Everyone is struggling to deal with the profound impact the Internet is having on virtually every aspect of our lives. Recent news accounts of the largely ineffective attempts to regulate, review, or otherwise police the

Internet are a sign of the times. There have been numerous congressional hearings on all sorts of Internet-related issues ranging from pornography and guns, to minors ordering alcoholic beverages in cyberspace. This has generated a lot of hot air in Washington but not much concrete action. Many government agencies can't even agree on who has jurisdiction.

In short, the Internet is more like a space western than anything earthbound. And there's a lot of territory out there pardner, just waitin' to be carved up—and not too many sheriffs to look over your shoulder, either. Naturally, this situation offers enormous potential for both good and evil—especially for issues like credit and debt. If there ever was a time and a place to be careful, it's now on the Internet.

In this chapter, we'll do some Web surfing of our own. I'll tell you about the rapidly expanding universe of electronic money and credit and how to navigate your way around it without getting lost in cyberspace. Then I'll download some tips into your memory banks about how to keep track of your paperless transactions—and correct mistakes if necessary. After that, we'll explore some of the many realms of the Web itself—the good, the bad, and the ugly. I'll offer some suggestions on how to avoid some of its worst perils and how to protect your credit and your identity at the same time. All set? Fasten your seat belt—and fire up your modem!

Instant money, instant debt

In 1998, online shopping in this country amounted to $13 billion (with an average order totaling $55), and this figure is projected to reach $30 to $40 billion by the end of 1999, according to the Boston

Consulting Group. That's up from practically nothing just a few years ago. One reason e-shopping is
growing exponentially is that it's so easy. I've given
it a try myself—a few books and some computer
software so far. Point. Click. Browse. Point. Click.
Done. All from the comfort of your own home. No
long, time-consuming drive. No hassles trying to
find a parking space. No crowded shopping malls
and long lines at the checkout counter. And delivery can be as fast as overnight if you're willing to pay
for the premium service. This is about as close as
you can get to instant gratification. Maybe it's too
easy. The temptation to e-shop yourself into oblivion is substantial, especially if you're a compulsive
spender (more on that in Chapter 8).

In any case, it should come as no surprise that
the majority of all this e-shopping is being paid for
by credit cards. Just a few years ago, most experts
were saying that consumers wouldn't trust their
credit card numbers to the insecurities of the
Internet. Again, they were wrong. Big time. Frankly,
you are probably more likely to have your credit
card compromised when you use it at some local
restaurant or convenience store than when you are
dealing with a reputable online business. According
to most accounts, there are no known instances of a
credit card number being compromised while it was
in transit between a buyer and seller via a secure
Internet connection. That doesn't mean there
aren't any online security risks; there are plenty.
We'll look at them shortly. But for the moment,
we'll focus on the positive side.

Books and computer products aren't the only
things going online. Take a look at any popular Web
portal such as Yahoo!, or Excite, or the dozens of
others, and you'll see listings for autos, classifieds,

auctions, music, real estate, and investing, to name just a few. There are probably hundreds, if not thousands, of possible sites related to each of these categories. It's mind-boggling.

Electronic fund transfers

Online commerce has huge implications for the credit and banking industry. As consumers become more accustomed to doing business online, the demand for online financial services of all kinds grows apace. The huge growth in the popularity of online brokerage firms in the last few years is just one example of where all this is leading to. Are we headed for a checkless or cashless society? Probably yes. But for the time being, we're definitely in a transitional period where a variety of electronic fund transfer (EFT) methods will increasingly become the method of choice for more and more people. At the present time, those choices include: ATMs, telephone transfers, debit cards, preauthorized transfers, PC home banking, online credit cards, and "smart cards." Let's take a look at each one.

Automatic teller machines

Automatic teller machines, or ATMs as they're popularly called, are nothing new. The first ATM in this country was introduced in 1971 at the Citizens & Southern National Bank in Atlanta. For many years, ATMs were viewed as a technological curiosity, but not any more. ATMs are now found almost everywhere, and ATM cards have become as ubiquitous as the machines they access. You can make deposits, transfer funds, check balances, and access cash 24 hours a day, seven days a week. No more rushing to the bank before closing time. ATM cards are used in conjunction with a unique personal identification number, referred to as a "PIN."

Telephone transfers

Bank customers have been able to transfer funds between accounts or make payments of specific bills by phone for many years. Now, most systems also allow you to access information about checking and savings accounts, as well as loans and certificates of deposit. You can also review recent transactions and leave messages. It's quick, convenient, and cuts down on trips to the bank. You can't make deposits or withdraw cash, however, which limits the usefulness of this strategy somewhat.

Debit cards

Debit cards can be used when shopping to deduct money directly from your bank account to make a purchase. Debit cards eliminate the need to carry a lot of cash. They also offer a self-limiting function—you can't run up a big debt, since once you have exhausted your bank account, your debit card won't work for additional purchases until you replenish your money supply. See Chapter 2 for more advantages and disadvantages of debit cards.

Preauthorized transfers

This increasingly popular method of EFT allows you to have deposits added to, or withdrawals deducted from, your bank accounts automatically when you authorize the bank or other party to do so. You can have wages, social security, dividend and interest payments, and other sources of income sent electronically to your account on a regular basis. The same arrangements can be made for the payment of ongoing routine bills such as mortgage, insurance, utilities, and even things like investments in mutual funds. This strategy eliminates a lot of checks, stamps, and envelopes, and also ensures that bills are paid on time. I've set up a number of preauthorized

Unofficially...
The average bank
cost of process-
ing a paper
check can run
anywhere from
45 cents to $1
(depending on
where you get
your statistics).
In contrast, the
average elec-
tronic fund
transfer costs
between 4 cents
and 20 cents.
Banks love EFTs.

transfers for my own accounts, and I love the convenience. Banks like it too because it eliminates a lot
of expensive hand-processing of checks. Disconti-
nuing automatic debits can be a bit of a hassle,
however, so you might want to find out what the procedure is ahead of time.

PC home banking

A recent addition to this list is PC home banking.
This option comes in two varieties: direct-dial pro-
prietary systems and, increasingly, Internet systems.
These systems allow customers to do all of the things
with their accounts that they can do with preauthorized transfers and telephone transfers—and
more—depending on the sophistication of the software they are using. About 5.8 million Americans
already step into an Internet bank branch regularly,
and this number is expected to increase 26 percent
annually through 2002, according to market
researcher INTECO. As recently as three years ago,
less than two million people banked online, according to the American Bankers Association.

Many consumers like the 24-hour convenience,
speed, and low cost of online banking. Banks like it
for largely the same reasons. It's a win-win situation
for banks and customers alike. I've used a dial-up
system for about two years, and I've grown to like it.
No more waiting until the end of the month to rec-
oncile your account. Want to know if that big check
has cleared your account yet? Dial up, log on, and
you'll know immediately. And with financial software like Quicken and Money, this online information can be instantly integrated into your personal
financial records at home.

The exponential growth of e-commerce in general, along with reduced concerns about security of

credit card numbers and other sensitive data, has encouraged consumer confidence in e-banking. Go to www.bankrate.com and check the online banking directory for a list of dozens of banks that offer online services and for details about the accounts. PC home banking has arrived. "It's definitely the wave of the future," says Sherry Shield, assistant vice president and manager of corporate banking services at the Vermont National Bank.

Online credit cards

The most recent entry of all in the field of electronic money is the online credit card. This phenomenon has seemingly come out of nowhere but is growing exponentially as card issuers chase customers and potential customers into cyberspace. Online credit cards make perfect sense. People who are buying online are going to be comfortable about paying their bills online in a paperless, totally electronic transaction. About 51.3 million U.S. adults are regular users of the Internet, and roughly 6.75 million credit card accounts have already been opened through Internet marketing, according to Brittain & Associates, an Atlanta-based market research firm.

The NextCard, issued by Heritage Bank of Commerce in San Ramon, California, introduced early in 1998, claims to be the "first true Internet Visa." Naturally, you can apply for it online. Your completed application receives a response in less than 30 seconds. That's right, seconds. Upon approval, you are presented with a number of card options with various terms based on your credit profile. It doesn't get much quicker or easier than that.

The NextCard already has lots of competition. The same profusion of choices that have been

Watch Out!
When you are looking for an online credit card, the same rules apply as when you are comparison shopping for regular plastic cards. Check the various fees and features carefully before you pick a card.

available in hard plastic are now increasingly popping up in their electronic versions. As you might expect, MBNA and First USA, two of the biggest plastic card issuers, are already staking their claims to a substantial segment of cybercard-space with a galactic army of offerings. Try www.bankrate.com for an up-to-date listing of online credit cards. Go to "Find the Best Rate for You." Click on Start. Then from the next menu of choices, select "Online Card" from "What Is Your Goal?" You'll be amazed by the choices (also try www.getsmart.com). You'll also be amazed at the huge differences in the various charges and features. Like plastic cards, all online Visa and MasterCards are not created equal. Choose carefully.

Smart cards

So-called smart cards are mainly used in this country in "closed systems," such as college or university campuses or hospital complexes where they are often used much like debit cards. However, you'll be seeing more smart cards soon—a lot more. By 2001, it is estimated 4 billion smart cards will be in use worldwide. Developed back in 1974, smart cards, which now come in various configurations, have an embedded chip that has the ability to store a broad range of information including, but not limited to, credit, debit, electronic cash, consumer loyalty programs, electronic ticketing, secure identification, drivers license, and health care records. I suppose you could consider smart cards to be phone cards on steroids, but we're really talking about a far more advanced and complex system with multiple capabilities. The technology is already widely used in various countries around the world, especially in France and Germany, where millions of these cards have been issued. Smart cards have been tested for general consumer use in this country, most notably at the 1996 Atlanta Summer Olympic Games.

Tests in other locations in the U.S. are ongoing. The potential that smart cards have for boosting electronic fund transfers in general, and Internet banking and commerce in particular, is enormous. Smart cards are the missing link that is needed to complete the electronic money loop. With the right hardware and software, your home computer suddenly becomes an ATM. And we all know how popular ATMs have been. Get the picture? If you'd like to learn more about smart cards, check out www.smartcardintl.com or www.smart-card.com for tons of information.

The Electronic Fund Transfer Act

Okay, with all this e-cash zipping around on fiber-optic cables, what laws offer you protection in the event of problems? The Electronic Fund Transfer Act (EFTA) is the place to look for answers. The law covers one big question related to electronic fund transfers—record-keeping. It points out that you receive a printed receipt for every EFT transaction, whether it's from an ATM or from a credit or debit card purchase at a retail business location. In addition, you receive a complete record of all EFT activity at the end of the month on your bank statement (or potentially every day if you use a PC banking system). Your monthly statement serves as proof of payment to another person or entity, as your record for tax purposes, and as your way of reconciling your transactions with your bank balance, according to the act.

What if your ATM or debit card is lost or stolen? Stuff happens. As I mentioned in Chapter 2, your

Moneysaver
If your bank charges a fee for ATM withdrawals, you'll save money by taking out larger sums of cash less frequently, since the fee is the same, regardless of the amount you withdraw.

liability is limited to $50 if you notify the bank within 2 days of the loss, according to EFTA. That liability jumps to $500 between 2 and 60 days. After that, you could be held liable for the loss of everything in your account, including overdraft protection. Not a pretty prospect. One way to safeguard your ATM and debit cards is to memorize your PIN. Don't write it down on the card or carry it in your wallet. And don't use your birth date or your Social Security number as a PIN. Those are some of the first numbers a crook will try.

So what do you do if you find a mistake on your statement or in your ATM or debit card transaction? The law is specific:

1. Write or call your institution as soon as possible, but at least within 60 days from the date the statement that contains the error was mailed to you. Give your name, your account number, the specific amount in question, and the date of the transaction; and explain why you think there is an error.

2. Your financial institution must investigate the error and resolve it within 45 days. If resolution takes more than 10 business days, your institution generally must credit your account for the amount in question until the matter is resolved.

3. Your financial institution must notify you of the results of its investigation. If there was an error, it must be corrected promptly. If the institution determines that there was no error, it must explain in writing why it feels this is the case. You have the right to ask for copies of any documents relied upon in the investigation.

There is one technical point I need to mention. If a thief makes a cash advance with your stolen credit card (as opposed to your ATM card) at an ATM machine, the governing law is the Fair Credit Billing Act, rather than the Electronic Fund Transfer Act. In this case, you would have to deal with the credit card issuer to resolve the billing problem, even though the crime took place on an ATM machine. (see Chapter 3.)

The Internet

Few people realize that the Internet had its origins back in 1969 as a Defense Department plan to maintain communications in the event of a nuclear attack. Ironically, it would probably take an all-out nuclear war to distract most Americans from using the Internet for what it obviously was really created for—shopping and spending money. This endless universe of electronic Web sites brimming over with everything imaginable (and some stuff that's hard to imagine) is open for business 24 hours a day, seven days a week. Want to buy a unique birthday present at midnight for that special someone? Or a rare book from a bookseller in England? You can. Or perhaps an Elvis painting on black velvet is more to your liking. You'll find that too. You can do it all while at home in your bathrobe. It's a merchant's dream come true, and the package delivery services are pretty happy about it as well.

Unfortunately, all this round-the-clock consumer spending can leave you without a shirt on your back if you're not careful. It's so easy to get carried away with Internet purchases. So while we're exploring the Web, we will not only check out some of the neat stuff that's available but also watch out

Unofficially...
Slightly more men than women shopped online in 1998. E-commerce spending overall was up: one-third of buyers spent $300 or more, according to an Ernst & Young Internet shopping study.

for the spiders lurking in dark corners. They can leave you entangled in debt if you're not careful.

Before we blast off into cyberspace, I'd like to add one slight disclaimer. Trying to write anything in print about the Internet is a perilous venture; things change so quickly. Web sites are notoriously ephemeral. Although I've taken every precaution to ensure that the Web addresses and other site information in this book are accurate, there will likely be a few that have moved, morphed, or just plain vanished by the time you read this. If you can't find something, try one of the many search engines like Yahoo!, Excite, Alta Vista, or MetaCrawler. They'll probably steer you in the right direction. Okay, it's time to climb aboard and strap yourself in. Let's kick this box of microchips we're riding into hyperdrive and see where we end up.

The good...

If you're looking for information about credit and debt, I can't think of a better place for gathering gigabits of data than the Internet. A few words of caution, however. As a savvy Web surfer, you have to realize that the quality of the information you will find online ranges from rock-solid accurate, to questionable, to flat-out wrong or deliberately misleading. You need to distinguish official government archives of laws and regulations from crackpot personal opinion sites, and reputable consumer help organizations from someone who has an agenda or something to sell. Usually the difference is fairly obvious, but sometimes it isn't. Just because you see it on the Net doesn't mean it's true. Having said that, let's look at some of the good stuff.

You don't have to pay a lot of money (or any at all in most cases) to find good, sound advice and information on credit and debt on the Internet. It's everywhere. Click on Money & Investing and then Banking & Credit on a Net portal such as Excite, and you (and your hard drive) will be on your way to information overload. Yahoo!, Alta Vista, and many, many other portals will lead you in the same general direction, although their key words may be a little different. There are simply too many sites to list all of them here, but I'll save you some time wandering around in cyberspace by listing a few of the better ones I've checked out:

- Bank Rate Monitor, at www.bankrate.com, has a wealth of information on current lending rates, auto loans, credit cards, home equity, mortgages, news, payment calculators, credit tips, and much, much more.

- GetSmart, at www.getsmart.com, is a free, objective information service that helps simplify your borrowing decisions. It offers lots of useful information on home loans, debt consolidation, credit cards, auto financing, and student loans.

- CardTrak Online, at www.cardtrak.com, offers extensive lists of the best credit cards, as well as consumer news and commentary.

- Credit Choice, at www.creditchoice.com, claims to be the most comprehensive credit card resource online. They have a lot of information about rates, rebates and offers, affinity cards, quick credit, and secured cards, as well as news articles and general information.

- Debt Counselors of America®, a nonprofit online resource located at www.dca.org, has an unbelievable wealth of information to help people who are in debt or who are trying to stay out of debt. They even host a chat room about credit, debt, and personal finance, and a live call-in Internet radio show.

- Federal Reserve Board, at www.bog.frb.fed.us, is overflowing with information about virtually every activity of the Federal Reserve. The most useful sections for the majority of folks are Consumer Information and Publications.

- Federal Trade Commission, at www.ftc.gov, contains a huge range of information on consumer protection and offers a vast selection of pamphlets on everything from automobiles to credit, and from e-commerce to telemarketing, and much more. Most of their dozens of publications are downloadable online.

- Public Interest Research Groups has a national portal site at www.pirg.org filled with great consumer information and links to most of the state organizations around the country.

- National Consumers League, at www.nclnet. org, is a private, nonprofit advocacy group representing consumers on marketplace and workplace issues. The site has lots of up-to-date consumer warnings and information, as well as an extensive archive of additional material.

- National Foundation for Consumer Credit, at www.nfcc.org, is the national umbrella organization for the regional Consumer Credit Counseling Services. In addition to offering links to local services, it has information on credit reports, bankruptcy, tips on getting out of debt, answers to frequently asked questions, and lists of educational programs.

■ National Institute for Consumer Education, at www.emich.edu/public/coe/nice, is a clearing-house for consumer, economic, and personal finance education that has good information on credit cards, avoiding credit card fraud, getting out of debt, and more.

If you haven't already exceeded your memory capacity with these sites, you can explore countless others and get a lot of great ideas in a relatively short length of time. Significantly, of all the hundreds of chat rooms and thousands of newsgroups I surveyed in cyberspace, practically none were specifically devoted to managing debt. The only ones I could find were the chat room and radio show just mentioned above at Debt Counselors of America®, and several chat rooms sponsored by Debtors Anonymous (see Chapter 11). There may be some others, but I'm not aware of them. People will gladly talk about sex on the Net (and there are lots of sites where you can do that) before they'll discuss their debt problems (more on that in Chapter 8).

The bad...

So far, we've been cruising through safe territory. Now it's time to explore some of the darker sectors of cyberspace. An increasing number of problems are associated with the Internet. I've already alluded to one: misinformation. Some misinformation is just honest error or uninformed opinion, but an enormous amount of absolute rubbish that is presented as fact is also floating around in cyberspace. This situation isn't a major problem for most people, but, unfortunately, enough folks are taken in to make it worrisome. And people who are deeply in debt are prone to believe anything that offers them

Moneysaver
If someone tries to get you to pay for credit advice up front when you're surfing the Internet, you should keep on looking, because good, free advice is plentiful.

the hope of a quick fix for their problems. This is as good a time as any to get one thing straight: There are no (legal) quick fixes to serious debt problems. As long as you remember that, you will be better able to protect yourself from some of the questionable advice that you will encounter on the Net (to say nothing of the ads you will see in other media).

Security issues

Two other issues are increasingly important to consumers: security and privacy. These issues are magnified tenfold online. We'll start with security. The security of online shopping has been a matter of ongoing concern for many years. Although most major reputable Web sites are generally safe, you can't be absolutely sure. There are some steps you can take, however, to increase your chances of avoiding trouble. Your first precaution is to make sure that the site you are visiting uses one of two security methods: Secure Electronic Transaction (SET) or Secure Socket Layer (SSL). Both Microsoft Internet Explorer and Netscape Navigator support these standards. SSL uses encryption to keep your credit card data safe while it's in transit. SET, on the other hand, uses digital signatures to ensure that merchants and Internet credit card users are actually who they say they are.

When you're trying to decide on the safety of a site, your next precaution is to check to see whether it lists customer service phone numbers and a real address (not a P.O. Box number). You should be skeptical about doing business with sites that don't have any obvious physical location. Also check for a country abbreviation at the end of the Web address. If you see something like .au (Australia), or .ru (Russia), or perhaps .vg (British Virgin Islands), for example, tacked on at the end, you might want to be careful because you've just landed offshore. This is especially important if you thought you were dealing with a company located in the U.S.

A Web-based merchant is required to deliver your ordered merchandise within 30 days, unless you are advised otherwise in advance. You should not have to wait for much more than a week. If your goods don't arrive promptly, you should inquire about the status of your order. And *always* pay for it by credit card—not your debit card. This gives you the full protections of the federal credit laws against billing errors and fraud. Check out the Better Business Bureau Online at www.bbbonline.org for more information about safe Web surfing. If you're still not sure about a business site, go to www.bizrate.com where you will find lists of customer evaluations of numerous Web merchants, including a star rating system.

Privacy

One of the Internet's greatest advantages is the vast store of information that is easily available online. At the same time, this gold mine of data is also one of cyberspace's most troubling issues. While much of this information has been around for years, the exponential growth of the Internet has made it far easier to gather (and exploit) that information. For a number of years, privacy rights and civil-liberties groups have decried the ease of access to personal data on the Net. The computer chip manufacturer, Intel, stirred up a hornet's nest of protest when it was revealed in early 1999 that its new Pentium® III processor contained a serial number that could be electronically retrieved upon command. The possibilities of people leaving an even wider electronic

Watch Out!
Pay attention to the two- and three-letter country abbreviations at the end of foreign Web addresses. Most U.S. sites don't have them. Remember that your federal legal protections against billing errors and fraud don't extend overseas.

trail behind them than they already do when surfing the Net was just too much. Intel backed off and essentially disabled the feature. "...Nobody wants to be tracked like a dog," noted *PC Magazine* columnist John C. Dvorak about the questions raised by the incident. "And being tracked is what will happen."

So what can you do to protect your personal data from thieves, hackers, and unscrupulous businesses? You can start by removing your name and e-mail address from your Web browser. Also have your browser warn you when 'cookies' are being deposited on your hard drive by a Web site. Cookies are electronic notations used to identify users, to help the site send a customized page or account information, and other purposes. It's the "other purposes" that worry some people. Some Web sites are very persistent about depositing cookies, and you may decide it's not worth the hassle of trying to defend yourself against them. It's up to you. Check out www.cookiecentral.com for additional information.

Unofficially...
Cookies were first developed by Netscape to make it easier for Internet surfers to visit their favorite Web sites without having to go through a lengthy identification process.

Cyber debt

Before we get into the really bad stuff, here are a few more observations about the perils of the Internet and debt. Some people rail against the Internet as The Source of All Evil. I suppose there's some justification for that view, but they also miss an important point. The Internet is another in a long series of advances in communication technology. It's neither inherently good nor evil. It just depends on how you choose to use (or abuse) it. What is available on the Internet is simply a reflection of the larger society as a whole. But one thing is true about the Internet. It's brought an awful lot of temptation right into your own home. If you're a compulsive spender, or gambler, or investor, or whatever, you need to be careful about your online activities. Using the Internet can become *very* addictive. With the simple click of the mouse, you can loose huge amounts of money in nanoseconds. Those same opportunities to lose money have always been available, of course, it's just more efficient now.

...And the ugly

In almost every spaghetti western ever made, the bad guys are really bad. On the Internet they can be downright ugly. Lon Chaney, the American film actor who stared in *The Hunchback of Notre Dame* (1923) and *The Phantom of the Opera* (1925), was known as "The Man of a Thousand Faces." He was particularly renowned for his ugly faces. Ironically, on the Internet you can't see the faces of the actors who are playing the roles of villains, but they play those ugly parts like the professionals they are. Unlike Chaney, it's the anonymity that makes contemporary cyber-criminals so effective. The Web sites they use as a lure may look enticing, but you need to be on your guard. Even though you can't see them, these slick operators can see you coming from a mile away. And they're ready and waiting.

We've already covered fraud and theft in Chapter 3, but now we're going to focus on the many dangers you need to specifically watch out for online. We're going to be cruising in the vicinity of some of the hungriest black holes in the cyber universe, and they're just waiting to swallow all of your money without a trace. I'll try to give you some navigational aids to keep that from happening.

The top ten frauds

With so many perils to watch out for, it's hard to decide where to begin. I guess we'll start at the top of the list compiled by the National Consumer's League for 1998. What's number one? Online auctions. Auctions were first on the list for 1997, too, at 26 percent of complaints. That figure rose to an alarming 68 percent for 1998. These statistics reflect the exponential increase in popularity of these sites. "More people are online, and more people are getting scammed," says Susan Grant, director of NCL's Internet Fraud Watch. "Consumers need to remember that con artists are everywhere—even in cyberspace." Especially in cyberspace, I would add. It's significant to note that most of the consumer payments that resulted in fraud were made "offline" by check or money order sent to the various businesses in question. "Requesting cash is a clear sign of fraud," warns Grant. Pay with a credit card, she advises, and you can dispute the charge if there is a problem.

Okay, so what is the entire list of top scams? Here they are from NCL, in descending order:

1. Auctions

2. General merchandise sales

3. Computer equipment/software

4. Internet services

5. Work-at-home

6. Business opportunities/franchises

7. Multilevel marketing/pyramids

8. Credit card offers

9. Advance fee loans

10. Employment offers

If most of this sounds familiar, you're right. It's the same old stuff that people have been falling for in telephone, TV, and direct mail scams for years. The crooks have simply adapted to the times and given their tired old schemes a fresh, new, digital look. Regardless of the medium, the basic problem is the ability of the scam artists to take advantage of people's gullibility—or greed. P.T. Barnum (or whoever actually made that famous comment about suckers) was right. Check out www.scambusters.org for lots of additional information about online scams. The dramatic growth of Internet fraud is obvious from this chart.

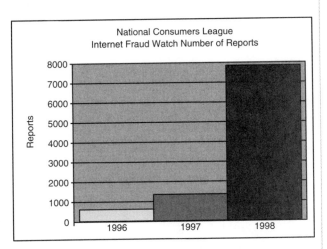

Growth of Internet fraud reports from 1996 to 1998. Source: National Consumers League

Fake Web sites

You might be tempted to think that the preceding top ten list must cover online fraud pretty thoroughly. Think again. The variations are endless. It's actually possible to lose sensitive information like credit card and bank account numbers at fake Web sites. That's right, sites set up specifically to steal your information. "It's easy to duplicate someone else's site and create your own bogus site," notes David Stewart, director at Global Concepts, Inc., of Atlanta in a *Bank Technology News* article. "I'm not a hacker, but in 10 minutes, you could build a site that replicates an existing Web site of a bank."

Here's how this scam works. You think that you're ordering something from a reputable business, but the product never arrives. Later, you discover that your credit card and other information has fallen into the wrong hands. By now, the site has probably vanished. Never, never give out your bank account numbers online. Especially via e-mail. Never. Unscrupulous merchants and other shady individuals can actually raid your accounts once they know those numbers. Some have.

The best way to avoid getting sucked into this black hole is to deal only with established, reputable merchants, especially those who use the Secure Electronic Transaction or Secure Socket Layer methods mentioned earlier. You should also look for a privacy seal of approval from online security organizations like the Better Business Bureau Online (www.bbbonline.com), HonorWeb (www.honorweb.com), or TRUSTe (www.truste.com). Be aware that some scams are very sophisticated.

Avoiding Internet fraud

Trying to steer clear of Internet booby traps can seem like an impossible task. It's not, but you do have to be constantly on guard to avoid getting into trouble. Here are helpful tips from the National Consumers League:

- Do business with those you know and trust.

- Understand the offer. Look carefully at all the information. If you don't understand something, ask for more information. A legitimate company will be glad to provide it.

- Check out the company's or individual's track record. Ask your Better Business Bureau or consumer protection agency for information.

- Ask to have written information mailed to you.

- Take your time. High-pressure sales tactics are often danger signs of fraud.

- Don't judge a Web site by its appearance.

- Beware of "friendly" tips about money-making schemes.

- Know that unsolicited e-mail (spam) is often used by con artists.

- Don't download programs to see pictures, hear music, or get other features from Web sites you're not familiar with. They may contain viruses or other unfriendly programs.

Watch Out!
Bogus credit card offers on the Internet usually want a fee paid up front or want you to send private financial information via e-mail. Don't do it.

This last tip is especially relevant to pornography sites. Some online porn sites count on the fact that most people are reluctant to admit they've visited the sites, to say nothing about being taken advantage of. This creates an ideal environment for scam artists. Whether you decide to visit these sites or not is up to you, but you need to be aware that you are putting yourself at greater risk of being scammed if you do. Don't be fooled by a pretty face.

Where to go for help

If you've been the victim of online fraud, or if you think someone was trying to scam you, report it right away. Your timely report may help others avoid being fleeced. The National Fraud Information

Center is the first place to go for help. The best way to contact them is to call their toll-free number at (800) 876-7060, where you can speak directly with their trained counselors. The NFIC accepts reports about attempts to defraud consumers on the phone or the Internet. Online fraud activity can include promotions found on Web sites, in chat rooms, in newsgroups and bulletin boards, as well as by e-mail.

The NFIC has a Web site at www.fraud.org where you will find an Online Incident Report Form.

You can also report online fraud to the Federal Trade Commission, Consumer Protection Bureau, or the Securities and Exchange Commission Complaint Center. See "Telemarketing and Online Fraud" in the Resource Guide, Appendix B, for more information. Happy surfing.

Just the facts

- Electronic fund transfers can save you a lot of time and trouble, and ensure that your bills get paid on time.

- The Internet can be a shopper's paradise—or a debtor's nightmare, depending on use.

- The Internet is a wonderful source of free information on credit and debt, if you know where to look.

- The possibilities for getting cyber-scammed on the Internet are substantial. Surf with care.

Your Credit History

GET THE SCOOP ON...
Bad reports on good people ▪ Credit bureaus ▪
Obtaining your credit report ▪ Making sense of
your report ▪ Where to go for help

PART II

Your Credit Report

Chapter 5

The first time you look at the information on your credit report, you may be tempted to think you are reading a foreign language and to throw up your hands in despair at the puzzling terms. You may even decide to stop trying to decipher the report and instead pour yourself a tall drink. But your credit report doesn't have to remain a mystery—or drive you to drink, either. If you understand a few basic things about it, your credit report can be quite informative. With a little more knowledge, it can be a downright useful tool to help you maintain, and even improve, your credit rating.

Now, I'm not suggesting that your credit report is scintillating reading. It's not. Reading a good novel (or even a bad one) would be more fun. Nevertheless, the details of your credit history that are reflected in your report are important. Here's why. Even if you always pay your bills on time, it's still possible to be denied credit because of an error (or several errors) in your report. You could even be turned down for a good job because of negative (but erroneous) information that your prospective employer sees in your report. A less-than-perfect

113

report can also mean higher interest rates for loans. If you don't check your report regularly, you have no way of knowing whether it's good or bad.

Gerri Detweiler, the education advisor for Debt Counselors of America® (www.GetOutOfDebt.org) and author of *The Ultimate Credit Handbook*, is adamant about the importance of credit reports. "These days, your credit report is truly one of your most important financial assets," she declares. "It really makes or breaks decisions when it comes to getting loans, mortgages, credit cards, and other types of credit. So, it really plays an important role in your financial life, and you want to make sure that it looks as good as possible." I absolutely agree with her.

In the pages that follow, I'll explain in more detail why your credit report is so vital. We'll also take a look at the "Big Three" reporting agencies—Experian, Equifax, and TransUnion—and see who they are and what they do. I'll explain your rights to review your report and give you details about the many ways you can get a copy. Then I'll go through all the different elements of your report, one at a time, and explain such things as account codes, status codes, and more. Most important of all, I'll help you understand and interpret your credit report. By the time we get done, you are going to know virtually everything you need to know about your report. Then you can settle down with it—and that tall drink—and enjoy both.

Importance of a good credit history

Linda, a woman from the Dallas area, signed up for a credit card offer mainly because of the free airline ticket that was being used as a come-on by the card issuer. Since she had never had any credit problems, she assumed she would automatically get the credit card—and the airline ticket. "Then I got a letter saying that 'based on information we got from the credit bureau, you're rejected,'" she said in a recent *Buffalo News* account of the incident. "I was flipped out."

Apparently, the credit bureau had made a little mistake—listing Linda as a bad credit risk after mixing up her information with someone else's. The problem was eventually resolved, but not without several months-worth of time-consuming and annoying phone calls and letters.

This is just one of hundreds of examples I could offer about why it's important to check your credit report regularly. In Linda's case, no serious, permanent damage was done. But the high incidence of fraud and theft that we looked at in Chapters 3 and 4 should provide an even more compelling incentive to check your report—and check it often. Once a year is probably best. Failure to do so can cost you higher interest rates for loans and make it difficult to rent an apartment, buy a house, or obtain insurance, among other things. Failure to catch a case of identity theft promptly could cost you your good credit rating.

Yet, despite the urgings of consumer advocacy groups, governmental agencies, and even the credit bureaus themselves, many consumers don't bother to check their reports. They wait until they have been denied credit and then they decide to find out why they were turned down. By then, it may be too late, especially if the reason for applying for a loan had a short time horizon associated with it.

Perhaps one reason for this general lack of interest is the fact that many people have only the haziest

Bright Idea
To avoid embarrassment and unnecessary delays, check your consolidated credit report before you make an application for a major loan such as a car or home.

idea about what a credit bureau or agency is. People tend to avoid things they don't understand. But if you're going to become an expert at beating debt, you need to understand at least the basics about credit bureaus.

Credit reporting agencies

First, let's make sure we're clear on the terminology. So far, I've used "credit bureau" and "credit reporting agency" interchangeably. I'll continue to do so, since they mean the same thing. Credit bureau is the more commonly used term.

Okay, what's a credit bureau? One dictionary definition for "bureau" is "a low chest of drawers for use in a bedroom." Obviously, this is the wrong definition. The right one, of course, is "a business establishment for exchanging information, making contacts, or coordinating activities." However, there is one interesting similarity between these two very different definitions. Like the chest of drawers, a credit bureau is a sort of storage place for information (rather than socks and underwear). And, as in the chest of drawers, that information is removed and replaced on a regular basis.

Thus, a credit bureau is essentially a clearinghouse for credit history information provided by credit grantors on how their customers pay their bills. The credit bureau also obtains information about consumers from sources of public record, such as courthouses. All of this information is assembled into a file on each consumer and placed in a computer database. This information is then made available to credit grantors. The information is constantly coming in and going back out again—just like your socks and underwear in the bureau drawers in your bedroom.

There are currently over 1,000 local and regional credit bureaus throughout the United States. Most credit bureaus are either owned by, or have a contractual arrangement with, one of the three major credit reporting agencies in the nation (more on them in a moment). These agencies maintain huge computer databases that contain the records of over 170 million Americans. Credit bureaus generate over a half-billion credit reports a year, according to TransUnion.

Unofficially...
The three major credit bureaus in this country process more than 2 billion items of information from credit grantors each month.
—Associated Credit Bureaus

Why they keep files on you

The credit bureaus gather and then disseminate their information to help credit grantors predict the future performance of potential creditors and to decide whether or not to issue credit. Creditors can include businesses that normally extend credit to individuals and other businesses, financial institutions, retailers, utilities, direct marketers, auto manufacturers, real estate brokers and agents, and many other entities as well.

Clearly, your credit report (or file, or profile, as it is also called) is used by many different businesses and institutions that you regularly come in contact with. That's why your credit report is so important. Technically, the credit bureaus do not "rate" your creditworthiness, although they do provide lenders with scoring that attempts to predict how likely you are to repay your bills. The individual lenders then use their own criteria in addition to the scoring to make a final decision. It's important to understand that the bureaus are not the ones who approve or reject your application for credit; they simply report the information that has been given to them by credit grantors.

Who can see your files?

Clearly, a ton of accurate (but don't count on it) and rather personal information about you is stored in credit bureau databases. Just who has access to your files? According to the Fair Credit Reporting Act (FCRA), a credit reporting agency may furnish a consumer report under the following circumstances:

- At your written request. This also applies to requests made by phone and, increasingly, via the credit bureaus' Web sites.

- When requested by a credit grantor that is considering extending credit to you, or in connection with the review or collection of an account.

- When requested by your employer or potential employer in connection with employment, promotion, reassignment, or retention.

- When requested by an insurance underwriter.

- In connection with a legitimate need for information associated with a business transaction initiated by you.

- In connection with the determination of eligibility for a government license.

- In response to a court order or a federal grand jury subpoena.

This last item could apply to a variety of circumstances but specifically includes cases of child support, where an enforcement agency needs the information in order to determine whether an individual has the resources to make payments. Ten days' advance notice must be sent to the individual via certified mail, however, before the information can be accessed and reviewed for this purpose.

There are also a number of circumstances under which people may *not* see your report. For example, your report cannot be used by attorneys, except in the case of an attempt to collect on debts. Your report may not be used to evaluate an insurance claim, nor can it be accessed by your ex-spouse. Finally, your report cannot be used for general marketing purposes. However, a gaping loophole exists in this rule, one that you could fly a jumbo jet through: prescreening.

Prescreening

In prescreening, a credit bureau compiles or edits a list of consumers who meet specific criteria provided by, say, a credit card company. The list is then provided to the company or, perhaps, a third-party mailing service (to circumvent some thorny issues about access), in order to solicit specific consumers for credit products (usually credit cards). This is where most of the zillions of preapproved credit card offers that fill your mailbox come from. Is this a legal use of your credit information? Well, more or less. It depends on who you talk to. The credit industry says yes. Some privacy rights and civil liberties groups are not convinced.

Whatever you may think of the practice, you can do something about prescreening. If you're tired of receiving the usual flood of promotional material, the most recent revision of the Fair Credit Reporting Act requires that credit bureaus publicize a toll-free number that you can call to block your file from prescreening for credit or insurance purposes. You need to be aware, however, that if you opt out of prescreening, you will not have the chance to compare credit offerings as often as you used to. It's your decision.

Information on how to opt out of prescreening is available at the credit bureaus' individual Web sites (see "Credit Bureaus" in the Resource Guide, Appendix B). You may also call the Option Out request line at (888) 567-8688. You will be given the choice of opting out for two years, resuming pre-screening if you previously opted out, or having your name permanently removed from the prescreening list. If you choose the last option, you will be sent a written confirmation form. Happily, this telephone number is good for all three of the major credit bureaus, so there's no need to make separate calls to each of them, which is a nice convenience.

One final point needs to be made about this sub-ject. Preapproved offers, once made, supposedly cannot be withdrawn by the lender arbitrarily, as long as nothing has changed in your credit report that would justify the withdrawal. A preapproved offer is a preapproved offer. Or at least that's what you'd think. The recent changes to the FCRA have muddied the waters somewhat on this issue, making it easier for credit grantors to wiggle out of what was originally supposed to be a "firm" offer. If you are turned down for a "preapproved" solicitation that you have accepted, and are unable to resolve the sit-uation with the credit issuer, you have the right to complain to the Federal Trade Commission (see "Federal Agencies" in the Resource Guide, Appendix B).

The big three credit agencies

As I mentioned previously, the three main credit bureaus in this country are: Equifax, Experian, and TransUnion. We'll look at all three. The oldest of them is Equifax, which dates from 1899 when two brothers from Tennessee, Guy and Cator Woolford, decided to set up their small credit information shop in Atlanta. They named it the Retail Credit Company, and it has been located in Atlanta ever since. The company became Equifax in 1975.

Today, Equifax is an international transaction processing and electronic commerce giant that does business in five continents and handles or facilitates more than 10 million online transactions per day for 300,000 customers around the world. Equifax employs more than 14,000 people in 18 countries and has sales in 50 countries. Annual sales are around $1.6 billion. The company claims to be the largest provider of consumer information in the U.S.

The second of the big credit bureaus is Experian, which was created when TRW sold off its Information Systems & Services in September 1996. The following month, the Great Universal Stores PLC purchased Experian and merged the company with the CCN Group of Nottingham, United Kingdom. The CCN Group was Europe's largest credit reference agency. The following year, the CCN Group changed its name to Experian.

Today, Experian, with its headquarters in Orange, California, is a major supplier of consumer and business credit, direct marketing, automotive, and real estate information services. The company says it is first or second in every market that it serves. Experian employs more than 11,000 people in the United States, the United Kingdom, continental Europe, Africa, and Asia Pacific. Annual sales are over $1.6 billion.

The third member of the triumvirate is TransUnion, which is headquartered in Chicago. TransUnion is a primary source of credit information. It offers risk and portfolio management services

Bright Idea
If you find incorrect information on your credit report from one of the main credit bureaus, it's a good idea to then get a copy from the other two bureaus as well. The information contained in these reports may not be the same, and you may have additional errors that need to be corrected.

to a broad range of industries and businesses that routinely evaluate credit risk or verify information about their customers. TransUnion lists financial and banking services, insurance agencies, retailers, collection agencies, communication and energy companies, and hospitals among its many clients.

TransUnion has offices nationwide, as well as regional consumer relations centers in Fullerton, California, and Springfield, Pennsylvania. More than 200 independent credit bureaus also operate in the company's network. In addition, the company has offices, either its own or through alliances and partnerships, in Canada, Chile, Italy, Kenya, Mexico, the Netherlands, Puerto Rico, and South Africa.

Before we move on, I should note that you can also get a consolidated credit report that combines the information offered by the Big Three. It can be ordered from credit.com at their Web site at www.credit.com at a cost of $29.95 (see "Credit Report Consolidators" under "Credit Bureaus" in the Resource Guide, Appendix B, for additional contact information).

Your rights to review your report

Okay, now we know who's got all your credit information. But how do you get your hands on it? Obtaining a copy of your credit report used to be a real chore. The credit bureau system tended to be very decentralized, which made it a lot harder to decide where to go and who to contact. Trying to review or fix your report was often a significant test of persistence and patience. The recent passage of the Fair Credit Reporting Act (FCRA), and changes within the Big Three, have improved the situation considerably.

Unofficially... Although hundreds of credit bureaus, generally known as "affiliates," are scattered across the country, getting your credit report is actually fairly easy. You need only request it from one of the "Big Three," either Equifax, Experian, or TransUnion, or from a credit report consolidator like credit.com.

The Fair Credit Reporting Act

The Fair Credit Reporting Act is your key to unlocking the credit bureau door that stands between you and your information. Before the passage of the FCRA, obtaining your credit report was difficult. Even after the FCRA, it was often a frustrating exercise. Happily, things have changed for the better. The Big Three have consolidated most of their customer service operations into a few large national centers and generally have made themselves far more accessible with features like toll-free numbers, more customer-service representatives, and extensive Web sites. The credit reports themselves have been simplified somewhat in an effort to make them more readable and useful.

The most recent update to the Fair Credit Reporting Act, which took effect in 1997, includes provisions that spell out your rights related to your credit report. Here's a summary of some of them:

- You must be told if information in your file has been used against you. Anyone who uses information from a consumer reporting agency to deny your application for credit, insurance, or employment must tell you and must give you the name, address, and phone number of the agency that provided the report.

- You have the right to find out what is in your file (more on this in a moment).

- You have the right to dispute inaccurate information. Inaccurate information must be corrected or deleted (more on this in Chapter 6, "Repairing Your Credit Report").

- You have the right to dispute inaccurate items with the source of the information (see Chapter 6).

- Outdated information may not be reported. A credit bureau may not use negative information that is more than 7 years old (10 years for Chapter 7 bankruptcies), although information that is not derogatory may stay on your report indefinitely.

- Access to your file is limited to those people having a need recognized by the FCRA— usually to consider an application with a creditor, insurer, employer, landlord, or other business.

- Your consent is required for reports that are provided to employers or for reports that contain medical information.

- You have the right to exclude your name from credit bureau lists for unsolicited credit and insurance offers (the prescreening mentioned earlier).

- You have the right to sue for damages in state or federal court if a credit bureau or (in some cases) a supplier of data violates the FCRA. You may also be able to collect legal fees and punitive damages.

In addition, when you close an account, the creditor must notify the credit bureaus, and they must report the account closed at your request. There are other provisions of the FCRA that relate mainly to correcting or adding information to your credit report. We'll look at them in more detail in Chapter 6.

How to request a copy

At your request, according to the FCRA, a credit bureau must give you the information in your file and must list everyone who has requested it recently.

There is no charge for the report if you have been denied credit because of information supplied by the bureau, and if you request it within 60 days. You are also entitled to one free report every 12 months upon request if you certify that (1) you are unemployed and plan to seek employment within 60 days, (2) you are on welfare, or (3) your report is inaccurate due to fraud. Otherwise, you may be charged up to $8 in most states.

However, if you live in Colorado, Georgia, Massachusetts, Maryland, New Jersey, or Vermont, you're entitled to a free report (two in Georgia) every year. Call Experian at (888) 397-3742, TransUnion at (800) 888-4213, or Equifax at (800) 685-1111 to get one. You can also request the free report by writing (see "Credit Bureaus" in the Resource Guide, Appendix B). The Web sites don't generally work for the freebies.

Regardless of how you request your report, you'll be asked to supply some basic information. This typically includes your full name (including maiden name or designations such as senior or junior or I, II, and so on); your spouse's name; your Social Security number; your current address and previous address, including zip codes; and your date of birth. You'll also have to sign your written request.

I conducted my own unofficial test to see how the Big Three would measure up. Equifax receives the prize for getting my report to me in eight days from the date I called and requested it. The one-page report was reasonably clear and was accompanied by a cover letter with specific additional information for Vermont residents. Also included was a sample credit file with explanations of the various codes

Watch Out!
When you request your credit report from a credit bureau, be sure to fill out your identifying data completely and, if appropriate, include your "generational information," such as Sr., Jr., I, II, and your middle initial. If you don't, you may receive the wrong report.

used in the report, as well as frequently asked questions with answers. A basic summary of billing rights and a Research Request Form (for notifying Equifax about errors) rounded out the packet. I didn't need the latter, since there were no mistakes in the report.

For obvious reasons, my major credit card account numbers (minus their last four digits) were included on the report to help identify which accounts were which. However, this is why you should never give out your card's last four digits (or any of them for that matter) to someone who is asking for some sort of "account or identity confirmation"—especially over the phone. If your credit report information has somehow fallen into the wrong hands, the thief has virtually everything needed to steal your identity (see "Identity Theft" in Chapter 3). I received my report from TransUnion (actually from an affiliate in Buffalo) 11 days after it was ordered. It was basically in the same format as the Equifax report but contained much more information and came to three pages. It had a listing for a Sears account that I hadn't used for seven years (which I have since closed) and for another account that wasn't mine. The report used fewer codes and spelled things out, so it was a little easier to understand. It was accompanied by the same sort of supplemental material as the Equifax report.

My Experian credit report arrived last—13 days after I ordered it. However, it was perhaps the most detailed of all, containing eight pages of data. Like the TransUnion report, the information was spelled out thoroughly and did not rely on code letters or numbers. The dormant Sears account was listed, as well as the account that didn't belong to me. The report contained basically the same supporting information that was supplied by the other two bureaus. Overall, I thought the Big Three did a pretty good job.

Standard credit report elements

Along with the centralization and consolidation that has taken place in the credit bureau arena in recent years, there has also been an effort to standardize the reports and bring a measure of uniformity to them. Consequently, this description of the standard elements of a credit report will generally cover a report from any of the major agencies. So, what will you find in your report? Let's take a look:

Consumer identifying information

At the top of your report, you'll see your personal identification information. This section includes your name, current and previous addresses, Social Security account number, date of birth, your telephone number, and your employment information.

Public records

Next, you'll see your public record information (if any) from local, state, and federal courts. This includes such unhappy items as liens, bankruptcies, foreclosures, judgments, and so on. Past-due child support may also be included.

Collection agency account information

The Collection Agency Account Information section details accounts (if any) that have been turned over to a collection agency.

Credit account information

This section lists your credit accounts and gets a little more complex, especially if you have a lot of open credit accounts. I've included a sample credit

Unofficially...
Your credit file doesn't actually exist on paper until someone requests it. Then the central computer searches its database and generates your report.

Sample credit file from Equifax.

How to Read Your Credit File

SAMPLE CREDIT FILE

This section includes your name, current and previous addresses and other identifying information reported by creditors.

Personal Identification Information

Your Name
123 Current Address
City, State 00000

Social Security #: 123-45-6789
Date of Birth: April 10th, 1940

Previous Address(es)
456 Former Rd. Atlanta, GA 30000
P.O. Box XXXX Savannah, GA 40000

Last Reported Employment: Engineer, Highway Planning

This section includes public record items obtained from local, state and federal courts.

Public Record Information

Lien Filed 03/93; Fulton CTY; Case or Other ID Number-32114; Amount-$26667; Class-State; Released 07/93; Verified 07/93

Bankruptcy Filed 12/92; Northern District Ct; Case or Other ID Number-673HC12; Liabilities-$15787; Personal; Individual; Discharged; Assets-$780

Satisfied Judgment Filed 07/94; Fulton CTY; Case or Other ID Number-898872; Defendant-Consumer; Amount-$8884; Plaintiff-ABC Real Estate; Satisfied 03/95; Verified 05/95

This section includes accounts that creditors have turned over to a collection agency.

Collection Agency Account Information

Pro Coll (800) xxx-xxxx

Collection Reported 05/96; Assigned 09/93 to Pro Coll (800) XXX-XXXX Client - ABC Hospital; Amount-$978; Unpaid; Balance $978; Date of Last Activity 09/93; Individual Account; Account Number 787652JC

This section contains both open and closed accounts.

1 The credit grantor reporting the information.
2 The account number reported by the credit grantor.
3 See explanation below.
4 The month and year the credit grantor opened the account.
5 Number of months account payment history has been reported.
6 The date of last payment, change or occurrence.
7 Highest amount charged or the credit limit.
8 Number of installments or monthly payment.
9 The amount owed as of the date reported.
10 The amount past due as of the date reported.
11 See explanation below.
12 Date of last account update.

Credit Account Information

Company Name	Account Number	Whose Acct	Date Opened	Months Reviewed	Date of Last Activity	High Credit	Terms	Balance	Past Due	Status	Date Reported
1	2	3	4	5	6	7	8	9	10	11	12
Department St.	32114	J	10/86	36	9/97	$950		$0		R1	10/97
Bank	1004735	A	11/86	24	5/97	$750		$0		I1	4/97
Oil Company	541125	A	6/86	12	3/97	$500		$0		O1	4/97
Auto Finance	529778	I	5/85	48	12/96	$1100	$50	$300	$200	I5	4/97

Previous Payment History: 3 Times 30 days late; 4 Times 60 days late; 2 Times 90+ days late
Previous Status: 01/97 - I2; 02/97 - I3; 03/97 - I4

This section includes a list of businesses that have received your credit file in the last 24 months.

Companies that Requested your Credit File

09/06/97 Equifax - Disclosure	08/27/97 Department Store	
07/29/97 PRM Bankcard	07/03/97 AM Bankcard	
04/10/97 AR Department Store	12/31/96 Equifax - Disclosure ACIS 123456789	

Whose Account	Status Type of Account	The following inquiries are NOT reported to businesses:
Indicates who is responsible for the account and the type of participation you have with the account. J = Joint I = Individual U = Undesignated A = Authorized User T = Terminated M = Maker C = Co-Maker/Co-Signer B = On behalf of another person S = Shared	O = Open (entire balance due each month) R = Revolving (payment amount variable) I = Installment (fixed number of payments) **Timeliness of Payment** 0 = Approved not used; too new to rate 1 = Paid as agreed 2 = 30+ days past due 3 = 60+ days past due 4 = 90+ days past due 5 = Pays or paid 120+ days past the due date; or collection account 6 = Making regular payments under wage earner plan or similar arrangement 7 = 8 = Repossession 9 = Charged off to bad debt	**PRM** - This type of inquiry means that only your name and address were given to a credit grantor so they could offer you an application for credit. (PRM inquiries remain on file for 12 months.) **AM or AR** - These inquiries indicate a periodic review of your credit history by one of your creditors. (AM and AR inquiries remain on file for 12 months.) **EQUIFAX, ACIS or UPDATE** - These inquiries indicate Equifax's activity in response to your request for either a copy of your credit file or a request for research. **PRM, AM, AR, Equifax, ACIS, Update and INQ** - These inquiries do not appear on credit files businesses receive, only on copies provided to you.

Form 102631-8-98 USA

file from Equifax to help explain the various elements.

Some credit reports, like the ones I received from TransUnion and Experian, spell out the explanations and don't use the code numbers and letters shown on the example. Regardless of which of the Big Three you get your report from, it will contain the same basic data. "Company Name (1)" is the first item and refers to the credit grantor who reported the information. The second item, "Account Number (2)," is self-explanatory. "Whose Account (3)" indicates who is responsible for the account and the type of participation you have in the account. This section may contain the following letter keys:

J = joint account

I = individual account

U = undesignated account

A = authorized user

T = terminated account

M = maker

C = comaker or cosigner

B = on behalf of another person

S = shared account

"Date Opened (4)" is the date the account was opened by the credit grantor. "Months Reviewed (5)" is the number of months that the payment history has been reported. "Date of Last Activity (6)" is the date of the last payment, change, or occurrence. "High Credit (7)" refers to the highest amount you have charged or the credit limit for the account. "Terms (8)" refers to the number of installments or monthly payments. "Balance (9)" is the amount you owed as of the date of the report. "Past Due (10)" is the amount on the account that was past due as of the date of the report. "Status (11)" refers to the type of account listed and how promptly you make your payments, sometimes described by a letter followed by a number—R1, for example. Here's what the codes for each type of account mean:

O = open account (the entire balance is due each month)

R = revolving account (payment amount varies)

I = installment account (fixed number of payments)

And here are the meanings for the timeliness of payment numbers:

    0 = approved but not used (too new to rate)

    1 = paid as agreed

    2 = 30 plus days past due

    3 = 60 plus days past due

    4 = 90 plus days past due

    5 = pays or paid 120 plus days past the due date, or a collection account

    7 = making regular payments under a wage earner plan or similar (credit counseling-type) arrangement

    8 = repossession

    9 = charged off to bad debt

Finally, the "Date Reported (12)" is the date the account information was last updated. There may also be a brief summary of your payment history at the bottom of the Credit Account Information section detailing the number of times you were late in making payments in the various timeliness categories just mentioned.

Inquiries

Inquiries, the final section of your report, gives a listing of the companies that have requested your credit file within the last 24 months for employment purposes and within 12 months for other reasons. It gives the date of the request, the name of the company, and the reason for the request. The letter codes for the three main categories are:

- PRM, or promotional—Only your name and address are given to a credit grantor so they can offer you an application for credit or other promotion (prescreening).

- AM, or account management; AR, or account review—This indicates a periodic review of your credit history by one of your creditors.

- ACIS or UPDATE (or name of credit bureau)—These inquiries are your credit bureau's activity in response to your request for a copy of your report or for research into errors.

PRM, AM, AR, ACIS, and UPDATE inquiries do not appear on the credit files that businesses receive. They are included only on the copies given to you by the credit bureau. I was appalled at the number of promotional inquiries that had been made on my report and have since opted out of pre-screening.

Your credit report will usually contain information on your charge accounts at large to mid-sized department stores and information on bank loans, auto loans, and student loans paid to a bank. In addition, your report will almost always include all your major credit cards, accounts at major retailers, and finance company loans. However, your accounts with gasoline companies, local utilities, landlords, physicians, hospitals, and lawyers will almost never appear unless they have been turned over for collection.

Understanding your report

Now that you know what's in your report, it's important to understand which elements are the most important—in both positive and negative terms—to prospective lenders. Frankly, your payment history is the main element that most lenders pay attention to. That's why it's so important to pay your accounts on time. But some of the other items listed on your

Watch Out!
If you don't recognize some of the names of companies who have made inquiries on your account, you might want to check for more information to make sure your account information has not been illegally accessed.

report count more than others. Here are some of the key items.

Positive information

Having a major credit card such as American Express, Discover, MasterCard, or Visa is probably the best credit report reference you can have. Having your account paid on time on a regular basis is better still. If you want to build a superior credit rating, getting one of these cards will be a big help—as long as you keep your account current.

Department store credit cards are not viewed as favorably by a prospective lender because they are easier to get and have lower credit limits. Gasoline company cards are hardly ever listed and aren't much use in establishing a good credit rating. Debit cards are never reported and do not help you build credit. See Chapter 1 for how to apply for a credit card.

Another item that lenders look for is stability. Paying your bills on time is considered a strong sign of stability. That's why it's so important for the status section of your credit report to show that you regularly make your payments "as agreed" or "never late," rather than 30, 60, or 90 days late. A black mark in this section will almost certainly cause you problems with your credit rating.

The length of time you have lived at your current address and the length of your current employment are additional aspects of stability that lenders pay attention to. If you are living a nomadic existence, you may have trouble establishing a good credit rating.

Lenders also may consider the type of employment you have, giving higher marks for a professional or managerial position over an entry-level manual job. As a practical matter, no one moves up overnight from flipping burgers at a fast-food joint to becoming an investment banker. So, the main item over which you have control is the steadiness of your employment history, and that will be reflected in the Personal Identification Information section of your credit report.

One final key area that lenders scrutinize on your report is your financial responsibility information contained in "Whose Account" or "Responsibility" in the Credit Account Information section. If you hold an individual or joint account, that will be a valuable credit reference.

Negative information

On the other hand, if you are merely an authorized user of an account, this won't help your credit rating, because you are not legally responsible for the repayment of the debt. See "Credit Issues for Women" in Chapter 1 for suggestions on how to fix this problem. There are some other items that may be on your report that won't be helpful when you are applying for credit.

One major item that prospective lenders don't want to see is delinquent child-support payments. They view this situation as a strong indication of financial irresponsibility. They're probably right. What's more, the fact that child-support payments take precedence in bankruptcy court over other consumer loans makes anyone with these delinquent payments on their credit report particularly unattractive to a lender. The increasingly aggressive stance that many states have taken in recent years regarding child-support scofflaws increases the

66
Judgments are a
particular prob-
lem because the
credit report
rarely lists, and
the scoring sys-
tem may not
take into
account, the
type or amount
of the judgment.
—Gerri
Detweiler, *The
Ultimate Credit
Handbook*
99

chance that this kind of information will end up on your report if you aren't staying current with your payments.

Finally, if your report contains recent listings of collection accounts, write-off or charge-off accounts, legal judgments, tax liens, or bankruptcy, you are undoubtedly going to have problems. These ugly stains on your record will follow you around like your dog when it has run into the wrong end of a skunk. A whole bathtub full of tomato juice won't be able to wash away the nasty odor they will impart to your credit report. Bankruptcy, in particular, will haunt you and your credit history for 7 years (for a Chapter 13 bankruptcy), and for 10 years (for a Chapter 7 bankruptcy). Regardless of the type of bankruptcy, you will have major problems reestablishing good credit for many years to come. See Chapters 13 and 14 for more on bankruptcy.

Need help? Contact the credit bureau

According to the FCRA, the credit bureaus are required to assist you in understanding your report. So, if you don't understand something or can't figure out how to deal with a situation on your credit report, check out the frequently asked questions (FAQs) at the credit bureaus' Web sites: Equifax, www.equifax.com; Experian, www.experian.com; TransUnion, www.transunion.com. If that doesn't resolve the matter, call one of the credit bureau's consumer assistance representatives. Contact Equifax at (888) 909-7304, Experian at (888) 397-3742, and TransUnion at (800) 916-8800. Your credit report may list a different customer service phone number, in which case you should use that one.

Just the facts

- It's important to check your credit report regularly.
- Getting a copy of your report is easy.
- Your payment history is the main item that lenders look at in your credit report.
- Collection and charge-off accounts, legal judgments, tax liens, and bankruptcy will severely damage your credit rating.

GET THE SCOOP ON...
What to look for when you review your report ▪
Credit repair services ▪ How to correct mistakes
on your report ▪ Divorce and your credit report
▪ When a credit monitoring service is useful

Repairing Your Credit Report

A standing joke in the credit industry used to be that "TRW," the name of a credit reporting company, stood for "The Report's Wrong." There was some justification. In 1991, for example, TRW mistakenly listed every property owner in Norwich, Vermont as being delinquent on their taxes. Norwich residents were not amused.

As the weeks went by, it became apparent that the problem was not confined to Norwich. All told, residents of 22 Vermont communities were affected by errors that were ultimately traced to a Georgia-based TRW subcontractor. The State of Vermont sued TRW. As the investigation into the matter continued, the problem spilled over into Maine, New Hampshire, and Rhode Island, as well. The lawsuits multiplied. TRW eventually removed all tax lien information from its records for each of those states, including Vermont.

TRW is no longer in the credit reporting business. Nevertheless, the phenomenon of errors in credit reports (regardless of who prepares them)

Chapter 6

137

continues to plague consumers and the industry. Some consumer groups have claimed for years that as many as half of all credit reports have mistakes in them. More recently, a U.S. Public Interest Research Group (PIRG) study concluded that nearly one-third of credit reports contain serious errors that could cause consumers to be denied access to mortgages, auto loans, and credit cards.

Not surprisingly, the credit industry disagrees. According to a 1992 Arthur Andersen & Co. study that reviewed 111,000 credit reports, only 0.2 percent of people had been denied credit because of inaccurate information. The Associated Credit Bureaus, a trade organization that represents credit reporting agencies, posted a response at its Web site concerning the U.S. PIRG study: "It stretches all credibility to conclude that these credit risk decisions are being made based on data that is as incorrect as U.S. PIRG would want people to believe." On the other hand, in an earlier study, Consolidated Information Services, an independent credit bureau, not a consumer lobbying group, turned up an overall credit report error rate of 42 to 47 percent.

So, who is to be believed? The actual figures probably fall somewhere in the middle of these various opinions. We could argue about the statistics until the cows come home, but the main point is that mistakes are made on credit reports all the time. And the increasing incidence of identity theft has exacerbated the situation.

In this chapter, we'll move beyond the statistics and I'll show you what specific problems you should look out for on your report. Then I'll tell you how to fix (and how not to fix) any errors that you might find. We'll take a look at the little-used, but potentially valuable, "consumer statement" section of your credit history, and we'll also revisit the topic of divorce and how it can affect your credit report. Finally, I'll give you the lowdown on credit monitoring services.

Reviewing your credit report

As I mentioned in Chapter 5, the Fair Credit Reporting Act (FCRA) gives you the right not only to review your credit report but to correct it as well. We've already gone over the basic elements of your report. Now we will look at the specific items lurking in your data that can actually cause you problems, and what you can and can't do about them.

Is it really you?

You know who you are. But does the credit bureau? Maybe. Maybe not. It's not unusual for portions of other people's credit information to get mixed up with yours, especially if you have a common name, or if there are several generations of people in the same family with almost identical names. This phenomenon is known as "comingling" in the industry, though you might be tempted to call it a pain in the butt. However you refer to it, the best way to avoid this problem is to be extremely careful when you fill out credit information; include your full name, with generational data, if appropriate. It's important to let the credit bureau know if this situation occurs on your report, so they can take steps to correct it and avoid the problem in the future.

Accounts that aren't yours

Incorrectly listed accounts are usually due to cases of mistaken identity. It's possible that an account you don't recognize may belong to a relative, or to a total stranger with the same name. It's also possible that a mystery account (or accounts) may be due to fraud. Regardless of the reason, it's important to question these entries promptly with the credit bureau before things get out of hand. Especially if the accounts are past due.

Legal actions that aren't yours

Occasionally, the information listed in the Public Information section of your report may be incorrect. Since this data is almost always negative in nature, you need to get this type of problem cleared up right away. Again, this may be a case of mistaken identity. Whatever the cause, you may have to petition the court in question to resolve the situation.

"Closed by consumer" accounts

It's not unusual for accounts that you have closed at some time in the past to simply be listed as "closed." As I've mentioned before, it's a good idea to have accounts that you have personally closed be listed as "closed by consumer," since too many closed accounts without any further explanation can become a negative factor on your credit rating.

Watch Out!
Correcting erroneous listings in the late payments section of your credit report is especially important because this information can have a serious negative impact on your credit rating and your ability to get a loan.

Incorrect late payments

If any information about late payments is wrong, make sure you correct it, especially if there are too many late payments listed or if the number of days past due is incorrect.

Duplicate submissions

Your credit report may show more than one listing for the same account. This is usually due to carelessness—such as a transposed account number—on someone's part, or confusion caused during a bank merger. Check all your account listings carefully to ferret out these kinds of errors.

Closed accounts

Another area that can be a real problem are accounts that have been paid off and closed but are still listed on your report. This is especially vexing if the account contains negative information, such as late payments or collections. The account has been paid in full, yet it's still there, coming back to haunt you. You may actually get rejected for credit because of an old account like this. Many people are under the mistaken impression that once an account is paid off, that's the end of it. Wrong. Legally, the credit bureaus may keep negative information, even on closed accounts, for up to seven years. And they probably will. Unfortunately, there is nothing you can do to remove this information, as long as it's accurate (more on this in a moment).

It's also possible that you may have had years of good payment history on an account, say a gasoline company credit card, that was never listed on your credit report. Then, when you had a temporary problem paying your bills for three or four months and were late on your payments, due to illness perhaps, this negative information promptly shows up on your credit history. "Not fair," you say. Maybe not. But it's legal. Creditors are not required to post positive information. You can ask them, but they don't have to. We'll cover this situation in more detail shortly.

Correcting mistakes

Considering the fact that creditors report billions of pieces of information, on tens of millions of people, to credit bureaus every year, it's not surprising that mistakes pop up now and then. Frankly, it's downright difficult to keep track of so many people who move, change their names, or get divorced. Mistakes happen. Correcting those mistakes used to be a major hassle, requiring that you track down and correct credit report errors with each of the major credit bureaus.

With the passage of the latest version of the Fair Credit Reporting Act (FCRA), however, making corrections is a lot easier. The law requires the credit bureaus to share disputed information. Thus, if your information is disputed and corrected on one report, it is supposed to be fixed on the reports of the other two bureaus as well. This is a vast improvement—in theory. In practice, it has not yet been fully implemented. Nevertheless, many of the current improvements are due to a system developed in 1995 by the Associated Credit Bureaus called Automated Consumer Dispute Verification. Disputes are now checked and cross-checked electronically.

Okay, so how do you fix your credit report? There are two approaches that you can take. One method makes sense; the other does not. This is one of those rare situations in which your choices are fairly clear. I've already briefly mentioned that credit repair services are not a good way to deal with your credit problems. I want to reemphasize that point before we get into the details of correcting your own credit report. The do-it-yourself method is the sensible approach. The credit repair company method makes no sense. Here's why.

Unofficially...
The new Automated Consumer Dispute Verification system employed by the major credit bureaus has cut the time for resolving consumer disputes from weeks to days.

Credit repair services

You've seen the ads on TV, heard them on the radio, read them in magazines, and removed them from your mailbox. "Credit Problems? No problem! We can erase your bad credit—100 percent guaranteed!" And now, increasingly, your e-mail inbox is filled with this junk too. And I mean junk.

The scam artists who promote this stuff try to convince you that they can magically erase negative information on your credit history so that you can get a credit card, auto loan, home mortgage, or possibly even a better job. Don't believe it. And don't waste your hard-earned money (that's already in short supply) on something you can do for yourself for free, or at very little cost. I've said this before, but it bears repeating: Only time and a deliberate, steady repayment history can correct a bad credit rating. No one can legally remove accurate negative information from your credit report. No one. And everything that a for-profit credit repair company or clinic can do for you legally, you can do for yourself. Or, if you do want help, you can turn to one of the many non-profit credit counseling services (see Chapter 11).

But that's not what you'll hear from the credit repair services. Most of these companies promise the moon but rarely deliver anything of real value. Worse yet, they're expensive. They sometimes charge hundreds, even thousands, of dollars. Consumer groups and state and federal agencies have been warning people about the perils of credit repair clinics for years. Yet folks with credit problems keep on getting taken for a ride. A few clinics may actually help some people rebuild their credit, but they are definitely in the minority. Fortunately, there are early warning signs that should tip you off about a questionable credit repair offer. According to the Federal Trade Commission, beware of companies that:

■ Want you to pay for credit repair services before any services are provided;

- Do not tell you your legal rights and what you can do yourself—for free;

- Recommend that you not contact a credit bureau directly;

- Suggest that you try to invent a "new" credit report by applying for an Employer Identification number to use instead of your Social Security number, or;

- Advise you to dispute all information in your credit report or to take questionable or illegal actions, such as creating a new identity.

The 1997 Credit Repair Organizations Act (CROA), which was designed to curb the worst abuses in this snake-infested field, stipulates that these organizations must give you a copy of your "Consumer Credit File Rights Under State and Federal Law" before you sign a contract. They also must provide you with a written contract that clearly spells out your rights and obligations. If you do decide to get involved with one of these companies (against my best advice), it's crucial that you at least carefully read and understand what you are signing. The law also says that credit repair companies cannot:

- Make false claims about their services;

- Charge you until they have completed the promised services; or

- Perform any services until they have your signature on a written contract and have completed a three-day waiting period.

This last point is especially important to remember. If you should have a change of heart during the three-day waiting period, you have an absolute right

Watch Out!
If you follow the advice of a credit repair clinic to alter your identification or take any other illegal action, you may be prosecuted. Sometimes the Feds will let unwitting dupes off the hook, but don't count on it.

to cancel the contract without being obligated to pay any fees. And don't let them convince you otherwise.

Finally, it's interesting to note that even the credit bureaus aren't thrilled about the proliferation of credit repair clinics because they tend to swamp the bureaus with repeated, spurious disputes about bad debts in the hope of simply overwhelming the bureaus' ability to effectively deal with them. Fortunately, the CROA has helped to cut down on this problem with a provision that allows credit bureaus to refuse to investigate "frivolous" disputes. In any case, my advice is to steer clear of credit repair clinics altogether.

If you have any questions about a credit repair offer, or if you have already been swindled by one of these scams, you should contact your state's consumer protection office or your state attorney general. You may also file a complaint with the Federal Trade Commission by contacting the Consumer Response Center at (202) FTC-HELP. You can also reach them by writing to the Consumer Response Center, Federal Trade Commission, Washington, D.C. 20580.

Do-it-yourself repairs

In life, certain tasks are best left to a professional—dentistry immediately comes to mind. Repairing your credit report, however, is not one of them. The only sensible way to fix your report is to do it yourself. Here's how. According to the Fair Credit Reporting Act, you have the right to dispute incorrect information in your report. If you do, the Act also says that the credit bureaus and the organizations that provided the original information are responsible for correcting it. This is an important distinction. They are responsible for fixing it—not you. But you *are* responsible for bringing the errors to their attention.

Let's say your report lists a department store bill as being delinquent even though it should have shown a credit for returned merchandise. That's bad enough. But let's also say you are listed as having a $2,689.27 balance on a Star Trek affinity credit card. The problem is, you don't have a Star Trek card. Never had one. You don't even watch the program. So, what do you do?

In the information packet that came with your credit report, the credit bureau should have included a form to make corrections. If it did not, ask for one or simply write a letter explaining the situation. Send the form or the letter, along with copies of any supporting documentation (not the originals) that you have, to the credit bureau.

In your letter or form, be sure to clearly identify each item that you are disputing in the report, explain why you are disputing it, and ask politely for an investigation. Be sure to include your name, address, Social Security number, and phone number(s). Keep a file copy of everything. Then mail the form or letter and documentation to the credit bureau via certified mail, return receipt requested. This will give you proof that the credit bureau received your request. Following is a sample dispute letter.

If you inform the bureau that your file contains inaccurate information, the bureau must investigate the items (normally within 30 days) by presenting your evidence to its sources of information. The

Bright Idea
If you are disputing a listing on your credit report, be sure to hang onto the original copies of everything related to the dispute. You may need them later if things don't go smoothly. Never send the originals.

Date

Your Name
Your Address
Your City, State, Zip Code
Social Security Number

Complaint Department
Name of Credit Reporting Agency
Address
City, State, Zip Code

Dear Sir or Madam:

I am writing to dispute the following information in my file. The items I dispute are also encircled on the attached copy of the report I received. (Identify item(s) disputed by name of source, such as creditors or tax court, and identify type of item, such as credit account, judgment, etc.).

This item is (inaccurate or incomplete) because (describe what is inaccurate or incomplete and why). I am requesting that the item be deleted (or request another specific change) to correct the information.

Enclosed are copies of (use this sentence if applicable and describe any enclosed documentation, such as payment records, court documents) supporting my position. Please reinvestigate this (these) matter(s), and (delete or correct) the disputed item(s) as soon as possible.

Sincerely,

(Your name)
Enclosures: (List what you are enclosing)

Sample Credit
Report Dispute
Letter
*Source: Federal
Trade
Commission*

source must review your evidence and report back to the bureau. The bureau then must give you a written report of the investigation and also a copy of its report if the investigation results in any correction or change. If the investigation does not resolve the dispute, you may add a brief statement to your file (more on that in a moment). Here are some additional provisions of the FCRA related to correcting your credit report:

- Inaccurate information must be corrected or deleted. The credit bureau must remove or correct inaccurate or unverified information from its files, usually within 30 days after you dispute it. This information may not be reinserted into your file unless the original source of the information verifies its accuracy. If this occurs, the bureau must send you a written notice of this action.

- If an item is incomplete, the bureau must complete it. For example, if your report indicates that you were late making payments but does not show that you are no longer delinquent, the bureau must indicate that you are current.

- You also have the right to dispute inaccurate items with the source of the information. If you tell a credit reporter—such as a merchant—that you dispute an item in your report, the merchant may not report that information to a credit bureau without including a notice of your dispute. Once you have notified the source of the error in writing, the source may not continue to report the information if it is incorrect.

- Outdated information may not be reported.
  A credit bureau may not use negative information that is more than seven years old.

However, there are some exceptions to this last point, according to the FTC:

- Bankruptcies can be reported for 7 to 10 years.

- Information reported because of a job application for a position with a salary in excess of $75,000 has no time limit.

- Information reported because of an application for more than $150,000 worth of credit or life insurance has no time limit.

- Information concerning a lawsuit or judgment against you can be reported for seven years or until the statute of limitations runs out, whichever is longer.

- Default information concerning U.S. Government insured or guaranteed student loans can be reported for seven years.

If an investigation into disputed information reveals an error, you may ask that a corrected version of your report be sent to anyone who received your report within the past six months. This is especially important if you were turned down for credit due to inaccurate information.

There is another situation where you may want to try to fix your credit report. It's not unusual for people to be turned down for a loan or credit account because of an "insufficient credit file" or "no credit file." You may actually have a credit history; but if it's mostly with local merchants, credit unions, or gasoline companies, it probably doesn't show up on the national credit bureau radar screen.

Moneysaver
Remember that there is no charge for correcting erroneous information on your credit report or for any investigations or reinvestigations associated with your dispute(s). Why pay anyone else to do this for you when it is free by law?

One way to solve this dilemma is to ask the bureau to add this type of information to future reports. You need to realize that they don't have to do this for you, so ask nicely. And they may charge you a small fee. You also need to be aware that since this information was not regularly reported in the past, it probably won't be kept up-to-date in the future either. But by then, hopefully you will have been able to build a sufficiently solid credit history elsewhere so that you won't need this temporary information any more.

How to use the "consumer statement"

Let's say that the credit bureau admits that they made a little mistake about the Star Trek credit card account and that they have removed your disputed listing for $2,689.27. Nevertheless, you are still going around and around with the department store about the charges for a coat. You returned the coat because it had hidden defective workmanship and you maintain that your account should have been credited. The store says no dice; you still owe them. This is where the consumer statement comes in handy.

The Fair Credit Reporting Act says that you can add a "brief statement" that explains an item you have disputed but that the lender has verified as accurate. This gives you an opportunity to tell your side of the story, and it will become a permanent part of your credit file. The statement is limited to 100 words. And the credit bureau will help you write a clear summary if you need assistance.

These statements are most effective when they are businesslike, straightforward, and specific, such as "I refused to pay for the coat and returned it because it had hidden defects in the sewing on the inside of the left sleeve. The store refused to credit my account." This is not the right place to vent your anger over the situation. If you have any documents or other evidence that supports your side of the dispute, you should mention in the statement that they are available.

I should note here that your FCRA right to add a consumer statement applies only when you are disputing the *accuracy* of the information in your file. It does not apply to explaining whatever *circumstances* may have caused your credit problems. However, Experian and Equifax go beyond the specific rights in the law and allow you to add brief statements explaining a general situation that caused problems with your credit. For example: "I missed making several payments on my account because I was sick for two months last year and could not work."

Now, you probably do not want a prospective lender or employer to know that you were sick last year, especially if you have a chronic ailment that keeps you from working. Does the advantage of the consumer statement relative to your credit report outweigh the possible disadvantage that some of the information might pose for your employment or other prospects? This is a judgment call that you have to make for yourself.

Admittedly, the consumer statement is not a cure-all, although in certain circumstances it may be genuinely helpful. In others, it may not do any good at all. Gerri Detweiler, from Debt Counselors of America®, www.GetOutOfDebt.org, explains: "For credit cards, most applications are reviewed by computer, so chances are that the consumer statement is not going to have much of an effect. But where it can help is if you have a situation where you can talk with the loan officer or the employer or insurance company representative and have someone actually review the report. And if the statement backs up what you have otherwise indicated as being problems with your credit, then it can be helpful." You decide.

Creating your own report

Here is yet another strategy that you might want to consider. Let's say that you have some serious disputed information in your credit report that is not being resolved promptly, and you are running out of time to apply for a car loan or perhaps a home loan. If you basically have good credit that is not being reported accurately by the credit bureau, you might try creating your own report.

I'm not talking about doing something sleazy, such as creating a new identity like some of the credit repair scam artists might suggest. What I *am* suggesting is that you ask some of your lenders who are not listed on your report to write positive letters of recommendation for you. A few may not be willing, but, if you explain your predicament, some will be happy to help. Car leasing companies will sometimes do this if you ask them. At the very least, you will be offering your potential lender some strong new evidence about your value as a new customer. The fact that you are making the extra effort may impress the right people. Deadbeats are not likely to go to this kind of trouble to get a loan. This approach is worth a try.

Your legal rights

In the event that you have tried every reasonable means to resolve your credit report errors—all to no avail—you have the final option of taking legal action. The Fair Credit Reporting Act gives you the right to sue the credit bureaus in the event they willfully violate the Act. This includes breaking the rules about who may see your credit records or not correcting errors in your file. If you have documentary evidence that the information is clearly wrong, you have a pretty good chance of winning your case. You may bring suit in a state or federal court. You are entitled to actual damages, plus punitive damages that the court may allow, if the violation is proven to have been intentional. You may also be entitled to damages and court costs (but not punitive damages) if you can prove negligent noncompliance, where the credit bureau failed to comply with the provisions of the Act.

You need to be aware, however, that these actions can be lengthy, expensive, and time-consuming. And there's no guarantee that you will win. Consequently, I recommend taking legal action only as a last resort. If you do decide to follow this path, I strongly advise you to get the advice of an attorney who is familiar with consumer credit protection laws. The attorney, incidentally, does not have to be from your home state in the case of a federal action. Consumer advocacy groups may be able to point you in the right direction.

Divorce and your credit report

I've already mentioned a number of major credit issues related to divorce in Chapter 1. Now, I'd like to briefly cover a few additional points regarding divorce that relate specifically to your credit report. Separation or divorce was number three on a list of the top ten reasons cited for credit file problems reported to the National Center for Financial Education (NCFE) in San Diego. In fact, about one-third of all calls received on the NCFE's

Unofficially...
If you can prove "willful noncompliance" in a legal action against a credit bureau, you are entitled to compensation for the actual monetary damages from $100 up to $1,000, plus attorney's fees and punitive damages.

credit-correction help line involved individuals whose credit rating had been damaged or whose credit files had problems caused by a former spouse after a divorce or separation agreement.

This number continues to grow, according to NCFE. "In most instances, these individuals allowed their former spouse to 'take over' responsibility for payment of jointly held debts and of future credit purchases as a part of the separation or divorce agreement—which is a mistake," says the NCFE. "The reason is that your creditors are not a part of the divorce agreement and in most instances probably would not approve of the arrangement anyway."

It's not unusual for a judge to divide financial obligations down the middle in a divorce agreement, but a late payment or default on the part of either party will damage the credit rating of the other ex-spouse. As I've already recommended in Chapter 1, pay off and cancel all joint accounts immediately after your divorce.

Credit report monitoring services

I don't know about you, but I've received a number of solicitations in the mail for credit monitoring services in recent years. Some came with the promise of a free credit report as an inducement to join. For a while I wondered if such an offer made sense. Then, I decided to try one. After reviewing the free report and carefully looking at the other benefits, I decided the service wasn't worth the cost.

So, should you consider subscribing to one of these services? It depends. Here's a little background. The first company to offer a service like this was TRW back in 1987. It was called Credentials, and it allowed you to get a copy of your report whenever you wanted to. The service also included a newsletter and other benefits. Credentials has since been sold to another company. A variety of these plans are available from other sources. Most offer a personal credit profile, quarterly updates, a research request form, and some sort of newsletter. Credit card and key registration are sometimes among the additional benefits. Costs vary but can be as high as around $60 a year.

Having explained my views on them, I nevertheless do recommend that you consider joining one of these monitoring services under certain circumstances:

- If you have been a recent victim of credit fraud;

- If you are trying to improve your credit rating quickly in order to buy a home;

- If you have recently been through a divorce and want to keep an eye on your credit report; or

- If you have cosigned a loan and want to make sure that the primary borrower is making payments on time.

If you don't fall into any of these categories and have no major credit problems but simply want to keep a watchful eye on things, you're better off waiting for your free annual report. Even if you live in a state where your report isn't free, the $8 charge is much less than the cost of a monitoring service. And there are cheaper ways to keep track of your credit cards and keys.

Just the facts

- Finding and promptly correcting mistakes on your credit report is important.

- The "consumer statement" can be a helpful tool to tell your side of the story.
- It's better and cheaper to correct your own credit report.
- Most people probably don't need a credit monitoring service.

In Over Your Head

GET THE SCOOP ON...
The common causes of money problems ▪ Debt
warning signs ▪ Your debt-to-income ratio ▪
Your current ratio ▪ The different kinds of
debtors

PART III

The Credit Crunch

Benjamin Franklin said "Beware of little expenses; a small leak will sink a great ship." When it comes to credit and debt, that advice is just as sound today as it was in Franklin's time. In fact, most people who are in over their heads financially didn't get that way overnight. For them, the small-leak analogy describes the process of getting into debt far more accurately than the one I used in the Introduction, in which I likened excessive debt in this country and a possible sudden financial crisis to the Titanic disaster—heedless free-spending consumers steaming straight-ahead toward a looming iceberg. Even if you're not one of those free-spending consumers but you have just lost your job, been through a divorce, or incurred unexpected heavy medical expenses, you may very well feel like you've been hit by an iceberg.

But for most folks, excessive personal debt is a gradual and insidious process that starts innocently enough with a charge account here (drip) and an extra purchase or two there (drip, drip). Then there's a new car, an unexpected major furnace repair, a weekend ski trip (drip, drip, drip), first-run

Chapter 7

159

movies, lunch out with your co-workers, new clothes for your new job, maybe even a second home (drip, drip, drip, gush). And on and on. By the time you realize that the lower decks are awash, you may already be in imminent danger of sinking in your own debts. But don't head for the lifeboats yet. There's still hope.

If it's any comfort, at least you're not alone. Millions of other Americans are also in over their heads. The good news is that you have decided to do something about it. In the next few pages, we'll take a look at some of the most common causes of money problems. Then we'll go through the long, unhappy list of danger signals that may indicate you are heading toward the Shoals of Financial Disaster. To help you get a solid fix on your present financial situation (whatever it may be), I'll explain how to calculate your debt-to-income ratio as well as your current ratio, and explain what their implications are for your particular circumstance. Finally, I'll profile the various kinds of debtors so that you can see how you got where you are and can put your current situation in its proper perspective. By the time we finish with this chapter, you will know exactly where you stand—even if it's up to your neck in debt. But don't give up the ship yet, you still may have time to plug those leaks before it's too late.

Frequent causes of money problems

Opportunities for getting into debt are endless. No one ever plans on falling into financial difficulty, yet debt happens to plenty of folks all the time. Basically, there are two broad categories of debt: voluntary and involuntary (or situational). And the two are not necessarily mutually exclusive. You may be suffering from one and suddenly get hit with the other. The effect of either (or both) is the same—you're in financial trouble. We'll take a look at involuntary first.

Divorce

I suppose you could argue that divorce is a voluntary, avoidable peril, but I'm going to give everyone the benefit of the doubt. When you first got married with all those beautiful flowers, pretty gowns, tuxedos, nice music, and visions of eternal bliss, you weren't planning on ditching your spouse the following week. In any case, as I've already mentioned, divorce and separation are two of the major reasons why people have financial problems.

Job loss

I'm afraid the old concept of a secure job for life at one company is about as dead as the dodo. People are the victims of mergers and downsizing all the time. Job loss is something that frequently comes out of the blue for folks that thought it would never happen to them. One day you are in pretty good financial shape, and the next you are up to your ears in debt—especially if you have been pushing your credit to the outer limits during the good times and don't have an adequate savings cushion set aside for the bad times (more on that in Chapter 16).

Medical bills

I don't think anyone would argue that unexpected medical bills are avoidable. I'm in favor of preventive medicine, but the fact remains that millions of Americans suddenly find themselves in financial distress every year because of unanticipated bills for medical care related to accident or illness. Medical insurance can help, but for most people it doesn't cover everything.

Other events

A death in the family or even the birth of a child can trigger financial difficulties. Then there are the more elemental, unpredictable disasters such as earthquake, fire, flood, and windstorm, to say nothing of man-made disasters such as burglary, theft, fraud, and so on. I'm sure you can think of many others. Perhaps they've happened to you. Some things cannot be anticipated or avoided, yet they can have a devastating effect on your finances.

So much for involuntary causes. Now let's take a look at the voluntary or avoidable ones. I'm not suggesting that people are deliberately going out of their way to get themselves into financial trouble. They're not. But many folks tend to make a series of conscious (or unconscious) choices that, taken together, ultimately lead them down the slippery slope of serious indebtedness. The emphasis here is on choice. You cannot choose to avoid being hit broadside by a driver running a red light—nor can you avoid the sudden huge medical expenses. Accidents happen. But you *can* choose not to charge another unnecessary purchase on your credit card. You can also choose to check your credit report to make sure it's correct, rather than waiting until you are turned down for credit.

> 66
> The surest way to ruin a man who doesn't know how to handle money is to give him some.
> —George Bernard Shaw
> 99

Frequent borrowing mistakes

Most of these voluntary causes of money problems are related to a variety of common, avoidable borrowing mistakes. Considering the traditional lack of basic financial training that most people in this country suffer from, it's not at all surprising that millions of Americans don't know how to handle money well. Give them some easy money (in the form of credit cards), and you don't have to be a

CPA to figure out what will happen next. Add to that the persistent, overwhelming pressures to spend, spend, spend from virtually every segment of our society, and it's no wonder that so many people are teetering on the edge of financial ruin.

To help you understand how people manage to get themselves into debt, let's look at the common borrowing mistakes. Over time, these seemingly minor errors can add up to a lot of money. A few of these mistakes may sound uncomfortably familiar:

- **Overuse of credit cards.** This is probably the number-one blunder that most people make when they are getting themselves into financial trouble. It's just so easy. "I love credit cards," says Howard Strong in his book *What Every Credit Card User Needs to Know.* "Properly handled, they can ease your way through life. Improperly handled, they can ruin your financial life...." A major trap that many people fall into when they use a credit card is that they forget that when they carry a balance it's a loan. If you wouldn't go to the bank and apply for a loan to make your purchase, then you probably shouldn't charge it on your credit card.

- **Paying too much for a credit card.** It's easy to pay too much in interest charges on a credit card because you didn't shop carefully for the right card for your particular needs (see Chapter 2). This sort of mistake can cost you anywhere from $50 to $500 a year. Over a lifetime that could come to anywhere from $2,000 to $20,000, according to Andrew Feinberg in his book *Downsize Your Debt.*

Unofficially...
The potential lifetime extra cost of a higher-than-necessary mortgage rate can run anywhere from $2,000 to $40,000 or more. That's no small change. Shop around for the lowest rate you can find.

- **Paying too much for loans.** This may sound like an obvious situation to avoid. Yet, as I've mentioned previously, millions of Americans pay too much for loans every year, placing an unnecessary burden on their finances and putting themselves at greater risk if other bills begin to pile up as well. This is especially important when you're talking about a home mortgage.

- **Inappropriate use of home equity loan.** This is an increasing problem because home equity loans are becoming so trendy. You've got to remember that you are putting your house on the line when you choose to follow this strategy. When economic times are good, it seems innocent enough. But what happens when the economy goes sour, as it inevitably will sooner or later? This great money-saving strategy with all of its attractive tax advantages won't look so great if you and your family are out on the street without a roof over your heads. Are you willing to gamble with your home?

- **Not cleaning up your credit history.** This may seem like a minor issue, but ignoring problems on your credit rating can cost you big time in higher interest rates and (as I mention in Chapter 5) even your chance at a new job. The potential cost over a lifetime could amount to thousands of dollars. Check your credit report, and fix it if it's wrong (see Chapter 6).

- **Living with perma-debt.** This sad condition occurs when you never seem to get caught up on your debts. Not only does it cost you enormous amounts of money that could be put to better use (like savings), it leaves you wide open to total financial meltdown in the event of an unexpected big expense. And such circumstances come along all the time. This is no way to live. The potential additional lifetime cost of this kind of lifestyle can be enormous.

The list of common borrowing mistakes goes on and on, but you get the general idea. The main thing to remember is that these are avoidable mistakes. Take the time to research and comparison-shop for credit, and you can save yourself hundreds, perhaps thousands, of dollars. If you don't, and some unexpected financial disaster should strike, you may suddenly find yourself in a severe credit crunch.

That sinking feeling

Sudden financial trauma isn't the only way to get into debt. As I mentioned earlier in this chapter, sliding into debt for many people is a gradual, almost imperceptible process. The case of Jef and Lorraine Murray, now living in Georgia, is a case in point. Married in 1982, the Murrays bought their first home, a $95,000 townhouse in the Washington, D.C. area, the following year. At the time, Jef was a well-paid engineer for a computer hardware manufacturer.

"It wasn't so much that we were piling up debt back then, it was just that we were totally unconcerned about accumulating any savings," Jef recalls. "We were operating under the school of financial management that says, 'Whatever comes in must go out.'" And it did. Then the couple moved to Atlanta, where they bought a new home. They also continued their previous spending habits.

Then the Murrays decided they needed a second home on the coast of Florida. "This is where things really began to get out of hand," Jef admits. But still, it was a gradual process. "We took our time doing this," he continues. "It's not like we suddenly went massively into debt."

It was now 1992, ten years after their marriage, and Jef and Lorraine were over $140,000 in debt. But the couple still had no savings and they now faced the expenses of maintaining two homes. As well as a boat. I almost forgot to mention the boat. On the positive side, the Murrays weren't carrying a heavy consumer debt load on their credit cards. "That wasn't our downfall; our downfall was the real estate," says Jef.

We'll check in with the Murrays later in the book to see how they made out. The point I'm trying to emphasize is that for most folks there's a fine line between just being in debt and being seriously in debt. Because almost everyone else you know is probably in debt too, it's hard to know what constitutes excessive indebtedness. Fortunately, these waters are not entirely uncharted. Some well-established danger signals exist that, if heeded in time, can help you steer clear of financial disaster.

Common danger signals

A number of different approaches can be used to tell whether you are carrying too much debt. Two are straightforward mathematical approaches: the debt-to-income ratio and the current ratio (we'll look at them shortly). Another is the less scientific, but equally useful, anecdotal approach, which is frequently used by debt counselors to try to determine how much trouble their clients are in. We'll start with the ancedotal approach for taking a hard look

Bright Idea
For many years, bankers have used the debt-to-income ratio to help them determine whether to approve a loan. This ratio is a helpful tool for you as well; from it you can learn how much debt you are actually carrying.

at your current financial situation. I'm going to present this in the form of a series of questions. Read them carefully, and try to answer honestly:

- Are you spending increasing amounts of your income to pay your bills?

- Do you put off paying your bills because you don't have enough money to cover them?

- Are you at or over the limit on your credit accounts?

- Have you been turned down for credit purchases because you're over the limit?

- Are you taking 60 or 90 days to pay your bills when you used to pay them in 30?

- Are you frequently making only minimum payments on your bills?

- Are you chronically late in paying your bills, including your mortgage or rent?

- Are you routinely paying late penalties on your bills?

- Are you constantly juggling your bills every month?

- Do you charge small, miscellaneous expenses because you don't have money to pay for them?

- Are you paying your bills with money that was supposed to go for something else?

- Are you borrowing money for things you used to pay for in cash?

- Are you using your credit cards to pay for normal living expenses?

- Are you paying half of your bills one month and half the next?

- Are you drawing down your savings in order to pay your bills?

- Are your current savings low or nonexistent?

- If you lost your job, would you be in immediate financial difficulty?

- Are you paying off one loan with another one?

- Have any of your credit cards been cancelled by the issuer because you have been consistently late or over your limit?

- Are you putting off medical or dental visits because you can't afford them?

- Have you had to cancel your auto, medical, or life insurance because you can't afford the premiums?

- Are you getting letters, phone calls, or collection notices from your creditors regarding late payments or unpaid bills?

- Are you working overtime or moonlighting in order to pay your bills?

- Have your utilities been shut off, or have you received shut-off notices?

- Are you repeatedly overdrawn at the bank?

- Are you living beyond your means?

- Are you frequently writing bad checks?

- Have you been threatened with repossession of your car?

- Do you have negative marks on your credit report?

- Have you been denied credit because of an adverse report from a credit bureau?

- Do you worry a lot about money?

- Do you and your spouse argue about money problems?

- Are you afraid that someone may find out how far in debt you are?

These questions are loosely based on a list published by the Money Management Institute back in 1987. I think it's significant that these queries are just as current today as they were over a decade ago. The more things change, the more they remain the same.

If you didn't answer yes to any of these questions, then you almost certainly are in good shape. Congratulations. But don't get complacent. Debt can creep up on you at any time if you're not careful.

If, on the other hand, you answered yes to one or more of the questions, you may or may not have cause for alarm, depending on the context of your answers. If you've just gone through a divorce or had to pay for expensive medical bills, the fact that you are temporarily behind may not be too serious in the long run. But if you are drawing down your savings to make minimum monthly payments on all of your credit card bills, then the alarm bells should be ringing loud and clear. If you answered yes to many or most of the questions, you definitely have a problem and should seriously consider getting help (see Chapter 11).

How much do you owe?

Regardless of how you fared in the previous quiz, it's a good idea to get a more exact measure of where you actually stand financially. Two methods will help you do that. The first, your *debt-to-income ratio*, takes a simple, quick picture of your current indebtedness on a monthly basis. It has one major shortcoming,

Timesaver
Knowing in advance the warning signs of excess debt will prepare you to take action should any of these signs pop up in the future. The sooner you act to reverse the trend, the easier it will be.

however. It does not take into account your long-term indebtedness or your assets or savings. The second method, your *current ratio,* does. We'll look at both.

Your debt-to-income ratio

For those of you who are mathematically challenged, don't worry; this is pretty basic. In order to figure your debt-to-income ratio, simply list all of your monthly debts, such as your auto loan, credit cards, and other loans (including student loans), in one column. In a second column, list the actual amount of your monthly payment. Check your monthly statements to be sure your figures are accurate. In a third column, list the actual amount owed (this should be your current balance, not your original loan amount). Do not include your home mortgage, home-equity loan, or normal living expenses such as rent, food, or utilities. Here's an example:

MONTHLY TOTAL BILLS

Lender	Monthly Payment	Total Owed
Car Loan	$250	$6,700
MasterCard	$95	$1,900
Visa	$20	$1,000
Dr. Sharp	$20	$175
Store Card	$15	$225
	$400	$10,000

Source: The Ultimate Credit Handbook

I want to note here that financial experts disagree somewhat on whether you should include a home equity loan in this calculation. I think the best rule of thumb is that if the loan is being used for physical improvements to your home, then it should not be included. If, on the other hand, you have consolidated some or all of your consumer debts or are using your home equity line of credit to pay medical bills or perhaps buy a car, then this loan quite properly belongs in your monthly debt-to-income ratio calculations.

The next step is to calculate your monthly income. If you receive a regular monthly paycheck that doesn't vary much, it's easy—that's the figure to use. On the other hand, if you get paid weekly, multiply that amount by 52 and then divide that figure by 12.

Experts also disagree about whether you should use your gross income (before taxes) or net income (after taxes). Using gross income will make your financial picture look better than if you use your net income. I'm going to follow the more conservative approach and use net income for this discussion. For the sake of this example, let's say your average net monthly income is $1,600.

Next, using the examples above, divide the total of your monthly debt payments ($400) by your monthly net income ($1,600). The resulting fractional figure is your monthly debt-to-income ratio. Here is how it looks: 400 ÷ 1600 = .25 (or 25 percent).

Okay, so what does this monthly debt-to-income ratio mean? Depending on which range your percentage falls into, you can tell how you stand relative to your debt. I should note, however, that these figures need to be viewed as general, rather than absolute guidelines. They tend to mean slightly different things to different people, depending upon their particular circumstances. Here are the ranges:

- Most experts agree that if your ratio is 20 percent or less, then you are in pretty good shape. At less than 10 percent, you really should not

Watch Out!
If your debt-to-income ratio is out of balance (too much debt—not enough income) you need to reduce your spending and/or increase your assets or income before the situation gets out of control.

have any problems at all. If you're pushing 20 percent, you should keep a watchful eye on any further indebtedness.

- The next range is 20 to 35 percent. You probably aren't in any serious danger in this range either, but you will not be able to save much money because you are spending so much of your income on paying your bills. If, as in the example shown in the above table, you're at 25 percent, you need to reduce that figure below the 20 percent level.

- Things start to get dicey when your debt-to-income ratio is between 35 and 50 percent. At this level, you definitely need to figure out ways to reduce your indebtedness. This is especially important if you are facing any issues that may cause you financial uncertainty, such as major new expenses (birth of a child, impending college bills, and so on) or perhaps uncertainty about your employment. Don't wait for those things to happen before you get your financial act together.

- If your ratio is over 50 percent, you definitely need help. See Chapter 11, "Where to Go for Assistance."

If your ratio is at the high end, it's important to take the matter seriously, but don't panic. However, I do advise you to take immediate steps to reduce your debt load as soon as possible before things worsen.

Your current ratio

As I mentioned earlier, your debt-to-income ratio does not take into account such items as your assets and long-term indebtedness. Your current ratio does, and consequently it gives you a more accurate picture of your actual overall net worth. We're going to use a few basic accounting terms here, but they're pretty simple, so don't worry. If you already know this stuff, bear with me.

In order to figure your current ratio, you need to list your present assets and liabilities. Your *assets* are the things that you own. Assets can include such items as cash; money in your checking, savings, and other bank accounts; stocks and bonds; the cash value of your life insurance; pension accumulations; real estate; automobiles; jewelry; antiques; works of art; and so on. You need to estimate or calculate the current market value of these items as accurately as possible in order for this exercise to work properly. For the sake of the discussion, let's say your total assets come to $60,000.

The next step is to tally your *liabilities*, which are what you owe. You already listed most of your liabilities when you figured your debt-to-income ratio (in the example, the total owed came to $10,000). Add to that list the remaining balance on your home mortgage (let's say $25,000) and any other obligations that you may have (let's say there aren't any). Then total your liabilities ($10,000 + $25,000 = $35,000). Still with me? Good.

The final step in calculating your current ratio is to divide your total liabilities ($35,000) by your total assets ($60,000). The resulting fractional figure is expressed as a percent. It looks like this: $35,000 ÷ $60,000 = .58, or 58 percent.

So how do you interpret these figures? Again, there are general (not absolute) ranges that indicate the relative strength or weakness of your financial position as expressed in your current ratio.

Here are the ranges:

- If your ratio is 30 percent or less, you're basically in pretty good shape.

- If your ratio falls between 30 and 50 percent, your financial position is relatively stable. The closer you are to 30 percent, the better. If you're pushing the other end of the scale and approaching 50 percent, you should consider paying off some of your debts before things get out of hand.

- If, like our example (58 percent), your ratio is somewhere between 50 and 100 percent, you are carrying too much debt. In this situation, you need to look at the kind of debt you are carrying. If you are like Jef and Lorraine Murray, the couple mentioned earlier in this chapter, and most of your indebtedness is tied up in real estate, you may be in trouble, especially if, like them, you don't have any savings to speak of. In this scenario, you are in a precarious position because you have little except your home to liquidate in an emergency.

- If your ratio is 100 percent or more, your liabilities exceed your assets. Loud warning bells should be ringing in your ears. You need to take immediate steps to cut your indebtedness and increase your assets. Keep reading this book, but especially see Part IV, "Time for Action."

Bright Idea
If your current ratio is just below 30 percent, you should not be having any serious debt problems. However, you may be carrying enough debt to make it difficult to save and invest. Consider reducing your debt level further to give yourself more money for savings and retirement.

How did you do with your current ratio? If you're in the under 30 percent range, congratulations. If you're somewhere in the middle, you need to pay attention to your indebtedness and start to reduce it. If you find yourself at the high end of the spectrum, it's not time to panic, but it is time to take decisive action to reduce your debt load before things get any worse.

What are realistic limits on your credit?

Now that you have some real figures to work with, what do they mean for you? This is another area in which opinions and answers differ, depending on your particular situation. The traditional view was that any amount of debt that pushed you above the 20 percent level in your debt-to-income ratio, or 30 percent in your current ratio, was too much. Over the years as debt levels have continued to climb, what was once viewed as imprudent is now viewed by many as acceptable, or at least tolerable.

I'd like to point out, however, that just because everybody else is dancing on the edge of a cliff doesn't mean you have to follow their foolish example. In fact, I'd recommend staying back as far from the edge as possible.

Here are additional factors that you should take into consideration when you are trying to figure out where you stand with your debt:

- If you are single, middle-aged (thus unlikely to incur large new debts), and have a good income, you can probably live successfully with a 20 percent or more debt-to-income ratio.

- If you are married and are a two-wage-earner family making a combined yearly total of $50,000 net income, you probably can handle a 20 percent debt-to-income ratio. But not with children. In that case, the ratio should be 15 percent or less.

- If you are retired and living on a fixed income, your ratio should probably remain below

10 percent. However, if in addition to a fixed
income, you have a regular supplemental
income, say from a part-time job, you might be
able to tolerate a little more debt. It just
depends.

As you can see, the ratio ranges mean different
things to different people, depending on their particular circumstances. Although these guidelines are
general, they are worth following.

Who gets into debt?

We've looked at *how* people get into debt. It would
also be helpful to look at *who* gets into debt. And
why. The simple answer to who, of course, is that
anyone can get into financial difficulties. Debt is an
equal-opportunity phenomenon. Anyone who has
attended a Debtor's Anonymous meeting (see
Chapter 11) knows that income level and economic
status don't make any difference. A millionaire can
just as easily slide down that slippery slope to financial woe as someone who barely earns $20,000 a
year.

Debtors fall into several categories that help to
explain how people handle their debts and how they
get into, or avoid, trouble in the first place. Of
course, if you understand how you got into debt, it's
easier to figure a way to get back out again. The categories are: responsible, situational, chronic, and
combination. We'll look at each one in turn.

Responsible

As I've mentioned previously, not all debt is bad, nor
are all types of debtors. Let me clarify that. Debtors,
per se, are not bad people. Some have just managed
to get themselves into a bad situation, even a really
bad situation. Responsible debtors, on the other

hand, undertake their debts carefully and manage their debt loads wisely. They make their payments on time and constantly strive to keep their debt within reasonable bounds. They view both credit and debt as useful tools, and under these circumstances, they are.

Situational

Earlier I noted that money problems can be due to many different kinds of involuntary or situational causes. These can happen to anyone at almost any time. An illness or death in the family, the birth of a child, accidents, job loss, legal problems, business reversals, even substance abuse—any of these events singly or in combination can send your debt load skyrocketing and your credit rating plummeting.

If you find yourself in this category, the good news is that your debt problem(s) stems from one (or several) easily identifiable causes. Once the cause of your problem has been resolved (which admittedly may not be easy), your position should begin to stabilize and you should be able to gradually bring your debts under control again.

Chronic

There are some people, especially those with addictive personalities, who simply cannot control their spending—or their debts. These individuals are compulsive or impulsive spenders who routinely buy things that they really don't need and in hindsight don't even want. Someone who is a chronic debtor is as helpless to stop their spending as an alcoholic is unable to quit drinking.

We'll look more deeply into the psychology of this problem in Chapter 8, but for now suffice it to say that a chronic debtor typically exhibits a persistent inability to make adequate financial plans and

Watch Out!
If you don't have an adequate savings cushion that will carry you through three to six months of living expenses, a situational money problem caused by illness or other unforeseen event can wreak havoc with your finances and your credit rating.

usually has a prolonged history of financial irresponsibility and excessive debt. Happily, there is
help for the chronic debtor. And it doesn't have to
cost a lot of money, either. If you might just possibly
fall into this category—even a little bit—you should
check out Debtors Anonymous (see Chapter 11).

Combination

Finally, there's the combination debtor who is usually struggling with several problems at the same
time. A typical example would be alcoholics or drug
addicts who have managed to drink or consume
themselves into serious debt. Even if the primary
addiction is resolved, these individuals may discover
that they also have a secondary addiction to overspending. Such combination problems are complicated to resolve. We'll look into this situation further
in Chapters 8 and 11.

Do you fit into one of these categories? If you are
the responsible debtor, that's good news. But if you
saw yourself in one of the other three, don't despair.
These categories aren't permanent. If you used to be
a responsible debtor but have fallen on hard times,
plenty of help is available to restore you and your
credit rating to their previous favorable status. It just
takes time, support, hard work, and determination.

Just the facts

- Getting into debt can be a gradual process.
- Some debts can't be avoided—others can.
- It's easy to calculate your debt-to-income ratio.
- Anybody can get into—and out of—debt.

Credit Problem Psychology

Chapter 8

You've heard the old saying, "Money is the root of all evil." That may be an oversimplification, but there's a good deal of truth to it. (I know, the correct quote from the Bible is "The *love* of money is the root of all evil.") Regardless of which quote you cite, neither is very complimentary about money. Of course, there's the other view that says the *lack* of money is the basis for all our problems. Take your pick. Any way you look at it, money causes grief for almost all of us at some point in our lives.

Ironically, money by itself has virtually no intrinsic value. It's just printed pieces of paper or non-precious metal coins or, increasingly, data stored in a computer's memory banks or on a plastic card. So why is this essentially worthless stuff so important to so many people? Used wisely, of course, money can be a creative tool for building better lives and a better society. Used improperly, it can destroy friendships, marriages, and entire families. And in extreme cases, even your life.

179

Unfortunately, in a country populated largely by financially undereducated citizens, the improper use of money seems to be epidemic. It's not surprising, then, that the desire for money and all the things that we can do—or think we can do—with it is such a problem. Those desires, encouraged by rampant commercialism, frequently exceed our ability to pay for them, but we try anyway. Severe consumer debt is often the unhappy result.

Now, if correcting this situation were just a matter of learning how to balance our checkbooks or live within our means, it would be a relatively simple matter. In many cases, however, spending and getting into debt isn't really about money at all. More often than not, it's about trying to buy happiness. Benjamin Franklin, as always, had an opinion on the subject. "Money," he observed, "never made a man happy yet nor will it. There is nothing in its nature to produce happiness. The more a man has, the more he wants. Instead of its filling a vacuum, it makes one."

Ben, as usual, was right. All the money in the world won't buy you happiness. In fact, it's a common phenomenon that many exceedingly wealthy people are exceedingly unhappy. Howard Hughes, the reclusive multimillionaire, comes to mind. Yet, many Americans continue to try to spend themselves into a state of contentment. Few succeed. What they do accomplish in the process, if they're not careful, is spending themselves into insolvency.

In order to develop a realistic plan on how to get out of debt, we need to understand the real reasons why we spend our money the way we do. In this chapter, we'll look at the psychological issues that lurk beneath many of our spending habits. Then we'll explore a variety of compulsive and addictive behaviors surrounding money. I'll explain the importance of breaking old, destructive habits and establishing new, healthier ones. We'll also touch on the importance of discussing your financial problems with others and on how to deal with the inevitable anxieties of being in debt. By the end of the chapter, I think it will be obvious that the improper *use* of money, rather than money itself, is the root of many evils.

Identifying the causes of credit problems

Whether you are a situational, chronic, or combination debtor (see Chapter 7), it's important to understand and deal with the underlying reasons for your being in debt. If you don't, all the budgets, counseling, spending plans, and best intentions in the world will not resolve your problems.

So why are you in debt? Are you unemployed or underemployed? For most people, this is one of the simpler issues to deal with. Getting a job, or a better job, or perhaps a second job while you pay down your debt may be the best strategy. Admittedly, improving your job skills may require some effort on your part, but in the long run your new skills will be helpful long after you have solved your immediate debt problem. It's a win-win strategy.

Perhaps your debt problem is due to a substance addiction, such as drugs or alcohol. Unfortunately, this is a very common scenario, and there is no way you can get out of debt—and stay out—until you deal with your addiction, or addictions. People with addictive personalities often suffer from multiple addictions. Organizations like Alcoholics Anonymous and related groups such as Debtors

> 66
> The desire to accumulate extreme wealth is irrational. Beyond a certain point, added wealth cannot increase the opulence of one's style of living or increase one's happiness. Yet the dream of having millions is common to most Americans.
> —Herb Goldberg and Robert T. Lewis, authors of *Money Madness: The Psychology of Saving, Spending, Loving, and Hating Money*
> 99

Watch Out!
Have you ever
been tempted to
cover up or lie
about your com-
pulsive spending
habits? To your
family, your
friends, or even
yourself?
Dishonesty is
one of the major
symptoms of an
addiction.

Anonymous (see the Resource Guide in Appendix B) can help.

You may suffer from a "process addiction," such as gambling, or a wide variety of other compulsive spending habits. In a process addiction such as gambling, the process eventually becomes more important than winning money, according to Anne Wilson Schaef, the author of *When Society Becomes an Addict.* "Like all addicts, compulsive gamblers use their addiction to keep them unaware of their internal feelings," she says in her book. "Their lives become progressively more unmanageable. Gambling can be as addictive as alcohol; although it does not destroy the body, as alcohol does, it is equally capable of destroying your life and of wreaking havoc with your relationships."

Are you a compulsive spender?

Compulsive spending, shopping, investing, and collecting—all can be addictive and can have the same destructive effects as a gambling addiction. If the addiction gets out of control, you can be in trouble. An addiction as defined by Schaef is any process over which you are powerless. It takes control of you and causes you to do and think things that are not consistent with your personal values. It leads you to become progressively more compulsive and obsessive.

You may be a recovering alcoholic who is doing well in an abstinence program. Suddenly you realize that you have a secondary addiction to compulsive spending. You will never conquer your financial problems until you recognize your secondary addiction and deal with it, too.

Melanie, 42, an independent marketing contractor who now lives in South Carolina knows all about addictive behavior. She's struggled with multiple addictions for years. Her debt problems started early. "I was very irresponsible from the first time I moved out on my own and rented a house," she recalls. She didn't pay her rent, partly because she was spending much of her money on alcohol and drugs. That was in Ohio.

In 1978, at age 21, she began an odyssey of moves through several Southern states, eventually ending up in South Carolina where she met and married an "ultra-responsible" man. She says that just being around her husband encouraged her to become more responsible with money. She settled down and paid the household bills. After about eight years, her credit rating had improved enough that she could get an American Express credit card. "I thought it was a godsend," she reports. She was wrong.

Although she regularly made more than the minimum payments every month on her new credit bills, she continued to add additional charges as well. In a few years, the number of credit cards Melanie was carrying had multiplied exponentially. And so had her unsecured debt, which now came to $25,000. "I couldn't figure out why my credit card debt kept growing because I was always paying more than the minimum payments, and yet it was still growing," she says. "Well, of course, if you charge more than you pay it just gets worse," she now concedes.

One important aspect of her compulsive spending habits that Melanie now recognizes is that she had always been vague about money. "I didn't know because I didn't *want* to know what I was doing," she admits. "I wanted to live in this illusion." Then one day, while she was paying her latest large pile of credit card bills, she finally decided to really look at the figures for the first time. She suddenly realized that out of the $130 payment she was about to make, $97 was for interest. "I was mortified," she admits. "And I was even more mortified that I had not known that. It was a real eye-opener for me."

While Melanie was working on her other addictions, she was introduced, through Alcoholics Anonymous, to Debtors Anonymous (DA). Some of her new friends in these groups suggested that she read *How to Get Out of Debt, Stay Out of Debt and Live Prosperously,* by Jerrold Mundis. She did. "And it just blew me away because it was me," she says. "I was all over the inside of that book, and it was the first time that I could see that this was not about money for me." The book was a turning point.

Melanie became active in DA and eventually decided to eliminate all of her unsecured debt. It took about four years and a lot of hard work and support, but she finally did it. Even though the debt is now gone, she remains vigilant. "Just because I don't have any unsecured debt doesn't mean that I am sober around money at all," she notes. "I use money to act out. And I've made enough money in the last 10 to 15 years that I can pretty much do what I want. If I see something that I want, I get it. I am so compulsive about what I want. I can go buy whatever, and I feel better. I use money to alter my feelings just like I used alcohol." In addition to cleaning up her unsecured debts, Melanie has also cleaned up the rest of her life. She's been drug- and alcohol-free for over five years.

So, how can you tell if you are a compulsive spender? There are no firm rules, since everyone is different. However, there are some general ways to differentiate between a money binger and someone who just enjoys a bargain. Here are some questions to ask yourself:

- Do you actually wear the clothes and shoes you buy, or do they just take up more and more room in your closets?

- Do you spend a lot of time thinking about shopping?

- Do you find yourself buying things that, in hindsight, you really don't need?

- Do you spend a lot of time actually shopping?

- When you get near a mall, do you just decide to stop in to see if you can find something that you need or to see what is on sale?

- A few days after you have bought something, do you feel slightly let down and unsatisfied?

If you answered yes to any of these questions, you may be a compulsive shopper. Or a compulsive shopper-in-training.

What motivates bad spending habits?

Before you can break bad spending habits, you need to know why they are happening in the first place. This requires that you look at what is actually happening in your life. If you are suffering from an addiction like Melanie's, or even if you are only mildly compulsive and feel your money trying to burn a hole in your pocket when you get near a shopping mall, the most important question to ask yourself is *why* are you spending so much money on whatever it is you are buying?

This may not be a simple question to answer. Let's assume, for the sake of discussion, that you have a weight problem, are divorced, and are looking for

"
Many compulsive spenders like charge accounts and time-payment buying even better than money itself, since this equates to temporarily unlimited spending power. The pleasurable excitement from spending exceeds the pleasure obtained from their purchases.
—Ernest Bornemann, author of *The Psychoanalysis of Money*
"

a new partner. To make matters worse, you feel
trapped in a stressful job that you despise. As a sub-
conscious compensation for your many woes, you
may go on a spending binge at the mall occasionally,
or maybe regularly. This could be one way that you
express your distress about the things in your life
that you are unhappy about. Like Melanie, your
spending may (temporarily) make you feel better.

The act of spending money or the items you buy
(or both) may be an attempt on your part to create
a substitute for other things that are missing in your
life, such as love, companionship, family, or even
community. It's also possible that you may be
attempting to prop up your self-esteem by your
spending habits. This can be a self-defeating strategy; if your spending drives you into debt, your self-
esteem is lowered even further.

Try to be honest with yourself, as painful as that
may be. Like Melanie, you may not want to know
what's going on. However, once you get clear in your
own head about what's really happening in your life,
you've taken the first important step to cleaning up
your act. If you can't sort it out, consider attending
a meeting of Debtors Anonymous. The people there
may be able to help you gain the clarity you need.
And you can't beat the price. It's free.

Is this really a money problem?

After carefully examining your situation, you may
realize that your weight problem, your loneliness,
and your miserable job are the real culprits.
Obviously, just reining in your spending will not
solve these underlying problems, and shopping may
seem easier than dealing with your painful emo-
tional issues. Nevertheless, you need to face your difficulties squarely and take some positive steps to fix

things—like find a new job, lose some weight, and try to figure out places to go to meet some new friends.

Maybe you're not overweight, lonely, and stuck in a crummy job. Perhaps the reason you are an overspender is that you have nothing better to do with your time and you are trying to fill a spiritual void in your life. Now, I'm not suggesting that you run out and "get religion." What I *am* suggesting, however, is that you might want to take a hard look at your spiritual side. It's possible to be a very spiritual person without adhering to any particular religion. If you find that a specific religious denomination meets your needs, that's fine. But if you have neither a spiritual nor a religious rudder to help steer your life, you may be drifting aimlessly on the Sea of Commercialism—and into debt.

Online addiction

There are lots of potential money-related addictions to watch out for, but one area requires particular caution—the Internet. In Chapter 4, I warned about some of the many dangers of the Internet. These warnings are especially relevant for people with addictive personalities. The ease of logging on in the privacy of your own home and being just a mouse click away from Shopper's Heaven puts you in grave danger of ending up in Debtor's Hell instead. This is true for almost any e-commerce site, but it's a serious problem with the wildly popular new auction sites. Evidence is mounting that these sites are regularly getting a lot of folks hooked.

"I know people who are nearly addicted to these sites, checking them out multiple times every day to track their bids, and buying things that they don't

Unofficially...
If your basic needs are unfulfilled, all the spending in the world will still leave you unhappy and dissatisfied.

really need," said editor-in-chief Michael J. Miller in a recent *PC Magazine* editorial. He's right.

Part of the problem is that these sites put compulsive spenders within easy reach of their "drug" without the usual restraints of friends or family members who might question an impulsive purchase while cruising a mall or flea market. Add to that the excitement and competition normally associated with an auction, and you end up with a potentially disastrous combination.

In a recent *New York Times* article, a woman from Texas named Jane admitted that her spending at an online auction site had become a real problem. "I am trying to stop this addictive cycle at the present time," she said, "as I've spent far too much money and now have a household of 'things' that I would probably be better off without." Jane estimated that she had already bought between 1,500 and 2,000 items, mainly antiques and dolls. "I've tried stopping, but I don't do too well," she added.

I've surfed some of the more popular auction sites myself, such as eBay, Auction Universe, and Onsale.com, and I was immediately impressed with the vast amount of stuff that was available. Everything from rare first-edition books to DVD movies, and antiques to power tools. I even found some obscure, discontinued computer accessories that I hadn't been able to locate anywhere else. I began to hear this little voice whispering in my ear, "Hey, you could really use some of this stuff!" I quickly logged off.

I'm not suggesting that you shouldn't visit these sites if you have a legitimate need to buy (or sell) something, especially something obscure that you might otherwise spend years searching for. But if you are already in debt, or are a compulsive spender teetering on the edge of debt, you have no business getting anywhere near these terrible temptations.

How to deal with your problems

One of the most important steps in solving your debt problems is to acknowledge that you have a problem. That may sound obvious, but it can be an incredibly painful and difficult step for many individuals to take. It's not unusual for some people to refuse to acknowledge that their family members or spouses are right about their unhealthy spending patterns. If you don't admit that something is wrong, you're going to remain stuck in the same behavior until you do. And the longer you continue your destructive behavior, the worse things will become. Getting past this step is crucial.

Accepting responsibility

The next important step is to accept full responsibility for your debt problems. In most instances, you are the one who got yourself into financial trouble. Now you must get yourself back out, since it's highly unlikely that anyone else will do it for you. In many cases, your problem stems from a long pattern of financial irresponsibility. If there are other family members in your household, this pattern has adversely affected them for a long time also. All the more incentive to finally get your act together.

Once you have taken these first steps, you may suddenly feel overwhelmed by the magnitude of your problems. That's normal. Like Melanie, you may have been living in a self-created illusory world. Now you may be facing reality for the first time, and you may not like what you see. Facing your problem can be a frightening experience, but it can also be a positive one. Although I hesitate to say that a situation like this "builds character," it almost certainly will help you discover some truly valuable lessons and give you some new perspectives on life after you have gotten through it all. So, aside from the purely financial advantages of getting out of debt, there should be some other, less tangible, but equally important benefits as well. It's definitely worth the effort.

Don't blame others

Accepting the blame yourself, rather than placing it on others, is another important part of the process of accepting responsibility. If you really were the one who has spent yourself into a hole, don't waste your time and energy trying to shift the blame to anybody else. Even if you weren't responsible for your debts, say in the case of a traffic accident, wallowing in blame and recrimination isn't productive.

The case of Jim and Jennifer illustrates this point. In June of 1990, they were just married and looking forward to an exciting new life together in Maine. Then, a week later, Jim was involved in an auto accident caused by another driver. He received severe injuries to his head and spine, which landed him in the hospital and later kept him from working for many years. The young couple suddenly found themselves over $70,000 in debt due to Jim's medical bills. Jennifer, who was a speech language pathologist at the time, eventually had to quit her full-time job in order to be at home to help care for her husband. This did not improve their financial situation any.

Eventually, after five years of wrangling with an insurance company, they received a $50,000 insurance settlement. That still left $20,000 worth of medical bills hanging over their heads. Jim says that he spent a lot of the time blaming his misfortune on the driver of the other car and the insurance company that had been so reluctant to cough up the money. But eventually he says that he realized this wasn't getting him or his wife anywhere. He finally simply acknowledged that they had a debt that needed to be paid off. "So what do we do now?" he recalls thinking at the time. "Looking at reality was important—that was a big shift for me," he says. It was a significant shift for both of them.

We'll come back to Jim and Jennifer in a moment. The main point here is the importance of not wasting your time and energy blaming other people for your problems. Just face them, and deal with them. If Jim and Jennifer, who had every reason to be angry with their situation, could get past it, so can you.

Making changes

When you are dealing with a long-established pattern of irresponsible behavior that has put you in financial jeopardy, it's vital that you make real changes in your life—and stick to them—if you hope to make meaningful and lasting improvements to your finances. I realize that this can be a traumatic experience because any departure from the status quo can be scary—even if the status quo stinks.

Actually, the bigger your financial problems, the easier it should be for you to take decisive action. If you are utterly sick of the hassles that you are struggling with, you may decide that anything is better than what you are currently going through. That's good. On the other hand, if things are bad, but not horrible, you may be tempted to slide along in familiar territory rather than strike out in a bold new direction. That's not so good.

Unofficially...
Trying to get out
of debt can be a
traumatic experi-
ence. But think
of it as shutting
the door on an
unhappy part of
your past and
opening the door
to a brighter,
happier future.

In this case, your choices may not be quite so
obvious. You will almost certainly have to deal with a
persistent batch of deeply entrenched defense
mechanisms that will provide you with an endless
stream of plausible-sounding rationalizations why
you should not pursue a path of radical change. "I
enjoy shopping; I'll just cut back a little on
nonessentials for a while," or "I'll only go shopping
when there's a sale," or "I'll go to the mall only once
a month." Plausible-sounding, but excuses nonetheless. You need to be alert to these mechanisms and
their attempts to torpedo your resolve to change.

Making dramatic changes in your life doesn't
have to be terrifying. It can also be exciting. You may
be leaving familiar territory, but that territory
includes compulsive spending, high stress, and
heavy debt; so it's time to move on anyway. Firmly
closing one chapter in your life and opening a new
one can be a liberating and empowering experience, and it can lead to many unanticipated
rewards.

For most people this process primarily involves
breaking old habits and creating new, healthier
ones. For Jim and Jennifer, this strategy was combined with literally leaving familiar territory in
Maine and moving out of state. With the new clarity
of thought that came with accepting responsibility
for their debts, the couple decided to move to
Vermont and start over.

"We learned from Jim's accident that life is very
precious and that we really needed to follow our
dreams and what makes us happy," Jennifer says.
And the poverty that we had been experiencing
taught us that we didn't want to experience it any
more. So, if we were going to have a meaningful life,

we were going to have to find some new goals, and we were going to have to learn how to manage money for the first time in our lives as well." And they did.

They sought out financial counseling and then took a number of financial courses for small business. They have learned how to manage their money, and they're gradually paying off their debts and beginning to build a good credit rating for the first time. It hasn't been easy, but Jim and Jennifer are now home-care providers for the developmentally disabled in a small Vermont town. "It's been very, very exciting," says Jennifer. "And empowering."

Breaking old habits

Now, I don't recommend that anyone who is in debt simply pack up and leave town. That, by itself, won't solve anything. However, if a physical move is combined with a significant psychological shift away from old, destructive habits, then it should be beneficial.

On the other hand, let's assume that you like living where you are but you still want to clean up your financial act. In that case, you must identify the habits that have gotten you into trouble and radically alter or eliminate them. Spending too much time at the mall? Stay away. Ordering too many things from mail-order catalogs? Toss out the catalogs before you're even tempted. Spending too much money on expensive lunches? Bring a bag lunch. We'll look at many more money-saving ideas in Chapter 9, but I think you get the general idea.

Creating new, healthier habits

Eliminating bad habits is just the start. Next, you need to substitute new, healthier patterns to keep from sliding back into the old ones. These new patterns could be anything from attending regular Debtors Anonymous meetings to spending more quality time with your family (*not* at the mall). Perhaps you could enroll in that yoga class you've always wanted to attend (but were too busy shopping to do). Getting involved in a self-improvement program or learning a foreign language might be both fun and useful.

Another approach might be to eliminate temptation by having your employer deduct from your paycheck an amount equivalent to what you used to blow on buying useless stuff, and have the money direct-deposited in your savings account or perhaps a mutual fund. If you don't have the money in hand, you can't spend it. Of course, this particular strategy won't work until after you have cleaned up your debts, but regular saving is one of the best habits you can establish (more on that in Chapter 16).

Keep an open mind

Since you are probably going to be exploring unfamiliar territory as you try to reorder your habits (and your life), it's important to stay open-minded to new ideas or approaches to dealing with your problems, even if they are not the way you have always done things in the past. A new strategy that you read about in a book or that someone suggests to you may have real merit. Besides, the way you did things in the past got you in trouble in the first place. There's no point in clinging to the past.

Now that you have chosen to get your financial act together, you can begin to take a positive, proactive approach to your debt problems. If you've been deeply in debt for some time, you have undoubtedly developed a reactive lifestyle that focuses on dealing with the latest crisis. Now you can seize the initiative and start to regain control of your finances—and your life.

Discussing your problem

One of the most pervasive problems associated with debt is the reluctance of most people to discuss it, even in private. I mentioned earlier in the book that people will talk, quite freely in some cases, about sex, but not about money and especially not about debt. There is a widespread taboo associated with discussing personal money matters. If the subject is brought up at all, it's usually discussed in the abstract. If the conversation gets too personal, the topic is usually dropped in embarrassment.

The psychological aspects of this quickly get complicated. Suffice it to say that when you are in serious financial trouble, you need assistance. Talking about your problems with family members or trusted friends can be extremely helpful. Outside support groups such as Debtors Anonymous and similar organizations can be invaluable. Not only do they provide an opportunity for you to vent your frustrations, they also offer a venue for an open exchange of ideas, experiences, advice, and suggestions from people who have been struggling with the same issues. Finding out that you are not alone in your problems can offer much comfort at a critical time. "Ask for support; don't try to do this alone," advises Melanie from South Carolina. "I feel we're meant to heal in community. It's important to reach out to other people."

Restoring your self-esteem

As I mentioned previously, if you've been struggling with serious debt for some time, your self-esteem has probably taken a big hit. This may be especially

> 66
> Money...is hardly spoken of in parlours without an apology.
> —Ralph Waldo Emerson
> 99

true if the reason you were spending was to prop up your self-image. It doesn't take too many months of being hounded by creditors and bill collectors before you start to feel like a hunted animal—a rat or maybe a mouse—trapped in a corner and feeling just as helpless.

By accepting responsibility for your debts and then actually making positive changes in order to resolve the problem, you have taken steps that should begin to restore your tattered feelings about yourself. Before too long, you will begin to see some positive results of your actions. The flood of calls and letters and visits from creditors or bill collectors should stop (see Chapter 10, "Dealing with Creditors"). As you begin to pay off your debts, you should be able to take some pride in the fact that you are turning over a new leaf and transforming yourself from an irresponsible debtor into a responsible, bill-paying member of your family and, by extension, your community. What's more, you are also taking an extremely negative situation and turning it into a positive one that should have a far more profound and long-lasting impact on your life than your previous indebtedness.

Dealing with anxiety

It's not unusual for people who struggle through this kind of situation to spend a lot of time worrying about it. And you *should* worry about your irresponsible behavior long enough to do something to change the situation. But once you have taken the steps outlined above to eliminate your debts, it's time to set your anxieties aside and focus on the positive aspects of what you are doing. Lying awake at night and fretting about the size of debt you are dealing with, or the length of time the payment is going to take, is counterproductive. And literally worrying yourself sick about it is worse yet.

In most cases, totally eliminating debt takes a number of years, so you might as well relax and take the process one day at a time. You probably didn't get into debt overnight, and you're not going to get out of debt any faster. This is one situation where patience definitely is a virtue, and be sure to celebrate the little victories as one small debt after another gets retired. Let every dollar you pay off be a reminder of the consequences of your previous behavior and a reinforcement of your resolve to never allow yourself to fall into the same trap again.

Maintaining a healthy sense of humor

One final observation. It's easy to take your debt situation, and yourself, far too seriously. You're only human. Humans have a habit of making mistakes, so don't be too hard on yourself. Try to find the humorous aspects of your situation (there are some) as much as possible. Live each day as lightly and optimistically as possible, with the expectation that things will continue to get better.

Just the facts

- It's important to understand and deal with the underlying reasons for being in debt.

- Acknowledging that you actually have a debt problem is a first crucial step.

- It's important to take responsibility for your debts.

- You need to make meaningful changes in your life if you are going to get out—and stay out—of debt.

- It's important to relax about the debt elimination process and to maintain a sense of humor.

Bright Idea
Paying off large debts takes time—usually years. The best thing you can do for yourself while you are actively working on paying off your debts is to relax and try to maintain a good sense of humor, and treat yourself to dinner out now and then.

GET THE SCOOP ON...
Changing your spending habits ▪ A realistic
budget ▪ Living on cash ▪ Slashing your
expenses ▪ Boosting your income

Getting Your Act Together

Chapter 9

I n the 1976 movie, *All the President's Men*, Deep Throat advises Bob Woodward (Robert Redford) to "follow the money... just follow the money," in his investigation of the Watergate scandal. Woodward and Carl Bernstein (Dustin Hoffman), the two young *Washington Post* reporters who were working on the story of the bungled Watergate burglary, took their anonymous informant's advice and followed bags stuffed with money, Mexican checks, slush funds, and a maze of financial records (that had escaped the shredder); and ultimately they put the pieces of the puzzle together. The money trail, and where it led, was crucial to their ultimate success. Their relentless investigative journalism broke the ugly scandal wide open and, in the end, was instrumental in bringing down the Nixon Presidency.

We're going to take Deep Throat's advice to "follow the money" too, although nothing as dramatic as the fall of the President is going to be the result. In our case, there's no mystery about where the money first came from—your paycheck. What our investigation *will* expose, however, is where your money went. And the spending habits that caused it to go where it did. Our goal will be to put your money to better use. In order to get your financial act together, you must know exactly where your money has been going before you can make intelligent decisions about where it ought to be going in the future.

In this chapter we'll examine your current approaches to dealing with credit and how to make significant changes in your spending. Then, we'll look at a number of strategies you can use to keep your debts from getting any worse. Next, we'll carefully follow your money trail and identify your monthly expenses. Then, we'll explore the ins and outs of budgets and spending reduction plans—how to prepare, evaluate, and use them. In addition, I'll offer you lots of proven ways to cut your expenses and increase your income. We'll even look at using cash—not the way Nixon's Committee to Reelect the President did with its infamous slush fund—but as an instructional tool to help you see the immediate consequences of your spending. All set? Let's follow the money—and see where it goes.

Changing your attitudes about credit

Before you start tracking the details about how and where you spend your money, you need to step back and look at the bigger picture. Assuming that your credit problems are significant, you will have to make some fairly drastic changes in your spending habits to get yourself out of debt. That means changing your attitudes about your spending and probably your lifestyle as well. If you have found that lifestyle to be somewhat shallow and unfulfilling anyway, the process may not be so difficult. On the other hand, if you have become accustomed to your lifestyle and really enjoy it, your task is going to be more challenging. In either case, you will have to make tough, but not impossible, decisions.

Once you get past this hurdle, you will have to set up a debt reduction plan. This plan will include specific goals, a means of tracking your current spending, and a method of reducing your future spending and paying off your debts. I'll spell this out in greater detail in a moment. But if the plan you set up is too strict, like any crash diet, you won't be able to stick to it over the long haul. You'll find yourself sliding back down to where you started from, only you'll be more depressed than ever because you failed in your attempt. I'd like to help you avoid that. So, as you go through this process, I'll tell you where you need to be firm and where you can give yourself a little slack.

I need to point out that if you have a family, it's important to discuss all the issues in this chapter with them and try to enlist their support as much as possible. They may not be thrilled, especially if you have adolescent children; but if you are honest with them and explain the importance of your current situation, they should see that it's in their own long-term best interests to participate. Uncooperative family members are a threat to the success of any debt reduction plan. Try to ensure that everybody is on-board.

I'd also like to note that even if you aren't deeply in debt, you can still save yourself huge amounts of money over time by reducing the amount of debt that you carry, even if you are well under your credit limits and always make your payments on time. That 19 or 20 percent credit card interest that you are

> 66
> Credit card debt can be like hand-cuffs. It really removes your freedom. It keeps you from doing things with your money that are productive.
> —Kay R. Shirley, author of *Live Long and Profit*.
> 99

paying every month can add up to thousands of dollars over 10 or 20 years. If you could invest that money, instead of paying it to a bank, you'd be far better off. So, just because you're not up to your ears in debt doesn't mean you should skip this chapter. There's something here for everybody.

Look at your lifestyle

Okay, back to changing your attitudes about spending. There are a number of important aspects to this, but right at the top of the list is your lifestyle. Chances are, the main reason you are in debt is that your lifestyle has been exceeding your means, perhaps for quite a while. It's time to change that pattern.

"Getting out of debt does require lifestyle changes," says Gerri Detweiler of Debt Counselors of America®. "This doesn't mean that you have to go on a crash budget," she continues. "Crash diets don't work; crash budgets don't either. You don't want to deprive yourself of everything that you enjoy. But I have yet to work with anyone who has tracked their spending carefully, who has not found some area where they were just wasting money and didn't even realize how much they were spending."

If you have been living fairly high on the hog, chances are you have been wasting a lot of money on things that were not essential. Consequently, you need to take a hard look at all aspects of your life to identify nonessential spending. Most people manage to find a remarkable number of areas in which they don't mind cutting back because the goal of getting out of debt has become more important. Later in the chapter, I'll offer dozens of suggestions on how to cut your expenses in small ways, but here's a few big ones that could save you a lot of money in a hurry:

- Fire the cook, the housekeeper, and the gardener. Do routine household tasks yourself.

- If you've got a vacation home or time-share condo, get rid of it. These are notorious money pits. Alternatively, you can rent your vacation home and gain some income and tax breaks if you just can't bear the thought of selling it.

- If you have a boat, other than a canoe or a rowboat, sell it unless you use it constantly. Big boats generate big expenses. You can always rent one for an occasional outing on the water.

- If you're driving one of those big, popular, four-wheel-drive gas hogs that you bought on credit, consider downsizing to something more economical and less expensive. Maybe something a few years old that's in good mechanical condition. You'll still be able to get where you need to go.

I know these suggestions sound obvious to some people but like complete heresy to others. You may also be thinking, "cook?" "housekeeper?" "gardener?" "What's he talking about?" Obviously, there are huge differences in lifestyles in this country, and what seems like unimaginable opulence to some is considered absolute necessity by others. As I've already mentioned, debt is an equal opportunity phenomenon. The main point is that you are going to have to decide what you can cut from your particular lifestyle in order to help bring your finances back into balance. Making these decisions may also turn out to be an interesting opportunity to learn what really is—and isn't—important in your life.

Forego short-term pleasure

Another key element to getting out of debt is chang-ing your attitude about buying things now and pay-ing for them later. For most folks, buying consumer products on credit is one of the most difficult temp-tations they face, because they are constantly inun-dated by advertising that promotes this financially unsound idea.

You know the pitch, "Special Offer! For Preferred Customers Like You! And So Affordable! For only $19.95 a month (plus shipping and han-dling), you can have this exquisite (fill in the blank). Act now and use your credit card." This promotional stuff clogs the airways, our mailboxes, newspapers, magazines, and now the Internet. It's hard to ignore. The theme has many variations, but all are seductive. And then you end up paying, and paying, and paying.

If you're going to make meaningful changes to your spending patterns, I can't think of a better place to start than consumer goods bought on credit. You need to stop buying things that offer short-term pleasures but keep you from achieving your long-range goal of financial responsibility. If you can't afford to pay cash for it, you can't afford it. Take a hard look at that flashy gizmo. Do you really need it? If you do, save for it.

Develop sound, long-range goals

One of the main reasons why many people get into financial difficulty is that their spending has been on auto-pilot for years and they have not been pay-ing attention to where they are heading—toward a financial crash landing. In many cases, this attitude is due to the fact that these folks have never learned

Moneysaver
One of the best ways to cut your debt load—and save money at the same time—is to stop buying consumer goods on credit.

the importance of planning ahead for their financial futures. Basically, planning ahead means establishing financial goals.

Ideally, these goals should be long-range because they will eventually have a profound, long-term impact on your financial well-being. But for now, we need to focus on an immediate goal—getting you out of debt. Once that has been achieved, we can look into the future and explore more productive ways to use your money (see Chapter 16, "Avoiding Future Problems").

Your goals should be realistic, or you'll end up failing to achieve them and find yourself back at square one. For now, paying off your debts is probably enough of a challenge without adding a bunch of other worthy, but secondary, goals. It's better to set modest goals that you can reach, or even exceed, than to take on too much at the outset. Set yourself up to succeed, not to fail.

This is also the time to decide exactly how far you want to take this plan. Do you want to get rid of your credit card debt only? Or do you want to pay off all your consumer debt except your mortgage and car payment? Perhaps you want to live totally debt free. These various goals are all achievable; some just take longer. This is one area where you have a lot of leeway in deciding how you want to proceed. You might decide to start with the credit cards. After that goal has been achieved, you may choose to press on and eliminate more debts. Whatever you decide, you need specific goals with a realistic time frame, such as six months, a year, five years, whatever. You have to decide for yourself what those goals are.

Eliminate your access to credit

You may or may not have considered having plastic surgery. It's expensive and must be performed by a specialist. But there is one kind of plastic surgery that you can perform for yourself. Instead of costing anything, this surgery will actually save you a lot of money—and help you get out of debt at the same time. Too good to be true? Not at all. Just take a sharp pair of scissors and carefully cut your credit cards into pieces. Then, to complete the procedure, return the pieces to the issuers. Be sure to include a note to the creditors asking them to list the accounts as "closed by consumer" on your credit report.

With this simple operation, you have eliminated the means of getting yourself deeper into credit card debt, and you have provided protection against your worst enemy—yourself. If you want to retain one credit card for identification purposes, keep a card that is near its maximum credit limit. This will give you the identification you want without the temptation of adding any large additional charges. Caution: Make absolutely sure that you don't use the card; otherwise you'll end up paying over-the-limit charges and getting yourself deeper into debt.

If you can't part with your cards. Fine. Lock them away somewhere, or give them to a trusted family member or friend who is aware of your situation and knows what you are trying to do. Don't ask to have them back until you have paid off your accounts or achieved your pre-determined goal. As with any addictive behavior, the temptation to fall off the wagon is tremendous, so you need to erect as many barriers between yourself and those cards as possible. That's why I recommend getting rid of them altogether. But I'll admit that you can make a convincing case for keeping just one card for emergencies and identification purposes, or if you travel on business frequently, for car rentals, airline tickets and hotel reservations.

Here's a quirky (but possibly helpful) strategy to limit your access to your one remaining credit card. Mary Hunt in her book *The Complete Cheapskate* suggests that if you don't trust yourself to carry a credit card, try freezing it. Fill a coffee can half-full of water and freeze it. Then put your credit card on top of the layer of ice, fill the can to the top with water and stick it back in the freezer. "The card will be available if you *absolutely* need it, but the time required to thaw your ice cube card will make it difficult to use and at least will give you time to reconsider any purchase you want to make with it," she says.

I would add that you shouldn't consider *any* additional purchases except for a true emergency. This is one area where you have virtually no room for maneuver. Sorry. If you want to succeed at eliminating your indebtedness, you simply must not add any more debt to your existing load.

If, after trying to limit your access to your credit cards, you find yourself repeatedly sneaking "just one more purchase" on them (regardless of the reason), it's time to admit you don't have the necessary self-control. Cut them up. Send them back. Once you get yourself out of debt, you can always apply for new ones.

Another area where you may be leaking money seriously is your overdraft line of credit on your checking account. Although these lines of credit may have a legitimate purpose for covering unexpected emergencies or other temporary situations

Bright Idea
If you can't convince yourself to cut up your credit cards but still want to limit your access to them, try locking them in your safe deposit box.

in which you have inadvertently overdrawn your account, they are just as perilous as credit cards in the hands of people with little or no financial self-discipline. If you find that you are constantly using your line of credit for nonemergency purposes, you should eliminate it.

Budgets vs. spending plans

We've covered most of the basics. Now it's time to start working with real numbers. Generally speaking, that means we need to look at "the budget thing," as it is sometimes less-than-enthusiastically referred to.

Right off, you need to know that experts in the financial counseling arena disagree about budgets. Some insist that they are absolutely essential. Others maintain that they're too restrictive and should be avoided, or at least modified. This second school of thought promotes "spending plans" or "debt diets" (or whatever you want to call them). These plans tend to be less rigid than traditional budgets. I'm going to cover both approaches and let you decide which is best for your needs.

If you are the kind of analytical person who loves to work with numbers and keep track of every possible detail, the budget method is probably for you. If you like a more flexible approach to things, the "spending plan" may be better suited to your personality. Whichever strategy you adopt, be sure to leave yourself enough room for maneuvering so that you can get past the inevitable tight moment without trashing your budget or plan altogether. And even more important, whichever strategy you decide to use, stick to it.

When the subject of budgets arises, people have one of two reactions. For many people, their eyes start to glaze over and their heads start to nod as the long lists of figures work their narcotic magic. The other reaction is panic-stricken flight as the long lines of figures march down the page toward you like an ant army from hell. I'll admit to being an occasional member of the first group.

Budgets don't have to put you to sleep or send you running as fast as you can for the nearest exit. A well-developed—and realistic—budget is one of the most useful tools that you can employ in your efforts to get yourself out of debt. Being on a budget doesn't necessarily mean total denial of the things that you enjoy. It just means enjoying those things in moderation for a while. When budgets don't work for people, it's frequently because they set unrealistic goals, especially when they don't follow the process in the right order.

Mike Kidwell, vice president and cofounder of Debt Counselors of America®, explains: "So many people think they can just sit down and make a budget for themselves and that will solve things," he says. "But they don't have any concept of where their money is going. Before you can do anything like that, you first need to evaluate where your money is going. Then, after you've tracked it for several months, you can create a budget knowing what your spending style is like. Everybody has their own unique spending style, and until you know what yours is, there's no way that you can give yourself a budget."

He's right. Whether you decide to use the budget approach or the spending plan approach, there is no disagreement on the importance of identifying and tracking your regular expenses first.

Watch Out!
Beware of trying to create a budget for yourself before you know what your actual monthly expenses are. It's almost guaranteed to fail.

Identify monthly expenses

Identifying monthly expenses is an absolutely essential part of any debt reduction plan. Without this information, you are merely thrashing around in the dark. Here is where we begin to "follow the money" in earnest. Sharpen your pencils.

To follow the money effectively, you need to keep track of everything that you spend, right down to the last penny. You'll need a small notebook that you can carry in your purse or pocket so you can write down every purchase, and you'll need to do this for at least a month. Record everything: convenience-store purchases, vending machines, automotive expenses (gas, parking, road tolls), meals, tips, coffee, candy, cigarettes, incidentals, and so on. This is admittedly a lot of trouble, but it's crucial and therefore worth the hassle. Just the act of writing down the figures will almost certainly raise your consciousness about your purchases. You can use your checkbook to determine recurring monthly expenses. That way you only have to track monthly cash expenditures.

You may be surprised at how much you are actually spending on some of these seemingly "minor" categories. Once you have collected irrefutable evidence about how much you are wasting on some of this stuff, you may decide you don't need it after all. Just one 75-cent vending machine soda at lunch on a regular workday will cost you $187.50 a year. That's a lot of money for carbonated sugar water. If you drink more than one soda a day, multiply out the cost on an annual basis to see what those sodas really cost.

However, remember that you're tracking all your expenses, not just the incidental ones. You need to write down everything. If you have a computer and a money management program such as Quicken or Money, this task is fairly simple. Be sure to enter all miscellaneous cash expenditures in addition to your checks and credit card purchases. If you don't have a computer, you can keep track of your spending in an accountant's notebook with preprinted columns. If you are using the notebook approach, begin by writing in basic categories for each column. For most people, these categories will include:

- Housing (rent or mortgage)
- Utilities (phone, electricity, heat, etc.)
- Household (supplies, maintenance, appliances, etc.)
- Food
- Transportation (auto expenses, public transport)
- Taxes (like property taxes)
- Insurance
- Children
- Clothing
- Medical/Health Care
- Education
- Personal
- Entertainment/Recreation
- Savings
- Charitable donations
- Miscellaneous

You may need to create other categories if you regularly spend significant amounts of money on items or activities not covered above. At the moment, if you are deeply in debt, savings and

Bright Idea
If you are regularly spending money on a special project or personal interest that does not easily fall under normal budget categories, create a special category to help you keep track of the expenses.

charitable donations are probably at or near zero. But they are important in the long run, so I've included them anyway. Now that your recording system is set up, use it to follow your money trail for a month, being careful to record everything.

Prepare your monthly budget

After you have tracked your spending habits for a month, you will have almost everything you need to develop your budget. There will still be a few items that you pay for on a quarterly, semiannual, or annual basis, such as some insurance policies and perhaps annual club fees or memberships. Be sure to factor these in. If you don't, the first time one of these periodic items pops up, it will throw your budget off. You may also find it advantageous to use your spending records (tax returns, check registers) from last year (assuming there have been no major changes) to help confirm the monthly figures you are developing for your current budget. The more accurate these figures are, the better.

Now add up all the figures in the various categories to come up with your total monthly expenses. To keep track of expenses, you might want to use a form similar to the sample shown here.

How to evaluate your budget

The first column in the worksheet lists the general expense categories mentioned previously. The second column is for your projected figures. The third column is for your *actual* expenses. The fourth column allows you to track whether you came in under or over your estimate and will assist you in making adjustments to future monthly budgets. Remember: A budget is not carved in stone. It's meant to be a flexible financial guide, not a straightjacket. If at

MONTHLY BUDGET WORKSHEET

	Projected	Actual	(+/-)
Housing (rent, mortgage)	$	$	$
Utilities	$	$	$
Household	$	$	$
Food	$	$	$
Transportation	$	$	$
Taxes (property taxes)	$	$	$
Insurance	$	$	$
Children	$	$	$
Clothing	$	$	$
Medical/Health Care	$	$	$
Education	$	$	$
Personal	$	$	$
Vacation/Recreation/Entertainment	$	$	$
Savings	$	$	$
Charitable Donations	$	$	$
Miscellaneous	$	$	$
Total Monthly Expenses	$	$	$

first you don't succeed, try, try again. You'll get it right eventually.

The final part of this exercise, as shown on the second worksheet, is to find out how much money you have available on a monthly basis to pay down your debts. You need to add up your salary or wages, investment income, Social Security/disability, pensions and annuities, alimony or child support payments, etc., to determine your total monthly income. Be sure to use net income figures (income minus taxes). Your last year's income tax return will help you come up with the right figures. Then subtract your total monthly expenses from your total monthly net income. The resulting figure is the money you have left over to use for repaying your creditors.

If you end up with a negative figure, you are still spending more than you are making. You need to cut your expenses immediately before you get any further into debt, or increase your income with a second job.

Use your budget as a guide

If you have money left after deducting your monthly expenses from your income (and you should), use it to begin paying down your debts. This money isn't all that you have to work with, however—here is where your budget really comes in handy as a guide.

MONEY REMAINING FOR CREDITORS	
Total Monthly Net Income	$
Total Monthly Expenses	−$
Money Remaining for Creditors	=$

Since you now know what you are actually spending on the various categories, you can trim the fat and apply this money to reducing your debts as well. How you decide to do that is up to you. The following hints will help you make some informed choices.

Moneysaver
A carefully planned budget can be one of your most effective debt management tools. It helps you identify many potential cost-cutting opportunities that can save you hundreds or thousands of dollars.

Your expenses basically fall into three broad categories: essential fixed expenses, essential variable expenses, and nonessential expenses. Your essential fixed expenses include your rent or mortgage, insurance costs, student loans, and perhaps child care, alimony, or child support. To reduce these expenses, you could decide to move to a less expensive apartment or sell your house and buy a smaller one, but those are drastic steps. We'll assume for the moment that you want to stay where you are.

So where else can you cut costs? There are other essential expenses that are variable, such as food, utilities, clothing, and transportation. You may be able to cut back in some of these categories, especially if you have been spending too much to begin with. I'll be listing dozens of suggestions later in this chapter. Here's a quick preview. Are you driving a fancy new car that you bought on credit? This is a prime candidate for pruning that will cut your transportation debt and also give you more money for reducing your other debts. Are you constantly buying new clothing? If so, your closets are undoubtedly overstuffed already. Make do with what you have for a while.

Reducing essential costs is important, but probably your biggest opportunity to cut expenses is in the nonessential categories, such as recreation and entertainment. Have you been eating out at fancy (or even not-so-fancy) restaurants? Those meals can

Watch Out!
Be careful not to
eliminate too
many things that
you enjoy from
your budget. You
may feel that it's
just not worth
all the pain,
and decide to
give up.

add up quickly. Some families spend $100 a week
(or more) at the pizza parlor! Have you been taking
expensive overseas vacations? Grab the pruning
shears again. Try visiting nearer to home, perhaps
camping or hiking in local state parks. You can easily save hundreds or even thousands of dollars this
way.

I'm not suggesting that you deprive yourself of
everything that you love to do. That's a sure-fire prescription for budget failure. However, you do need
to reign in your spending, and the nonessential categories usually have the most fat to trim. You decide
what you need to keep—and what you can do without. Think about what you are gaining from this
exercise—financial responsibility and peace of mind
(at the very least)—rather than about what you are
giving up.

Your spending plan

If the budget approach leaves you cold, you can
try a spending plan instead. Frankly, it's the same
general idea as a budget. You still have to track
your expenses and figure out how much money is
available for the various monthly categories, but
it's somewhat simplified and maybe a little more
flexible.

As in the budget method, you need to come up
with basic expense categories. For the sake of simplicity, you can combine some of them. In Gerri
Detweiler's *The Ultimate Credit Handbook*, she uses the
following condensed categories:

- Home—rent or mortgage, utilities, maintenance costs, etc.

- Food—food you eat at home or during work
  hours

- Transportation—all automotive expenses including car payments and/or public transportation fares

- Medical Expenses—doctors, dentists, prescriptions, eyewear, etc.

- Clothing and Personal Care—clothing, shoes, jewelry, toiletries, haircuts, etc.

- Entertainment/Recreation—movies, video rentals, dining out, vacations

- Loan Payments—credit cards, lines of credit, etc., excluding mortgage and car loans (already listed)

- Miscellaneous—create your own categories as needed

You don't *have* to use these exact categories, but they should work for most people. As before, you keep track of every penny you spend in a little notebook that you carry with you and then transfer those figures to your money management software or accountant's notebook at home (no escaping this part, I'm afraid). Also, be sure to figure in tax payments or other expenses that occur only at certain times during the year. Now add up all the figures. It should come to no more than your total monthly net income (which we calculated earlier). Again, if it exceeds your monthly income, you need to cut your spending immediately.

Assuming, however, that the total figure is at or below your monthly income, you now need to decide how to spend the money you have available in each of your categories. There's no right or wrong way to do this. Just a way that works for you. However, the less you spend in all the categories except the seventh (loan payments), the more you will have available for those loan payments, and the quicker you will reduce your debts. There are various strategies on how to pay off those debts. We'll cover them in Chapter 12, "Climbing Back Up."

As in the budget method described earlier, don't make too many drastic cuts right away—unless you are teetering on the edge of bankruptcy. As you work with your spending plan over a period of months, you will begin to identify more ways you can cut your expenses without seriously impacting the important things in your life. You may even begin to wonder why you were spending so much money on so many things that weren't vital.

Tips for reducing expenses

First the bad news. Generally speaking, when compared with people in other parts of the world, Americans spend so much money on so many things that we are inevitably wasting a lot of our money on nonessentials. Now the good news. This means that you probably don't have to be a CPA in order to find lots of ways to cut your spending.

If you have a family, you should enlist their support in finding ways to trim expenses. Focus on one expense category at a time, and see what kind of imaginative strategies you can come up with. Remember to maintain your sense of humor. Make the process fun by turning it into a contest. You can even offer modest, non-monetary rewards like a special meal or perhaps a hike to a favorite spot for the best ideas.

Here are some great money-saving tips, organized by spending plan category, to get your "little gray cells" working. We'll start with home:

- Comparison-shop for the cheapest telephone rates. There are a wide variety of carriers available.

- Refinance your home mortgage if interest rates are lower than what you are currently paying.

- Swap babysitting duties with friends rather than hiring someone.

- Save on your hot water heating bill by lowering the setting on your hot water heater from around 140° to 120°.

- De-clutter your home. You'll be amazed at how much stuff you don't really need. Sell it, and apply the money toward reducing your debts or toward your savings. Unsold items can be donated to charity, and you can take a tax deduction.

- Rent carpet-cleaning equipment, and do it yourself.

- Substitute a down comforter for your electric blanket.

- Learn to make minor home repairs yourself.

- Consider energy-efficient light bulbs.

- Buy your heating oil off-season. Pre-buy arrangements can save you a lot of money (firewood prices tend to be lower during the summer as well).

- Consider moving to a smaller, less expensive house or apartment. The savings could be substantial, especially if your current home is really too large for your needs. If you have extra space, you may be able to take in a boarder for extra income.

Moneysaver
The $5 a day that you spend on eating out at work comes to $100 a month. For about $40 a month, you can buy more than enough food supplies for a brown bag lunch. You save $60 per month.

Here are some money-saving tips for food:

- Shop with coupons, but carefully. Use coupons only for things you would buy anyway.

- Bring a brown bag lunch to work.

- Never shop when hungry.

- Make a shopping list, and stick to it.

- Avoid buying convenience foods.

- Cook more than you need for one meal, and then refrigerate or freeze the rest to save time (and money) later.

- Keep a list of prices on the food items you normally buy; then you will know a deal when you see it and can stock up.

- Shop at a farmer's market.

- If you do eat out at a restaurant, save half of it for a future meal; this effectively cuts the cost of the meal in half.

Here are some suggestions for ways to save money on transportation:

- If you own a big, expensive gas hog, trade down.

- Consider buying a secondhand vehicle in good mechanical condition.

- Carpool to work.

- Walk or bike to work if it's not too far.

- Check fluid levels, and consider doing minor maintenance chores yourself.

- Keep tires inflated properly. This will optimize your gas mileage and reduce tire wear.

- Follow regular, scheduled maintenance plans. They will pay for themselves in the long run.

- Keep your vehicle longer. If properly maintained, it should easily last 10 years.

- Slow down. Not only will you get better mileage, but you also may avoid costly speeding tickets or accidents.

- If you live in an area served by public transport, use it.

Here are some money-saving tips on medical expenses:

- Carefully check your hospital bills. Studies have shown that over 95 percent of these bills have errors in favor of the hospital.

- Practice preventive health maintenance. Have your teeth cleaned and checked regularly and have a general physical exam every year, for example.

- Exercise by regularly taking walks (they're free) instead of paying for expensive health club memberships.

- Never be without health insurance coverage of some sort, even if it has high deductibles. Consider it as catastrophic accident/illness protection.

- Keep your kids' immunizations up to date.

- Ask for generic medicines.

- Don't smoke.

Here are some ideas on ways to cut costs on clothing and personal care:

- Buy fewer items, but buy classics. Avoid trendy, short-lived styles.

- Buy clothes off-season at substantially reduced prices.

- Avoid "dry clean only" items. They're expensive to maintain over the life of the garment.

- Buy clothes at thrift shops and consignment stores. The money you spend may benefit worthy causes, and you'll save money at the same time.

- Avoid shopping at the last minute. Plan ahead for the best deals.

- Learn to cut your kids' hair.

- Get your own hair done at a beauty school. The prices are low.

- Stand bottles of shampoo, hand lotion, moisturizers, and other creamy stuff on their caps so that you can get the last drop.

Finally, here are some ways to save money on entertainment and recreation:

- Eat out only on special occasions.

- Entertain your friends at home. Consider a potluck meal.

- Avoid vacation time-shares—they tend to be expensive.

- Take an off-season vacation when rates are lower.

- Rent videos instead of going to first-run movies.

- Don't watch the shopping channel.

- Stop buying lottery tickets.

- Check out your local library. In addition to books, you'll find newspapers, magazines, videos, CDs, and various programs for children and adults. And it's normally free or comparitively inexpensive.

- Don't join record, CD, or book clubs. You don't need to be constantly tempted.

- Take advantage of inexpensive family entertainment. Outings for hiking, biking, picnicking, or visiting parks and playgrounds are free or very inexpensive.

- Many communities, churches, schools, colleges, and universities offer free concerts and other cultural events, especially during the summer months. Check them out.

- Consider purchasing local entertainment books that offer discount coupons for things you normally do.

This is only a sampling. I'm sure you can think of many more possibilities. Although the savings involved with some of these ideas may amount to only a few dollars, taken together with all the other ideas, they can really add up. And this can actually be fun, once you get your creativity working on it and the rest of your family involved.

Try using cash

There is yet one more strategy that may help you curb your spending, especially if you are in financial trouble mainly through the imprudent use of credit cards. After you have removed your credit cards from your wallet, instead of resorting to your checkbook for your miscellaneous spending, use cash for a while. Pay by cash for your nonessential items but also for regular purchases such as groceries.

This can be a remarkably therapeutic experience. You can see the immediate consequences of your spending. There's nothing quite like counting out a fistful of one dollar bills into the hand of a store clerk to drive home the reality of what you are

Bright Idea
As you find more and more ways to cut your spending, you may soon discover that besides saving a lot of money, you are actually improving various aspects of your life at the same time.

doing. It may even make you think twice about doing it.

Tips for increasing your income

So far, we've focused mainly on cutting expenses. But what if that still isn't enough? Or perhaps you want to speed up the debt reduction process more than your current income level will allow. Several strategies are available for increasing the income side of your budget or spending plan:

- If you are not currently employed and are able to work, the solution is obvious—get a job. If there is another member of your family who is currently unemployed or underemployed, consider having this person take a full-time job, even if it's just on a temporary basis until your debts are paid off. This strategy can give a welcome boost to your family income.

- If you are already fully employed, the choices are not quite as obvious. You might be able to apply for a better job with your existing employer, but be aware that this choice may involve additional training or schooling and is more of a long-term strategy than an immediate one. Avoid going back to school for a degree unless that field is going to provide you with enough money to satisfy your current debt load, new student loans, and leave you with more money each month.

- You might consider getting a better-paying job somewhere else. Obviously, don't give up your old job before you are absolutely certain you have a new one, or you'll quickly be even deeper in debt. Before you make a move like this, be careful to look at every aspect of your prospective new position to be sure that you really will come out ahead in such areas as pension plans, health benefits, and leave policies. Check out such factors as transportation costs and commuting times as well. And don't forget about your long-term potential for advancement.

■ Moonlighting at a second job is another possibility. Before you decide to follow this strategy, you need to weigh the possible disadvantages of too much work and not enough time to spend with your family (unless your second job is home-based). It's very easy to burn out in this scenario. However, if you can combine a second job with something that you really enjoy doing, or think you would like to do, consider trying it out for a while as an experiment. You'll also be earning a little extra money at the same time. You may even find a new career in the process. You'll never know unless you try. Another advantage of the second job strategy is that cutting down on leisure time also reduces potential shopping time.

Whatever you decide, any additional income should be used primarily to pay down your debt, not to buy yourself things to boost your sagging morale due to overwork. That's just chasing your tail around in circles.

Don't give up

As I mentioned earlier, regardless of which debt reduction strategy you are using, it's important to stick with it. One of the best ways to ensure your long-term success is to remain as flexible as possible. Murphy's Law will almost certainly come into play

Watch Out!
Resist the temptation to use the money budgeted for loan payments for anything else. If you succumb to the temptation, it will slow down your debt reduction plans and may even put them in jeopardy if it happens too often.

somewhere along the way, and you'll suddenly find yourself facing an unexpected expense. Don't panic. See if you can shift some money temporarily from one or more of your budget (or spending plan) categories to the one that needs the extra money. The only category that is "untouchable" is your loan payment category. Only dip into that one as an absolute last resort.

If you find that you occasionally have a little money left over at the end of the month, shifting it into your savings category as a small cushion to protect against Murphy's Law is an excellent idea. Or you can apply it to your loan payment category. Regardless of what may come along, maintain your sense of humor. If you stumble badly one month, pick yourself up, dust yourself off, and keep on going. It's not the end of the world. And don't give up. This isn't forever.

Just the facts

- You need to make substantial changes to your spending habits in order to get out of debt.

- You may need to make some changes to your lifestyle as well.

- It's important to develop realistic financial goals.

- A good budget or spending plan is one of your most powerful tools for helping you to reduce your spending—and your debt.

- A lot of small cuts in spending can add up to big savings.

- Stick to your plan—and don't give up.

GET THE SCOOP ON...
How to deal with your creditors ▪ How to negotiate lower payments ▪ What your creditors
can—and can't do ▪ Your legal protections ▪
Dealing with bill collectors ▪ How to deal with
the IRS

Dealing with Creditors

Chapter 10

B eing in debt is bad enough, but being hassled by your creditors or by bill collectors is
even worse. If you've managed to spend
yourself into a financial hole, you've basically got no
one to blame but yourself for the consequences of
your actions. Still, receiving a constant stream of
dunning notices and calls about past due bills is an
embarrassing, degrading, and disruptive situation.
If you're in debt because of circumstances beyond
your control, then being hassled just adds to the
stress. In either case, it's no fun.

Instead of facing the situation squarely, many
people waste a lot of time and energy trying to avoid
their problems—and their creditors. This only
makes matters worse. Learning how to deal with
creditors and bill collectors effectively is not unlike
learning basic self-defense techniques. The main
goal of a good self-defense program is empowerment
rather than technique. And that's what I'm going to
focus on in this chapter—your empowerment.

In the following pages, I'll help you deal with your creditors and offer some suggestions that should make a stressful situation a little easier. First, if you are having trouble making even the minimum payments, I'll tell you how to restructure your debts by negotiating lower payments. Then we'll go over the legal weapons that your creditors can use against you in trying to collect your overdue accounts, and the legal rights you have to defend yourself. I'll tell you about bill collectors, what they can and can't do, and offer suggestions about what you should and shouldn't agree to do when they contact you. Last, but by no means least, I'll offer some tips on dealing with the IRS when you owe them money. If nothing else, by the end of this chapter, you will know how to stand up for yourself when debt collectors pay you a visit. Don't let them push you around.

Determining your current debt situation

Fortunately, the days when people were tossed into debtor's prison are long past. You don't have to worry about languishing in jail on bread and water if you begin to fall behind on your bills. However, that doesn't mean you can ignore the situation; you should definitely pay attention to the little reminders that you will be receiving from your creditors. Before we go into detail about this, it is helpful to look at the various stages of credit distress to see what kind of response is appropriate for each level. There are basically three stages. For lack of better terminology, I'll call them early, middle, and late.

Early stage

In the early stage of credit distress, you are probably a month or so behind in your payments, you are being charged late fees, may be at or over your credit limits, and probably don't have any serious marks against your credit. In this scenario, you don't need a CPA to tell you that you should be able to straighten things out fairly quickly by reducing your spending for a few months and allocating more of your income toward paying off your bills until you get your debts under control.

Even in the early stage of credit distress, it's important to contact your creditors promptly to explain what's going on. If you are a good customer and normally pay your bills on time, they may be willing to work something out. They may set up a revised payment plan or make other concessions for you until you get caught up. Once you have made an agreement, however, be absolutely sure that you live up to it. Failure to do so will be reflected on your credit report and will also make it harder for you to work things out with these creditors in the future if you get into difficulty again.

Middle stage

By the time things have progressed to the middle stage of distress, your task has become far more difficult. Your bills are months past due, and you are probably hearing about it on a regular basis from your creditors. Nevertheless, it's not too late to face the problem squarely and deal with it. The longer you wait, however, the harder time you'll have.

If you act promptly, before your creditors take collection action against you, it's still possible to deal directly with them. As difficult as that may be, it's better than dealing with collection agencies. Having your account turned over to a collection agency leaves an even worse blemish on your credit record than a late payment, so you want to try to

Watch Out!
The absolute worst thing you can do when you are in debt is to try to avoid your creditors. Doing nothing to resolve the problem only makes things worse.

avoid this if possible. Depending on how deeply in debt you are, you may need to contact a debt counseling service or support group (see Chapter 11, "Where to Go for Assistance").

Late stage

By the time you reach the final stage of credit distress, you are in so deep that it's going to be very difficult to extricate yourself. Difficult, but not impossible. Your accounts have been turned over to collection agencies, you are probably facing court proceedings, some of your possessions may have been attached, the repo agency may have taken your car, and your wages may be subject to garnishment. Not a pretty picture.

This situation could have been avoided if you had taken action sooner to work with your creditors, or perhaps with a credit counseling service. Yet, even at this stage there's no need to give up entirely—you still have several options. We'll look at them later in this chapter.

My next point belabors the obvious, but I need to say it to make sure that we're all on the same wavelength. Regardless of which stage of debt you find yourself in, you absolutely should not continue your prior spending habits. Cut your expenses to the bone, and watch every purchase carefully. If you are in the middle or late stage of credit distress and you skipped over Chapter 9, go back and read it now, especially the section on changing your attitudes about credit.

How to negotiate with creditors

Now that you have a clearer idea of the various levels of credit distress, you need to figure out where you fit into that picture with your particular debt situation. If you are in one of the first two stages, it's important to understand that you still have room to negotiate with your creditors, especially if you are having trouble making your minimum payments. If this is the case, then negotiating lower monthly payments is a viable short-term option. A word of caution: there are a growing number of creditors who are not willing to negotiate, but many still do, so it's definitely worth a try.

Of course, by taking longer to pay off your bills, you will pay more in interest charges. The extra cost may be worth it, however, if the damage to your credit rating can be minimized, but you need to contact your creditors promptly to keep things from getting any worse. The longer you wait, the more limited your options become.

Develop a plan

Before contacting your creditors, you have to develop a plan of action. In Chapter 9 we figured out what your income and expenses were. If, after subtracting your expenses from your income, you ended up with a negative figure, you have to either reduce your expenses or increase your income (or both) to bring your income and expenses back into balance. Assuming that you have already trimmed your spending to the bone, have no immediate prospects for increasing your income, and are still having trouble meeting your minimum payments, your only viable option is to negotiate with your creditors to reduce your payments. The negative figure mentioned above should serve as a target for that reduction. For example, if the negative amount is $70, you need to reduce your total monthly bill payments by at least $70.

Before you begin negotiating with your creditors, however, you need to sort through your

Bright Idea
If you can't make your minimum monthly payments, try negotiating lower payments with your creditors. This strategy may allow you to keep your accounts current and protect your credit rating.

obligations to determine which ones are fairly negotiable and which ones are not as negotiable. As I
mentioned in Chapter 9, not all bills are equal, especially your essential fixed obligations like mortgage,
rent, child support, and income taxes. Most of your
other bills probably are negotiable, at least on a temporary basis until you can get caught up. Actually,
even your mortgage and income tax payments can
be negotiated to some extent (more on that later),
but I suggest that you start with your other bills first.

The first step in developing your plan is to list all
of your debts in one column. In the second column,
add up the monthly payments that you currently
make on your debts. In the third column, list the
payment amount that you think you can afford to
make, taking into account those items that are not
easily negotiable and those that are. A simplified list,
for example, might look something like the one
shown here (your actual list would probably include
many more items):

LIST OF MONTHLY BILL PAYMENTS

Creditor	Monthly Payment	Amount You Can Afford
Mortgage	$450	$450
Child Support	$200	$200
Credit Card 1	$75	$60
Credit Card 2	$50	$40
Car Payment	$220	$175
Total	$995	$925 ($70 reduction)

Note that the mortgage and child support payments remained unchanged between columns two
and three, while the credit card and car payment
amounts were reduced to what you felt you could

afford. If, by making these adjustments, you have reduced your total monthly payments by the amount needed to balance your income and expenses ($70), then you've targeted the accounts requiring negotiation. In the example, the figures in the last column for your credit cards ($60 and $40) and your car payment ($175) would be your negotiating targets.

An alternative approach would be to figure your nonnegotiable bills first in one list and then make a separate list of your negotiable accounts. The negotiable list might look like this sample work sheet:

PAYMENT PROPOSAL WORK SHEET				
Account	Balance	Minimum Payment	Proposed Payment	Agreed Payment
Credit Card 1	$1,095	$75	$55	$60
Credit Card 2	$750	$50	$35	$40
Car Payment	$4,500	$220	$160	$175
Totals	$6,345	$345	$250	$275

The first column lists your bills, and the second column is the remaining balance in the account. The third column lists your current minimum payments; the fourth column is your proposed payments. The fifth column lists the payments you actually agree to with your creditors. Again, for the purposes of this example, the reduction comes to $70, the amount you need to bring your income and expenses into balance.

Once you have your target reduction amounts, you need to figure out how long you will need to get your debts under control and resume making full payments again. It might be a few months, perhaps

Moneysaver
Try negotiating lower monthly payments with your credit card issuers first. These loans are unsecured, and that may give you a little bargaining power.

a year, depending on the amount of your indebtedness. Your creditors will want to know how long you think the process will take. (Be aware that the longer it takes, the more your creditors will make on interest, so this isn't a bad deal for them.) You shouldn't have too much trouble getting most creditors to agree to a few months of reduced payments. While you're at it, you may be able to get them to lower the interest rate as well. It's worth a try. After your information is organized, you are ready to put your plan into action.

Implementing your plan

When you're ready to begin negotiations, one of the best places to start with is your credit card accounts. Although the credit card companies will certainly try to collect the money you owe them, they aren't holding any collateral, such as your car or house, on the loan. Many of these companies would rather work out a reasonable repayment deal with you directly, than incur the time, trouble, and expense of turning your account over to a collection agency. Some companies, however, may not be willing to negotiate.

Assuming that you have a proposed repayment plan, the next step is to take the bull by the horns and call your creditors, one at a time, and explain the situation. You may find this step extremely difficult, especially if you are not accustomed to being assertive. Take a deep breath—and do it. After a little practice, you may discover that you aren't as much of a wimp as you thought you were.

The fact that you are calling should make a difference to your creditors. Your call means that you are serious about paying back your debts. There is a lot of competition in the credit card field these days, and card issuers want customers who carry a balance from month to month—like you—so they really do want your business. Consequently, you should have your creditor's undivided attention at this point. Make the most of it.

After you have explained that you are not able to make your present payments, tell the creditor that you have developed a realistic repayment plan that will allow you to keep your account in good standing while meeting the needs of your other creditors as well. Have your specific proposal in hand for reference during this discussion.

Let's say that (from the preceding example) you owe $1,095 on your Credit Card 1 account, with a minimum payment of $75. You might propose to make a minimum payment of $55 and eventually agree to make a payment of $60 with the credit manager. Just remember, no matter how hard-nosed they may sound, most of your creditors probably would prefer to make a deal instead of resorting to collection. Be persistent. If you are having a hard time arriving at a negotiated amount, you simply may have to ask what is the minimum payment that will keep your account in good standing.

Let your creditors know the details of your particular situation, especially if there are some extenuating circumstances, so that they can take those circumstances into account while developing a plan that will work. Be polite but firm. Don't let anyone intimidate you. Throughout this process, it's important to remain calm. Getting into a shouting match is not helpful.

Make sure you keep careful records of whom you talked to, the date and time of your conversation, and what was agreed to. It's probably best to speak with a supervisor or manager, or who-ever is authorized to negotiate terms on accounts. It's also important to follow up your conversation with a letter (sent via certified mail, return receipt requested) to the person you spoke with. This should eliminate any possible misunderstanding or lack of communication between you, your creditor, and any of the creditor's various departments. As always, keep a copy of the letter, along with the return receipt card showing it was received, for future reference.

Regardless of the total size of your debts, it's important to let your creditors know that they will be treated equally and that your payments will be on a pro rata basis. Large account balances will receive proportionately larger payments, and smaller bal-ances will receive smaller payments. During the negotiating process, you should not agree to giving one creditor a larger payment that will adversely affect your payments to your other creditors. Whatever you agree to, be sure it's realistic and that you will be able to follow through on it. Never agree to a payment that you can't afford to make.

Fixed loans

If you have negotiated new, lower payments on your credit cards and you are still in negative financial territory on your monthly budget, you need to turn your attention to your fixed loan payments for items such as appliance and furniture loans and, perhaps, student loans. Follow the same strategy that you used on your credit card accounts, being sure to talk to the appropriate loan officer or credit manager. Propose a specific reduction for your payment and suggest the number of months that this plan will remain in effect.

Watch Out!
Once you have negotiated agreements for lower monthly payments, it's extremely impor-tant to live up to them. You'll be in even more trouble if you don't.

With fixed loans, you also have the option of asking to extend the term of the loan in order to lower your monthly payments. A 12-month loan, for example, could be extended to 18 months. Again, this will cost you more in interest payments, but it's probably a fair trade-off if it gets you through your current crisis. With student loans, it's possible to receive a deferment or forbearance on the loan if you are temporarily in financial difficulty (see "Student Loans" in Chapter 2 for more details).

How to keep your car

If you are struggling to deal with a temporary financial shortfall and you regularly use your car to get to work, the last thing you need is to have your car repossessed. Although auto loans are fixed loans, their relatively unique aspects warrant a separate discussion.

First of all, in some states if you miss only one payment, your car technically may be repossessed (depending on the terms of your loan and your state's laws on "default"). Should this occur, you may receive a letter saying that you have 10 days in which to pay your loan in full, or your car will either be kept by your creditor or be sold (sometimes at auction). In some cases, you may not even get the benefit of the 10-day written warning. Fat chance of paying off the entire loan when you couldn't even afford the monthly payment. The ultimatum is bad enough, but it gets worse.

If your car is auctioned off, it may receive only a wholesale bid based on its current, depreciated value. The proceeds of the sale are deducted from the remaining balance on your loan. You will then be responsible for paying the difference between the auction price and the remaining loan balance, plus any repossession costs or penalties. This amount is known as the "*deficiency balance.*"

At this point, you no longer have a car and you are facing yet another bill that you can't afford to pay. Even if you decide to give the car back to the lender ("voluntary repossession"), you will still be responsible for the deficiency balance, and perhaps other fees as well. It's a lousy situation. But there are several alternatives.

You may be able to refinance the remaining balance of your loan for a longer time period. Failing that, you may be able to get the finance manager to extend your loan for two or three months. In effect, this will allow you to skip a few months' worth of payments without damaging your credit rating. It's a short-term fix, but if your credit crunch is a temporary one, it may gain you the financial breathing room that you need.

You might also explore the possibility of trading your car in for a less expensive one. Look carefully at all aspects of this strategy, including any extra fees that might be involved, to be sure you will actually come out ahead. Trading down could reduce your monthly payments and allow you to continue to drive to work. If you are a homeowner, you can see about replacing your auto loan with a home equity loan that has lower monthly payments.

The next option is a last resort. Assuming that none of the strategies just mentioned work, and you see default looming as a certainty, you may be better off selling the car before your creditor can repossess it. Then pay off the loan. The down side is that your transportation for work is gone, but at least you have avoided the extra costs of repossession and the potential black mark on your credit report.

How to keep your home

If you are struggling with a severe credit crunch, you may also be worried about losing your home. That's a justifiable concern. If you miss a mortgage payment, you will receive a notice that your payment is past due. On most mortgages, if you miss three payments, your lender must report your delinquency to a credit bureau and may initiate foreclosure proceedings against you.

Fortunately, most legitimate lenders will try to help you get back on your financial feet. Your best course of action is to immediately contact your lender when you first realize that you are going to have trouble making your mortgage payments. If you do this before you actually fall behind on your payments, you will have more options and more time to think about them. Most lenders are willing to work with you to come up with a solution as long as your financial difficulties are temporary and you are making a good faith effort to resolve them.

A few lenders may reduce or suspend your mortgage payments for a short time. However, when you resume making payments, you may have to pay an additional amount toward the total past due, as well as the interest that has been piling up. Other lenders may agree to change the terms of your mortgage by extending the repayment period—from 15 to 30 years, for example—to reduce your monthly payments. Find out what fees would be assessed for these changes and how they would affect you in the long run.

If you have mortgage insurance, another strategy is the so-called PMI technique. Contact your private mortgage insurer, explain what your situation is, and they may be willing to help you keep your

Watch Out!
An auto repossession is one of the worst blemishes your credit report can receive. Try to avoid it if you possibly can.

mortgage payments current. Most insurers would rather do that than pay a claim on a default.

If your are unable to work out a new payment plan with your lender, contact a housing counseling agency. They may be able to assist you. Call the local office of the Department of Housing and Urban Development or the housing authority in your area to help you locate a counseling agency near you.

Charged-off accounts

Earlier in this chapter, I mentioned that even in the late stage of credit distress you still have some options. Attempting to resolve charged-off accounts is one of those options. A *charge-off account* is an account that has remained unpaid for at least 90, and sometimes as long as 180 days, at which point the creditor gives up on receiving payment and "charges it off" as a bad debt. The account is then turned over or sold to a collection agency or other party.

You should know that when this happens, creditors dramatically reduce their expectations of ever receiving the full amount that was due on the account. Collection agencies collect only about 20 percent of the accounts placed with them, and they keep a hefty percentage of what they do collect as compensation for their time and effort. Thus, the creditor ultimately ends up with very little, if anything, on so-called collection accounts.

This situation can work to your advantage. In the past, a popular strategy was to get the creditor to remove the bad mark on your credit rating in exchange for your paying off the debt for less than the full amount. Unfortunately, this strategy is now widely frowned upon throughout the industry. Nevertheless, you still may contact the creditor (or collection agency) and offer to settle the account for less than the original balance due. You actually have some bargaining power, even at this late stage. Decide in advance how much you can afford to pay, and don't go over that amount.

You might try offering 25 percent of the original balance due to satisfy the account. This proposal probably won't fly, but it's a good place to begin your negotiations. To settle, you may have to agree to monthly payments if you don't have the cash on hand for a lump-sum payment. However, if you can handle the monthly payment, the settlement may be worth it in order to get the account paid off. If you decide to try this strategy, ask to speak with the credit manager—someone who has the authority to negotiate this kind of a settlement. This won't be easy. You'll have to use all the patience and diplomacy you can muster, but it's probably worth the effort.

In all likelihood, you'll receive a counteroffer. Continue to press for the best deal that you can get. Be sure that the creditor understands that first you will pay creditors who are willing to agree to a compromise and that the others will just have to wait.

There are some disadvantages to this strategy, however, that you need to be aware of. If a collection agency or creditor forgives an amount in excess of $600 they have to report the figure to the IRS, and you will then be liable for paying taxes on that amount (unless you are insolvent). Also, while the portion of the debt that you pay will be listed by the creditor as "paid as agreed," the remainder of the debt most likely will be listed as "settled" or "written off," which is considered a negative mark on your credit report. While you do at least get the account settled for less than the full amount, it does-n't help your credit rating much. Still, a settled account is better than one that has not been paid at all; it's a matter of degree.

Assuming that you come to an agreement, it might be a good idea to try to get the creditor or collection agency to send you a letter that releases you from the debt. This will give you a written record of the fact that the account has been settled. If you do arrive at a settlement, be sure to let your creditor know how much you appreciate their cooperation.

Your creditors and their options

Your front doorbell rings. You open the door. Three burly men in dark clothing push their way into your home. "Pay up the money you owe, or we're gonna break your legs," the biggest and ugliest of them growls menacingly. You struggle to get away, but it's no use. The ugly one leans closer. You begin to sweat. Then you wake up. Fortunately this kind of B-movie nightmare scene is not the sort of thing that most people who are in debt have to worry about. Not only is it unlikely, it's also illegal. Your creditors can't use this sort of tactic to "encourage" you to pay what you owe. At least they're not supposed to.

Nevertheless, your creditors do have an arsenal of legal weapons at their disposal, and they almost certainly will use one or more of them to try to collect the money that you owe. These weapons include turning your account over to a collection agency, taking you to court, garnishing your wages, repossessing the collateral for secured loans (your furniture, appliances, or perhaps your car), and, in extreme cases, foreclosing on your home.

The decision on which of these weapons to use—and when to use them—largely depends on how far

Unofficially...
According to the Nilson Report, 2.95 percent of consumer debt was charged off as a loss in the United States in 1997. That comes to about $1 out of every $34 owed.

past due your accounts are and how hard you have tried to avoid payment. If your creditors have had to pursue you across the country for years like bloodhounds while you tried to cover your financial tracks behind you, you should not be too surprised if they come down hard on you when they finally do catch up with you.

On the other hand, if your debt problems are still in the early stages and you honestly have been trying to sort out your finances, you almost certainly will find that your creditors are willing to work with you. I've said this before, but it bears repeating: The sooner you contact your creditors and establish a dialog, the easier it is to work things out. The longer you wait, the harder it gets. Now let's look at your creditor's arsenal so you'll know what you're up against.

Informal collection

Informal collection is a strategy used in the early stages of an overdue account. Initially it consists of a polite reminder that your account is past due. This first reminder will generally be followed by increasingly pointed requests for payment that eventually become demands as your account slides further and further into arrears. If you respond to these requests soon enough, this is as far as the process goes. This is the best solution.

If you don't respond within about 60 days, your creditor may temporarily freeze your account or shut off your line of credit until you pay what you owe. Your account may even be closed altogether if you don't settle up.

Bill collectors

The next step, bill collectors, occurs when your creditor decides you aren't going to pay willingly, and your account is turned over to a collection department or agency. At this stage, it's important to know what kind of bill collector you are dealing with.

Many larger banks and creditors have their own in-house collection departments. If you are dealing with your creditor's collection department, you will find that your options for a settlement are still pretty good because your creditor would prefer to keep you as a paying customer. If you work out an arrangement on your bill at this stage, you can probably avoid having your account listed as being officially turned over for collection. But if you procrastinate, your account will almost certainly be turned over to a third-party collector. By then, the damage will have been done to your credit history.

Be aware that in-house collection departments can be more aggressive than third-party collectors because they are not subject to the same stringent rules that third-party collectors are under the federal Fair Debt Collection Practices Act (more on that in a moment).

Once your account has been turned over to a third-party collector, your options become considerably less attractive. At this point, you are limited primarily to paying off your debt (or a negotiated settlement amount). Your credit rating has now been damaged, and you probably won't be able to deal directly with your original creditor any more.

Third-party collectors generally fall into three categories: primary, secondary, and tertiary. The primary collectors get the easiest (and most recent) accounts and keep about a third of the money they collect as their commission. After about six months, if the primary collector fails, the account is generally

Unofficially...
Bad debt costs every adult in the United States over $680 per year. Looked at another way, this means that bad debt costs an average non-supervisory worker nearly 54 hours of labor (before taxes) on an annual basis.
—*American Collectors Association*

turned over to a secondary collector. The secondary collector, if successful, keeps up to 45 percent of the money collected. If the attempts of the secondary collector also fail, the account may be turned over to a tertiary collector, who may keep as a fee 50 percent or more of the amount collected. A tertiary collector may pursue an account for years.

Court proceedings

The threat of court proceedings is one of your creditor's most powerful weapons. A court judgment against you is a very serious blemish on your credit report. Try to avoid it. If you are threatened with being hauled into court, attempt to resolve your credit problems before the actual legal process begins. If it's already too late to stop the process, try to reach an out-of-court settlement before you have to appear in court. This is especially important if you really do owe the money in question and don't have any viable mitigating circumstances. If you do reach a settlement, the case can be dropped or dismissed before a judgment is actually handed down, thus saving your credit history yet another black mark.

The type of court you will be dealing with depends partly on the amount of your debt and the laws in your state. Cases involving disputes for less than $3,000 are generally handled in small claims court. Cases for larger amounts normally end up in civil court. You don't need to hire a lawyer for small claims court, so that's generally the least expensive and quickest route. If you end up in civil court, you'll need a lawyer.

If you believe that the claims of your creditor are incorrect, you will almost certainly want to mount a defense. Whether or not you are going to contest the suit, be sure to show up in court when summoned. If you don't, even if your creditor is totally wrong, the judge will take a dim view of your failure to show up and almost certainly will issue a "default judgment" against you. Once the judgment is issued, you will have to pay. If you can't make it to court on the specified date, call the court clerk and ask for a postponement or alternate date. But make sure you show up on the new date.

If you do end up in court, bring any evidence with you that could substantiate your side of the story, such as cancelled payment checks or receipts. On the other hand, if you really have no defense, try to get the judge and your creditor to agree to a repayment plan instead of a final judgment. By asking the court to stay (or delay) the final judgment, you will hopefully give yourself enough time to pay off the debt. Then you can petition the court to dismiss the case against you. This is admittedly a last-ditch defense, but it's still better than having a judgment handed down against you that will stain your credit report for at least seven years.

Bright Idea
In some states, mediation or arbitration is offered as an alternative to a court appearance. Check with your state's attorney general to see what is available in your state.

Judicial weapons

Another weapon in your creditor's arsenal is a lien. Basically, a *lien* is a legal ownership or interest in your property that must be satisfied before the property (or the proceeds of the sale of your property) can be used for other purposes. There are a variety of liens, but the type we're talking about here is a judicial lien. A judicial lien can result from either prejudgment or postjudgment collection efforts on the part of your creditor. A prejudgment lien, for example, might be a court-allowed attachment of your property while a lawsuit is pending. A postjudgment lien, on the other hand, might be a court-approved garnishment of your wages that remains in place until your debt obligation has been paid off.

Wage garnishment (also known as "wage attachment") cannot occur without a court judgment against you, and it is not imposed before you have been given an opportunity to pay your creditor the amount of a judicial judgment, or at least set up a payment plan. If you don't pay, your creditor will certainly go back to court and obtain a "*Writ of Garnishment*" (or "*Writ of Attachment of Wages*" as it is referred to in some states) that allows the creditor to forcibly take a portion of your disposable income. *Disposable income* is what is left of your paycheck after such items as Federal income taxes, Social Security taxes, and state and local taxes have been deducted.

Most of your earnings, such as wages, salaries, commissions, and bonuses, as well as regular payments from pension and retirement plans, are subject to garnishment. Unemployment compensation, welfare payments, veteran's, disability, Social Security benefits, and income tax refunds are not subject to garnishment. Generally speaking, garnishment may not exceed:

- 25 percent of your disposable income for the week (additional wages may be garnished to enforce child support agreements), or

- The amount by which your disposable income for that week exceeds 30 times the federal minimum hourly wage, whichever is less.

For example, if your disposable income for a week totals $250, then 25 percent of your disposable income is $62.50 ($250 × 25 percent = $62.50). If the federal minimum wage is $5.15, multiply that figure by 30 (30 × $5.15 = $154.50). Then take your disposable income of $250, subtract $154.50, and you get $95.50 ($250 − $154.50 = $95.50). Consequently, in this example the maximum amount subject to garnishment is $62.50, since it is less than $95.50.

Once your creditor has obtained a Writ of Garnishment, your employer is notified that they must withhold the applicable portion of your disposable income before you are paid the remainder. The process continues until the debt has been paid in full. In addition to federal laws, most states have garnishment laws of their own, which are even more favorable to the consumer. Check your state's laws to see what your rights are.

The Fair Debt Collection Practices Act

Now that you've seen most of the weapons at the disposal of your creditors, it's only fair that you get a little self-defense training. Your best defense against unfair collection practices is the federal Fair Debt Collection Practices Act. Passed in 1978, the FDCPA provides protection against abusive, unfair, and unreasonable collection activities on the part of third-party bill collectors (note: the FDCPA does not apply to the original creditor, just third-party collectors). The protections also extend to your spouse, parents (if the debtor is a minor), guardian, executor, or administrator.

Debts covered under the act include personal, family, and household debts, such as money owed on the purchase of a car, medical care bills, or personal charge accounts. The act, of course, does not erase any legitimate debt that you owe—paying off the debt is the only way to accomplish that.

How collectors may contact you

According to the FDCPA, if the collector knows that you are represented by an attorney, the collector must deal with your attorney. In this case, the collector is prohibited from contacting you or anyone else besides your attorney about the debt. If you do not have an attorney, the collector may talk with others in order to try to locate you. While making these inquiries, collectors must identify themselves and say that they are simply confirming or correcting information about your location. This information is confined to your residence, home phone number, and place of employment. It does not include your business phone number or the names and phone numbers of your supervisors, or any other information related to your job or pay.

During these inquiries, collectors may not indicate that they are from a collection agency or that they are attempting to collect a debt that you owe. When they are making inquiries, collectors are prohibited from discussing your debt with anyone else—even members of your own family—unless they are joint applicants or cosigners on the account in question.

Collectors are allowed to contact you in person, by mail, phone, telegram, or fax, but these contacts may not be made at inconvenient times. Unless you specifically tell them otherwise, collectors may not call you before 8 A.M. or after 9 P.M. at your location. A bill collector is also not supposed to contact you while you are taking care of routine activities away from your home, such as shopping, going to a day-care center, eating at a restaurant, and so on. They are also prohibited from calling you at work if your employer does not allow incoming personal calls.

What they must tell you

According to the FDCPA, when you are contacted by bill collectors, they must identify themselves and tell you that they are trying to collect a debt. They also must inform you of the following:

- The amount of the debt
- The name of the creditor
- What you can do if you don't think you owe the debt

After an initial contact with you, the collector is supposed to send you written notification within five days confirming the information in the initial conversation and stating that the debt is assumed to be valid unless you dispute it within 30 days. If you don't owe the debt or if the amount of the debt is in question, be sure to write to the collection agency within 30 days (certified mail, return receipt requested) and carefully explain your position. In the case of a disputed amount, request a verification of the figure. Do not call. It won't protect your rights.

How you can stop them

If you are tired of being hassled by a collection agency, you can actually tell them to stop. Write them a letter (certified mail, return receipt requested) and explain either that you can't afford to pay the bill at the present time or that you refuse to pay—perhaps because the bill in question is disputed—and by law they must stop. The only further contact they are permitted is to notify you that they are ending their collection activities, or that they are going to take you to court or pursue other legal remedies. Be forewarned that there is a strong probability they will sue.

What bill collectors can't do

The Fair Debt Collection Practices Act is very specific about the kinds of activities that are prohibited. Bill collectors may not harass you, make false statements to you, or engage in unfair practices. That eliminates the goon squad at the front door scenario I mentioned earlier, and a lot of other activities as well. Let's look at each of these categories in greater detail.

Harassment

According to the law, collectors may not harass, oppress, or abuse you or any third parties they come in contact with. Debt collectors specifically may not:

- Use threats of violence or harm;
- Publish a list of "deadbeats" who refuse to pay their debts (except to a credit bureau);
- Use obscene or profane language; or
- Repeatedly use the telephone to annoy you.

False statements

Debt collectors may not use any false or misleading statements when they are trying to collect a debt. For example, they may not:

- Falsely imply that they are attorneys or government representatives;
- Falsely imply that you have committed a crime;
- Falsely represent that they operate or work for a credit bureau;
- Misrepresent the amount of your debt;
- Misrepresent the legal status of any papers being sent to you.

In addition, it's important to know that debt collectors cannot threaten you with arrest if you don't pay your debt. They also cannot tell you that they will seize, garnish, attach, or sell your property or wages unless it's legal and they actually intend to do so. Finally, debt collectors may not use a false name or fictitious business name when they contact you about a debt.

Unfair practices

Debt collectors may not engage in unfair practices when they try to collect a debt. According to the law, they may not:

- Collect an amount that exceeds your actual debt, unless your contract with the creditor or your state law permits such a charge;

- Take or threaten to take your property unless this can be done legally;

- Use deception to get you to accept collect phone calls or pay for telegrams;

- Contact you by postcard; or

- Deposit a postdated check before the date written on it.

It's illegal for a debt collector to force you to send a postdated check in order to initiate criminal prosecution. Also, if you do decide to send a postdated check, it's a good idea to write "void until date shown" above the date.

Tips for dealing with bill collectors

Your best strategy, when dealing with bill collectors, is to take the initiative and propose what you can do, rather than allowing them to push you into agreeing to something that is unrealistic. It may be tempting to agree to a payment plan just to get a collector off your back, but that may not be such a good idea. If later on you can't make the payments, you're in

Watch Out!
Never pay a debt collector with a check that you know is going to bounce. In addition to your other problems, you'll almost certainly end up in court on a bad check charge.

worse trouble than you were to begin with. If you really can't pay them anything, say so. Your honesty may help to persuade them to focus their energies on more promising accounts.

In any event, you should take your time to consider any settlement proposals that are made to you, even if that means you have to call the bill collector back after you have thought about it. Upon reflection, you may decide that the proposal won't work, but you might want to make a counteroffer that is within your means.

If you do have enough cash on hand to pay a reduced amount on your bill, as I mentioned earlier, try making a lump-sum offer to clear the entire account. It may not work. But, then again, maybe it will. You won't know unless you try. If you're no good at negotiating on the phone, you can write your proposal on paper and send it to the collector (certified mail, of course). Keep a copy for yourself. In fact, as I mentioned earlier, keep good records of everything that takes place in case there are any disputes later about who agreed to what.

Your rights and how to protect them

Finally, like anyone who has taken a self-defense course knows, being alert and constantly on guard for possible problems is one of your best defensive strategies. Watch for any activities on the part of a bill collector that seem to be questionable. If you know in advance what they can and can't do, you are in a better position to take action against them if necessary.

The Fair Debt Collection Practices Act says you have the right to sue a collector who has violated the law in a state or federal court within one year of the time the violation occurred. If you win, you may recover money for damages you suffered plus up to an additional $1,000. You also may recover court costs and attorney's fees.

If you think a collector has done something illegal, write a letter that describes exactly what happened in detail. Send a copy of the letter to the Federal Trade Commission and to your state attorney general's office or consumer protection office. Be aware they will not assist you in your claim, though your letter might help them to identify trends that need attention. In addition, send a copy of the letter to the legal department of your original creditor as well as to the collection agency in question (certified mail, return receipt). At the very least, this should take the wind out of the collection agency's sails for a while. If you have a strong case and want to pursue it in court, go ahead. You have the right to do so.

The IRS

Finally, there is one more creditor that you should not ignore—the Internal Revenue Service. Few things strike more terror into the hearts of even law-abiding taxpayers than a little note from the IRS. If you're already struggling with other debts and the IRS begins to wonder where your tax payment is, whatever you do, *don't* ignore their letters. The IRS reacts to being ignored just like any other collection agency, only they are far more effective at getting their money.

Your best strategy is to immediately reply to their first letter and ask for more time to pay. Rest assured, you will be contacted by an agent. Truthfully explain your financial predicament, and the agent will probably try to work out a payment plan with you. The agent may even agree to reduce the amount you have to pay if your financial situation is really dire.

If you owe less than $10,000, negotiating a payment plan won't affect your credit rating. Unfortunately, if you owe more than $10,000, the IRS must put a lien on your property, which will hurt your credit report. Trying to hide from creditors is not a good idea. Trying to hide from the IRS is just plain stupid.

Just the facts

- Don't try to avoid your creditors; it just makes matters worse.

- If you can't meet your minimum monthly debt payments, you should be able to negotiate lower payments.

- Your creditors have a wide assortment of weapons they can use to legally collect the money you owe.

- Try to avoid being taken to court for your debts.

- The Fair Debt Collection Practices Act offers you many protections against unfair debt collection activities.

- The IRS is a creditor you don't want to ignore.

Help is on the Way

GET THE SCOOP ON...
Whether you need help or not ▪ Finding the
right counseling service for you ▪
A Twelve-Step approach ▪ Other counseling
alternatives ▪ Help that doesn't help

PART V

Chapter 11

Where to Go for Assistance

If you're deeply in debt, it's unlikely that you're running around town bragging about it. In fact, most folks are so embarrassed about their debts that they won't admit the fact to anyone unless they absolutely have to. Often, the situation is more subtle than that, however. Many debtors won't even admit to themselves that they have a problem. And if you don't have a problem, why do you need help?

In 1990, Peg, who now lives in Butte, Montana, started attending meetings of Debtors Anonymous. "I went, not because I thought I had a problem with money, but because someone else suggested that I might," she recalls. "And I went to the program to prove them wrong and to gather information so that I could build a case and show them that it wasn't true."

After attending a few meetings, Peg changed her tune. "I found, in fact, that I had a lot of issues with money," she now admits. "Debtors Anonymous has 13 signposts on the road to becoming a compulsive debtor, and I had a lot of them." We'll pick up Peg's story a little later in this chapter. For now, the point I want to make is that asking for help can be a very difficult thing for most people to do—especially when they're convinced that they don't need it.

Asking for help is not a sign of weakness. In fact, it's a sign of courage, and it shows that you are willing to face your problems squarely and honestly—whatever uncomfortable things they may reveal about your habits and lifestyle. In this chapter, I'll start off by trying to help you decide whether you need outside assistance to get your financial house in order. Then, we'll look at some of the most popular nonprofit counseling services that are available and examine why they are so popular. If your spending is borderline compulsive or addictive, I'll explain what Debtors Anonymous is and what they can offer you that most other services can't. Then we'll look at some less well-known counseling options you might want to try. We'll also briefly discuss for-profit counseling services. Finally, I'll review what services to avoid.

Need help?

Some people know when they need help. Others are too embarrassed or are afraid to ask. Some like to think of themselves as strong, silent, self-reliant types who don't need help from anybody for anything. Still others are just confused and don't know what to do. Regardless of where you fall (or where you think you fall) within this spectrum, it's important to know that a lot of assistance is available for people like you who are struggling to get their debts under control. You don't have to do this alone.

The more credit distress you are suffering from, the greater the likelihood that you are going to need some sort of assistance. If you're in the early stage of distress (see Chapter 10, "Dealing with Creditors"), you may be able to sort things out on your own. But if you are in the middle or late stage, it is increasingly likely that you will need professional assistance.

Realize that the longer you wait, the harder it's going to be to straighten things out—even with outside help. Don't let your embarrassment about your debts keep you from asking for help. Debt counselors and support groups have heard it all before. No amount of debt is too shocking. Many counselors routinely have clients that are carrying $25,000 or $30,000 on their credit cards. Even $100,000 is not that unusual.

Now, perhaps you're in the early stage of credit distress and you want to handle the problem on your own. I've already given you many of the basic tools you need to do this (and more are coming up in later chapters). Not everyone needs counseling, but do consider that much of this counseling is free, or almost free. You are foolish to ignore it entirely when it might make your task a little (or a lot) easier. You have to make up your own mind.

It's also important to understand that there is no single right approach for everyone—just the right approach for you. There are, however, a number of wrong approaches. We'll get to them at the end of the chapter. For now, we'll focus on the good stuff and where to go to get it. Even if you are convinced that you don't need help from anybody, I urge you to read about your options anyway. You may change your mind before we're done.

Nonprofit services

You can spend a lot of money on credit counseling services, but you don't need to. Some of the better counseling options are free or nearly free. If you feel that you could use some help with your credit problems, your best bet is to try one of the many non-profit groups that are ready, willing, and able to assist you. This is not to say that free help is always the best choice, but there is a lot of it available, and you need to shop around and make your own decision about what is right for you and your particular situation.

First, however, I want to offer a little perspective—and some unofficial advice. Most nonprofit counseling services are able to offer low-cost or no-cost assistance to consumers because they receive financial support from a number of different sources. For many, an important source is contributions from creditors for the payments that are made by consumers who participate in their counseling programs. This helps to keep the costs of these programs down for consumers.

As mentioned earlier in this book, debt counseling is a huge growth industry in this country. But the growth of the customer base has not kept pace with the number of services that are available. The result has been increased competition among counseling services. Another result has been a reduction in the creditor rebates that the counseling services receive. This figure was about 15 percent in the past and is now as low as 6 percent. These reductions have been due to a wide range of issues, but essentially are part of a larger ongoing trend in business to cut expenses wherever possible. The lower contributions have caused problems for some of these services.

Be aware that some counselors have resorted to recommending a formal debt-repayment plan, even though you might actually need only basic budget advice. At the very least, the continued reduction in creditor rebates may cause an increase in the fees charged to consumers who receive counseling services. Don't get me wrong; I'm not suggesting that you shouldn't use these services. Not at all. What I am suggesting is that you shop around carefully before you choose a counseling service and that you trust your instincts. If the service doesn't feel right, keep looking. You will likely find a better match. In the pages that follow, we'll explore your many options among the nonprofit counseling agencies.

National Foundation for Consumer Credit

One of the first places you might want to start looking for help is at the National Foundation for Consumer Credit (NFCC), headquartered in Silver Spring, Maryland. The NFCC is the umbrella group for a network of about 1500 nonprofit agencies that offer money management education; confidential budget, credit, and debt counseling; and debt repayment plans for individuals and families nationwide. Many of the member agencies operate under the name Consumer Credit Counseling Services and are often identified with the regions or states that they serve (Consumer Credit Counseling Service of New Hampshire and Vermont, for example).

The NFCC maintains an extensive and informative Web site at www.nfcc.org. On the Web site, you'll find information on what the organization has to offer. You'll also find basic advice on bankruptcy, on how to obtain and correct your credit report, and on a variety of educational programs offered by member agencies. There's even an online debt test you can take to help you decide if

Unofficially...
About 42 percent of credit card holders pay off their cards in full every month. That compares with just 22 percent in 1992. As a result, card issuers compete intensely for consumers who carry monthly balances.

you are in trouble. The site provides an office locator to find a member agency in your area. In addition, you can call (800) 388-2227 with a touch-tone phone to be automatically connected to the affiliated counseling agency in your area.

NFCC's funding comes from a variety of community resources, but the majority is derived from voluntary contributions from creditors who participate in NFCC/CCCS Debt Management Plans. For debt repayment plans, you may be charged anywhere from $5 to $25 a month. The NFCC and its affiliates refer to these charges as "voluntary contributions," which are deductible on your tax return. If you decline to make the contribution, you can remain in the program anyway. Fees for other services vary. Three-quarters of the offices do basic budget counseling for free, according to NFCC spokesperson William Furmanski. The remaining offices charge anywhere from $2 to $50.

Consumer Credit Counseling Services

The Consumer Credit Counseling Services (CCCS) scattered across the country (and in Puerto Rico and Canada as well) are the NFCC-affiliated offices where you actually go for counseling assistance. In most cases, these offices have been in existence for many years. Use the same phone number as for the NFCC to locate the nearest CCCS office in your area: (800) 388-2227. Although there may be minor variations in some of the program details or fees, most CCCS offices offer the same basic group of services. Here is an overview, based on CCCS literature.

What they offer

For starters, all CCCS offices provide fundamental financial advice to get you on the right track, and they will assist you in the repayment of your debts. Key elements included in CCCS services are confidential budget counseling as well as creditor repayment planning through a Debt Management Program. These services are conducted through in-person interviews or phone interviews at most locations.

In addition, CCCS offices provide a wide range of financial education programs. CCCS education departments develop, coordinate, and implement programs for people of all ages, as well as different economic and social groups. The workshops can be adapted to many different business and school settings to meet the varying needs of the participants. Contact your local CCCS for more details.

Who's eligible?

Confidential budget counseling is available by appointment. To be considered eligible for the Debt Management Program, you must be of legal age, consent to closing all your existing unsecured credit accounts, refrain from new credit requests, and demonstrate an ability to stick to the budget plan and creditor payments that are developed between you and your CCCS counselor.

Your budget

A CCCS counselor will develop a budget with you in roughly the same manner that I've already outlined in Chapter 9. During that process, your regular living expenses will be identified. If you are working with CCCS, you will be responsible for taking care of those expenses on your own. CCCS recommends the use of a savings account to assist you in your budgeting.

Watch Out!
CCCS has a specific prohibition against the use of a checking account with an attached line of credit for people who are enrolled in their Debt Management Program. This violates the program agreement. A regular checking account is fine, however.

The debt management program

In CCCS's Debt Management Program, a monthly deposit amount will be determined, with the help of a counselor, for payments to your creditors. Depending on your particular mix of creditors, the potential benefits of the program may include reduced monthly payments, reduced or waived finance charges, and the "re-aging" of accounts to bring them to a current status. When you enter a DMP, you will sign an agreement that stipulates a schedule of deposits to be disbursed to your creditors. All of the money that you deposit is used to reduce your debts; no fees are deducted from the deposits. The DMPs serve the dual role of helping you repay your debts and assisting your creditors in receiving the money you owe them. On average, DMPs run for about 48 months.

Your responsibilities

CCCS is very up-front about the fact that your debts are your responsibility and that ultimately you are the one who needs to solve your own problems. But CCCS acts as a facilitator and advisor in that process. As a participant in a DMP, you are responsible for ensuring that all your deposits in the program are made on time. You also have to agree that you will not make any credit purchases of any kind without first consulting with CCCS. You are also responsible for reviewing all your creditor statements and for reporting any problems with them to your case manager. You also have to keep CCCS apprised of any changes in your income and expenses.

Your rights

As a program participant, you have a variety of specific rights, not the least of which is to ask for a reevaluation appointment if you experience difficulty maintaining your budget or monthly deposits. You also have the right to express your dissatisfaction with any part of the program through a complaint resolution process. Last, but not least, you can terminate the program at any time by written notice.

Should you get involved with a CCCS program? Frankly, most of the features of the Debt Management Plan are things that you theoretically could do for yourself. We've already covered much of it in this book. However, CCCS is well organized, has a system that works, and has all the right connections with creditors already in place. It's those connections allow them to negotiate deals with your creditors that you might not be able to wangle for yourself. In fact, some creditors won't negotiate with you at all unless you are enrolled in a CCCS/NFCC (or similar) program.

You need to know that you will have to surrender your credit cards if you enroll in a Debt Management Plan (you may be allowed to keep one card if your employer requires you to travel). Giving up your cards is not the end of the world. Considering how much trouble your plastic has probably gotten you into, it could be a liberating experience. You also need to be aware that your participation in a debt management program will be noted on your credit history. Some of your creditors may even list you as late if you are making lower monthly payments.

One final advantage of participating in a CCCS program is the availability of one-on-one counseling to help you establish a realistic budget for the present and to help you avoid problems in the future as well. If you're feeling overwhelmed with the task confronting you, and especially if you need

Unofficially...
The fact that you have been through a debt management program may be viewed negatively by some of your creditors in the future, but it's still not as bad as having charge-offs or a bankruptcy on your credit report.

structure to help you follow through with your plan, then CCCS has a lot to offer.

Debt Counselors of America®

Another excellent option is Debt Counselors of America®. DCA, which was started in 1994, offers a wide range of financial services. Unlike other counseling organizations, they are primarily Web-based. Point your browser at www.GetOutOfDebt.org and you'll find their extensive Web site. Check out their huge list of online publications ($2.50 each, with discounts offered for multiple purchases of different titles). You'll also find listings for various strategies to help you get out, and stay out, of debt; the latest-breaking debt news stories; and a unique online chat room, plus many other interesting and informative features.

What they offer

Budget counseling is free. Unlike other counseling services, Debt Counselors® has lawyers and certified financial planners on its staff. DCA's debt-repayment plan, their ONE-PAY® Program, helps stop collection calls and may help you avoid bankruptcy. The plan also reduces or eliminates interest, and it consolidates your debts into one monthly payment. Participants in the ONE-PAY® Program have access to DCA's On-Track® Web site. This special limited access site allows users to create a custom spending plan. You are asked for a voluntary contribution of $2.90 per creditor per month for the ONE-PAY® service, which covers both secured and nonsecured debt. Most other agencies focus on nonsecured debt. DCA is also a bit unusual in that it sets no minimum amount of debt in order to qualify for their service. They won't turn you away if you don't have enough debt, as many other counseling offices do. In their view, if you're in debt, you're in debt. Period. And they'll help you.

DCA also offers a Crisis Relief Team. The team is staffed by debt professionals, a certified financial planner, a certified public accountant, staff attorneys who serve as a resource for the team, and several nationally recognized personal finance experts. The team is ready to try to help people who have been turned away by other counseling services and told to file for bankruptcy. "That doesn't sit well with us," says Mike Kidwell, vice-president and cofounder of DCA. "Bankruptcy is not always the answer," he continues. "We'll step in and try to find out what solutions are available. Once these consumers know what solutions they have available, they can make a better-informed decision on which way to go." The team also provides an in-depth examination of the circumstances that led to the problem in the first place. The fee for the Crisis Relief Team is $425.

Another unique feature is DCA's Debt Eliminator® Program for people who are current on their bills. The main idea of the plan is to help people organize their debts in order of priority so that if they have a little extra money, they can direct it to pay off the most pressing or important debts first. DCA also offers a weekly call-in radio show that you can listen to via their Web site. You can also view clips of recent television programs featuring DCA.

Something special

Perhaps the most unique feature of all is the DCA Chat Room hosted by Chatmaster Tina between 8:30 A.M. and 5 P.M. (eastern standard time) Monday through Friday. Tina will help you get answers to your credit, debt, and personal finance issues. The response to the Chat Room has been wildly enthusiastic. "It's great," says Mike Kidwell. "People enjoy being able to come in and ask questions and see the other questions and share their experiences. It helps them realize that they're not alone in this." (Note: Debtors Anonymous also sponsors several chat groups. See the discussion on Debtors Anonymous later in this chapter.)

Debt Counselors of America® has put together a list of questions that you should ask any credit or debt counseling agency before you make up your mind about using their services. Here is the list, with Debt Counselor's® answers (somewhat edited—check their Web site for complete answers):

Bright Idea
A debt counseling chat or discussion group can be a valuable tool to help you gain better perspective on your problems. You'll soon discover that you are not alone in your difficulties.

1. Will you send me information on your agency and programs?

    There is no reason that you should be required to provide account numbers and balances or any information other than your name and mailing address before an agency will agree to send you information.

2. Do you pay referral fees?

    Outside resources can be beneficial to the consumer. However, you should make sure that the agency you are working with does not maintain quotas and does have quality control and monitoring policies in place to ensure that you are receiving the best assistance possible.

3. What should I do if I can't afford the minimum payment?

    A good agency will not quickly dismiss you or tell you to file for bankruptcy simply because you cannot meet the minimum debt management program payment.

4. What kind of training do you have that makes you qualified to assist me?

   Ask any agency that you are considering going to for help what type of trained professionals they have on staff.

5. What kind of security measures do you take to protect my information?

   At a minimum, outside parties should not have access to any information that you send to a counseling agency without your permission. If your information is stored electronically, it should be protected by redundant servers and storage media, secure encrypted Web servers, daily backups with off-site storage, security firewalls, etc.

6. Can I get up-to-date, regular reports of the status of my accounts?

   Ask the agency you are considering how you can get regular updates on your account. If it is only by telephone, will a knowledgeable person be available when you call to give you the information you need?

7. Will you answer my general questions, even if I am not in your repayment program?

   Ask any agency you are considering if they can assist you with advice, education, and publications even if you are not going to enroll in their debt management program.

8. What kinds of educational programs and services do you provide?

   And how frequently is it provided? The more information you can access immediately, the better.

9. Is there a minimum amount of debt I have to have in order to work with you?

   The answer should be "no," according to DCA.

10. Will you help me with all my debts?

    Many agencies offer little assistance with secured debts like car payments or mortgages.

11. Is there a mandatory up-front fee?

    Some agencies charge up-front fees of $250 or more.

12. Will you sell my name or address to outside parties?

    They shouldn't.

13. How often do you pay my creditors?

    Make sure that the agency you go to for help sends out payments at least weekly.

So, should you make use of Debt Counselors of America's® services? Although they do charge fees for most of their publications and some services, their rates are not out of line for the industry, and they're lower than some agencies, even though they don't receive any contributions from outside sources or creditors to offset their costs. Participating in a debt management program anywhere has the same potential downside of creating a somewhat negative mark on your credit history, but again it's better than having listings for collection accounts and bankruptcy.

DCA's cutting-edge Web site, with its many innovative features and resources, is one of the best I've seen. Admittedly, if you don't have easy Web access, your options are limited, but you can always go to your local library to get online. The fact that DCA will work with just about anyone who has a debt problem is a real plus that sets them apart from the rest of the crowd. You could do a lot worse, and you can't do much better.

Genus Credit Management

Headquartered in Columbia, Maryland, Genus Credit Management is a nonprofit, community service organization that offers confidential and professional credit counseling, debt management, and financial educational information to consumers nationwide. The organization is dedicated to providing free services that help financially distressed consumers effectively manage their personal finances.

Genus was founded in 1992 and has grown rapidly since then. They now claim to be the nation's largest credit counseling organization, reaching more than 500,000 individuals every year, more than the next five largest credit counseling services combined. Genus is supported by voluntary contributions from creditors, businesses, community organizations, and private individuals. Genus has an extensive Web site at www.genus.org. You can also contact them at (888) 436-8715.

What they offer

"It's not a loan. It's a way out of debt," the company's slogan declares. Genus offers a wide range of information and services, including credit counseling and debt management, mortgage counseling, and educational material. Their Web site offers a lot of information about their many services. Be sure to check out their Personal Finance Calculators section, which offers an assortment of interactive online calculators that can help you develop a spending plan and assist you in getting out of debt.

Unofficially...
Because many of the major credit counseling agencies receive some of their funding from credit card issuers, they are trusted by these issuers to negotiate a repayment plan for you. In the issuer's view, even a reduced payment is better than no payment at all.

Their "Debt-to-Income Ratio" and "Budget Calculators" help you get a handle on your current financial situation. The "Credit Card," "Loan," and "Comparison Calculators" help you determine how long it will take you to get out of debt and to find the most affordable and efficient path back to financial stability.

Genus's Debt Management Program is similar to the plans I've already described. It allows you to consolidate your unsecured debts into one monthly payment. Through its established relationships with creditors, Genus is able to negotiate lower interest rates and waive late fees for many accounts; thus you have more money to apply toward reducing the principal on your debts. There is a voluntary charge of $3 per month per creditor.

According to their literature, Genus's state-of-the-art infrastructure offers you fast, dependable, accurate, and confidential service. On average, Genus clients are able to pay off their debts within 48 to 60 months. Genus works only with unsecured debt, in amounts exceeding $2,000.

Genus's Credit Management Educational Services department offers information on a wide variety of subjects, including budgeting, managing cash flow, interpreting credit reports, using credit cards effectively, and avoiding bankruptcy. In addition, Genus has a toll-free hotline, (888) 394-3687, that offers recorded tips on budgeting, effective credit card management, how to get out of debt, and improving your credit rating. Finally, Genus offers a mortgage counseling service for prospective homebuyers and for people who are facing default or foreclosure problems with their existing homes.

Is Genus for you?

Should you take advantage of Genus's services? They certainly offer a wide range of information and help. Their Web site is comprehensive and offers a good deal of free advice and assistance. Their credit counseling professionals are available by phone 24 hours a day, six days a week, and on Sundays from 9 A.M. to 6 P.M. (eastern standard time).

Again, as I've mentioned with all of the major counseling services we've looked at, it's possible that some of your creditors will view your participation in a debt management plan as a negative. However, that is a small price to pay for getting yourself back on track financially. Genus has a lot to like, and it doesn't cost you anything to take a look at what they have to offer.

Debtors Anonymous—for compulsive spenders

You may recall Peg from Butte, Montana, whom we met at the beginning of this chapter. She was convinced that she didn't need Debtors Anonymous, but after attending several sessions she discovered that she did. Perhaps you need it as well. "Not me," you say. "I keep my debts under control—usually." That's what Peg thought too. What I find intriguing about Peg's story is that it's not unusual; she could just as easily be describing you or me.

Peg attended college in the mid-1970s and ended up carrying a student loan. After graduation, she eventually became a program manager and consultant for a number of nonprofits in California. Over the years, she bought a series of cars, but nothing very extravagant. Then she got a credit card. "I

Watch Out!
Getting all the basic details you need to decide on the merits of a credit counseling program shouldn't cost you anything except your name and address. If it does, look elsewhere.

felt like I was coming of age because I was given a credit card," she recalls. "I went right out and bought things on it, but overall it was a gradual process."

"The process of debting seemed very normal," she continues. "The people around me were doing it too; it was like breathing. It's what people do in this society—incur debt. It seemed like a status symbol to have credit and to be able to buy things with it. And I remember feeling a 'high' from using a credit card; I felt like I was getting away with something. I was buying all this stuff, and it wasn't real that I'd have to pay for all of it eventually."

Peg was living closer to the edge than was prudent. She almost never put any money aside for a rainy day. When the inevitable emergency came along, she was not prepared. So, she charged it. She began to sink further into debt, yet even at her worst moments she wasn't more than $10,000 in debt. "But it was like a black cloud hanging over my head," she reports, "something that was always there. And I was mad that I had taken it on—and had nothing to show for it."

Then, she was prodded into attending Debtors Anonymous (D.A.). "I had decided to take a year off from work and had saved a few thousand dollars and had a credit card so that if I got into an emergency I could use the credit card," she relates. "So I would go to D.A. meetings and explain my situation, and I remember at some point someone else said 'This is a place where we come to learn to live without debting, this isn't a place to come to learn how to debt carefully.' That really spoke to me. I suddenly realized that I was like a maintenance drinker, believing that I could control my debting and that I was in charge of the show."

That was a defining moment for Peg. She decided that her life might be better if she wasn't carrying a load of unsecured debt. It took her from 1990 to the middle of 1998 to do it, but with the support of her D.A. friends she finally eliminated all of her unsecured debts—even the student loan. She gives much of the credit to those friends. "Don't try to do it on your own," she advises.

Best of all, there have been some unexpected additional benefits for Peg. "For me, what has been the real bonus is that not only am I not in debt, but I have a great life!" she declares. "My experience is that doing things soberly around money is a whole lot more fun, and that there is abundance possible without using debt. I guess I didn't believe that at first, but now, nine years later, I'm living it."

What is Debtors Anonymous?

What exactly is Debtors Anonymous and how does it work? First, some background, gleaned from the D.A. Web site (www.debtorsanonymous.org). Debtors Anonymous was started in 1968 when a group of recovery members of Alcoholics Anonymous held their first meeting to discuss the problems they were having with money. Initially, they called themselves the "Penny Pinchers" and later the "Capital Builders," and they made daily deposits into savings accounts because they believed that their financial problems stemmed from their inability to save money.

As time passed, the group realized that their problems were not due to an inability to save, but rather to their inability to let go of their debting habits. The group had already experienced the effectiveness of the Twelve Step Program in Alcoholics Anonymous and decided to use it to help

Unofficially...
Today, there are over 500 Debtors Anonymous meetings throughout the United States and in 13 other countries worldwide.

them resolve their debt habits as well. After a few years, the original group disbanded, but another group reemerged in 1976 in New York City. Within a year, another group was organized, and Debtors Anonymous was reborn.

The organization's purpose is straightforward. Debtors Anonymous is a fellowship of people who share their experience, strength, and hopes with each other in order to solve their common problem and help others to recover from compulsive debting. The only requirement for membership is a desire to stop incurring unsecured debt. There are no dues or membership fees. D.A. is self-supporting through participant contributions. D.A is not allied with any sect, denomination, politics, organization, or institution. The group does not engage in controversy and does not endorse or oppose any cause. The group's primary purpose is to stay solvent and help other compulsive debtors to achieve solvency.

Is D.A. right for you?

It's pop quiz time. If you answer yes to at least 8 of the following 15 questions, you may be a compulsive debtor:

1. Are your debts making your home life unhappy?
2. Does the pressure of your debts distract you from your daily work?
3. Are your debts affecting your reputation?
4. Do your debts cause you to think any less of yourself?
5. Have you ever given false information in order to obtain credit?
6. Have you ever made unrealistic promises to your creditors?

7. Does the pressure of your debts make you careless of the welfare of your family?

8. Do you ever fear that your employer, family, or friends will learn the extent of your total indebtedness?

9. When faced with a difficult financial situation, does the prospect of borrowing give you an inordinate feeling of relief?

10. Does the pressure of your debts cause you to have difficulty in sleeping?

11. Has the pressure of your debts ever caused you to consider getting drunk?

12. Have you ever borrowed money without giving adequate consideration to the rate of interest you are required to pay?

13. Do you usually expect a negative response when you are subject to a credit investigation?

14. Have you ever developed a strict regimen for paying off your debts, only to break it under pressure?

15. Do you justify your debts by telling yourself that you are superior to "other" people, and when you get your "break" you'll be out of debt overnight.

How did you do? If you answered yes to 8 or more questions, you might want to check out D.A. They may be able to help you.

Tools

How does Debtors Anonymous achieve its goals? The program uses a number of different tools. Some will sound similar to the tools used by other debt counseling groups; others are unique to the D.A. program. Here's an overview of its Twelve-Step approach, based on D.A. literature:

- Abstinence: Participants practice abstinence by not incurring unsecured debt one day at a time.

- Meetings: Participants attend meetings at which they share their experience, strength, and hope with one another.

- Record Maintenance: Participants maintain records of their daily income and expenses and of the retirement of any portions of their debts.

- Anonymity: Participants practice anonymity, which allows them freedom of expression.

- Telephone: D.A. members exchange phone numbers in order to maintain contact, especially before and after difficult times.

- Pressure Relief Groups and Pressure Relief Meetings: After you have gained some familiarity with the program, Pressure Relief Groups consisting of you and two other members of the group convene in a series of meetings to review your financial situation.

- Spending Plans: The Pressure Meeting normally results in the formulation of a spending plan and an action plan for resolving your debts and taking the first steps toward solvency.

- Sponsor: Frequently a sponsor, an abstinent member of D.A. who is usually more experienced in working the Twelve Steps, is selected to help you to implement your action plan.

- Business Meetings: Business meetings are held monthly. Participation in running the business of the organization is encouraged as a vehicle to help learn responsibility on various levels.

- **A.A. Literature:** Alcoholics Anonymous literature is used to help understand the nature of compulsive disease. "Compulsive debt" is substituted for "alcohol."

- **Awareness:** Participants maintain awareness of the danger of compulsive debt by taking note of bank, loan company, and credit card advertising and by reading accounts of its effects.

- **Service:** D.A. participants perform service at every level. "Only through service can we give to others what has been so generously given to us," D.A. says.

As mentioned in Chapter 7, some people suffer from multiple addictions. Some are primary; some are secondary. Sorting things out can be a time-consuming and arduous task when you have more than one addiction, and support groups like Debtors Anonymous can be enormously helpful. However, Debtors Anonymous focuses only on its one area of expertise—debt. If you have other issues that you also need to work on, D.A. will try to point you in the right direction.

How to contact Debtors Anonymous

You can contact the D.A. General Services Office by phoning (781) 453-2743. Depending on when you call, you may get a recorded message. Their Web site www.debtorsanonymous.org has a list of e-mail addresses and other resources as well, including phone numbers for about 30 local meetings scattered across the country.

The Web site has links and instructions to help you sign up for a number of online e-mail, discussion, or chat groups. These D.A.-sponsored groups are the only other online debt forums I've been able

66
Debtors Anonymous' source of strength lies in our singleness of purpose.
—Debtors Anonymous
99

to find besides the Debt Counselors of America®
Chat Room mentioned earlier. You don't have to be
an active participant in D.A. to sign up, although
some familiarity with the program is helpful. Some
groups are moderated, and some are not. Check
them out.

Should you turn to D.A.? Obviously, that's a personal decision that only you can make. D.A. may not
have the extensive connections with creditors that
many other services offer, but for the compulsive
debtor it's hard to find a better match. Think of this
as a group self-help approach. It doesn't cost anything to check out the Web site or attend a local
meeting or two. You decide.

Money 2000

Money 2000 is another program that has a lot to
offer. Originally launched by the U.S. Department
of Agriculture in 1996, Money 2000 is essentially a
self-directed home-study course of financial education that is now available through many state extension services.

For $10 to $15 a year, you can learn basic money
management strategies by mail, with the assistance
of quarterly newsletters, a variety of financial work-
sheets, and free analysis, all of which point you
toward the quickest way to pay down your debts. The
program will help you figure out where you are
financially at the present time and assist you in making informed decisions about where you would like
to be in the future, specifically by December 31,
2000—thus the program's name.

As a program participant, you learn how to:

▪ Make a spending plan that really works;

▪ Keep good records;

- Invest a part of your savings for additional earnings;
- Enhance your financial standing by paying off creditors.

One of the best features of the program is that you can essentially create your own parameters. Whatever your goals are, the program will help you to meet your financial educational needs. You are never asked to report your financial situation—just your goal and your progress toward your goal.

Individuals and families may enroll with their nearest participating extension service office. Many states have active Money 2000 programs, or at least someone you can contact for further information. Check out the Web page at www.human.cornell.edu/extension/money2000/nys for general information about the program and links to various other state coordinators.

Money 2000 probably won't be much help if you are in the late stage of acute credit distress. Also, this program is obviously a more self-directed and general kind of approach to sorting out your debt problems. However, if you are a self-starter and don't feel that you need a lot of hand holding, Money 2000, in conjunction with what you have learned in this book, may be just what you need. Check it out.

Other free (or inexpensive) advice

In addition to the organizations we've already covered, help is available from a number of other potentially worthwhile financial counseling and educational options. Universities, military bases, credit unions, or even housing authorities may offer low-cost or no-cost programs. Your state consumer protection office and state attorney general's office,

Watch Out!
With some debt repayment plans, your first month's payment, which you assumed would go to your creditors, ends up in your counselor's pocket as a commission instead. Check your agreement carefully before you sign.

as well as your local Legal Aid or Better Business Bureau, may also offer various kinds of financial advice or assistance programs. You may have to hunt around a bit to find some of them, but don't overlook these possibilities.

For-profit counseling services

Although for-profit debt counseling services are prohibited in some states, there are still zillions of them across the country. I'm sure that many actually provide valuable services to their customers. But when you consider how much low-cost or no-cost advice and assistance are available in this country, I frankly can't imagine why anyone would want to take the for-profit route. If you want to spend more money than you have to—go ahead. It's your choice. Whichever route you decide to follow, here are a few general guidelines to keep in mind:

- If your state has licensing or accreditation of debt counseling firms, deal only with approved services.

- Unless you're dealing with a nationally recognized counseling agency with a solid track record, stick to local, in-state companies. Your state's laws may not protect you if you send your money out of state.

- Before you actually sign up, make sure you understand what you are signing up for. Read all the fine print and ask a lot of questions. If you get evasive answers, look elsewhere.

- If you're asked to pay an up-front service charge of $250 or more, or if your monthly charge for a debt repayment plan is more than $50 or so, that's too much. Go elsewhere.

What to avoid

At the risk of repeating myself, I want to say that you should almost never consider responding to direct mail, telephone, television, newspaper, magazine, or Internet solicitations for credit counseling or credit repair. A possible exception might be one of the major nonprofit counseling services that I've mentioned in this chapter. Otherwise, ignore such offers. Always beware of any offers for a "quick fix." You'll just get yourself into a bigger fix.

Just the facts

- Asking for help can be difficult for many people.
- There are lots of excellent nonprofit counseling services to choose from.
- Debtors Anonymous can help compulsive debtors.
- Avoid responding to unsolicited promotions for credit counseling services.

GET THE SCOOP ON...
Where you are now and where you'd like to be ▪
Payment strategies ▪ The advantages of restructuring your debts ▪ Your debt consolidation
options ▪ What makes sense and what doesn't

Climbing Back Up

Chapter 12

F riends of mine live in a beautiful old farm-
house at the western base of the Green
Mountains in Lincoln, Vermont. One win-
ter's day, they were somewhat startled to find several
snowboarders in their backyard who were wondering where the base lodge was. This is an interesting
question because there *is* no base lodge in Lincoln.
In fact, there isn't a base lodge anywhere along the
western side of the mountain range.

It seems the hapless snowboarders had somehow
managed to stray from a trail at the ski area located
on the other side of the mountain and had ended
up not only on the wrong side of the mountain but
in a different county as well. They reported having a
great run coming down, but now there was no easy
way back to the top. In the end, they had to hitch a
ride on a lengthy and roundabout road route in
order to get back to the place they had started from.

Being deeply in debt is not unlike the young
snowboarders' experience. If you're not paying
attention to your spending, you can easily go astray.
The ride down is exhilarating for many people, but

then there's that rude awakening at the bottom and no easy way out of your dilemma. Whether you decide to climb back up to the top on foot or take the long way around, you are in for a tedious and time-consuming journey.

Assuming that you are standing dejectedly at the bottom of your mountain of debt, holding your slightly battered snowboard, with no obvious way back up, we'll begin this chapter by figuring out how you can get from where you are to where you'd like to be. Then I'll tell you about the advantages of restructuring your debts and about your many debt consolidation options. We'll even do a little credit card surfing (but no snowboarding) along the way. By the time we get done, you should be well on your way to getting back to the top of the mountain.

Before we start, I want to emphasize that I will be focusing here on strategies for helping you repay your debts. Bankruptcy is, of course, another way of climbing back up out of your financial woes. Generally speaking, though, it's a lousy way. We'll get to that in the next two chapters. For now though, we'll focus on more positive approaches.

Getting started

In Chapter 9, I covered the basic tools you need to get a handle on your income and expenses, and suggested ways to reduce your spending. In Chapter 10, you learned how to deal with your creditors, and in Chapter 11, I explained where to go for outside assistance if you need it. Now it's time to put all this knowledge to work and actually get yourself out of debt. I want to caution you, though, that it's going to be a long, slow process. You probably didn't get into debt overnight, and you won't get out overnight either.

The good news is that being in debt and having bad credit isn't forever. The sooner you start climbing back up, the sooner you'll reach your goal. How long will it take? If you're somewhere in the early or middle stage of credit distress, it will probably be a year or two before you have retired your debts. If you're in the late stage, it could take four years or more before you're out of the woods.

In Chapter 9, I also mentioned the importance of developing goals but said that getting out of debt was probably enough to tackle at first. Getting out of debt is what we're going to focus on here, but you may want to start thinking about where you would like to be in the future when you are debt free. After all, if you don't know where you are going, how will you know when you get there? Having experienced the distress of indebtedness once, you don't want to slide down the slippery slope of debt again. We'll revisit this issue in Chapter 16, but for now put it on the back burner and let it simmer.

Let's focus on getting you out of debt. We already know where you are at the moment—at the bottom of a mountain of debt. It's safe to say that you want to climb to the top of the mountain of financial responsibility. The main question is, How can you get there without the help of a handy ski lift? What you need is a good plan.

Payment strategies

Actually, you already have a pretty good plan in the form of your budget (or spending plan) from Chapter 9. Instead of haphazardly paying the creditor who is screaming the loudest at the moment, you should have a basic repayment plan in place by this time—or should be working on one.

There are some additional strategies that you may want to add to your plan, ones that will help you decide where to direct your limited resources to the best advantage. This involves a number of options we haven't examined yet. Prioritizing your debt payments is the first one we'll look at. This differs somewhat from the pro rata approach mentioned in Chapter 10, where every creditor received a proportionate payment. As I've said before, there is no one right way to eliminate your debts. Just the right way for you.

Pay off smaller debts first

There are several possible strategies you can use. The first is to pay off your smaller accounts first. If they are truly small, you may be able to gain a significant psychological boost from eliminating a large number of accounts quickly, allowing you to focus your attention on the few remaining larger accounts. It's not a bad strategy, but there's a better one.

Pay off high-rate debts first

The other approach is to pay off your high-rate credit cards first. Although this method may not give you the immediate short-term psychological lift of the small account strategy, in the long run it is the better option because it saves you both time and money.

Here's how it works. Start by trying to negotiate lower interest rates, as this may affect which cards come first in your payment strategy. Next, you examine your credit accounts to determine which one has the highest interest rate. Then, you decide how much extra, above the minimum payment, you can manage to pay every month on that one account. It could be just $10 or $15 or $20, whatever you decide

Moneysaver
By first paying off those accounts that carry the highest interest rates, you quickly free up more cash to pay off your remaining bills.

CREDIT CARD PAYMENT CALCULATOR

If You Paid Minimum Payment		If You Paid $20.00 Extra Per Month	
Current Balance:	$2,000.00	Current Balance:	$2,000.00
Minimum Monthly Payment	$75.00	Minimum Monthly Payment	$95.00
Annual Percentage Rate (APR):	20.90%	Annual Percentage Rate (APR):	20.90%
Total Number of Monthly Payments Until Payoff:	102	Total Number of Monthly Payments Until Payoff:	49
Time Until Payoff:	8 Years, 6 Months	Time Until Payoff:	4 Years, 1 Month

Source: Genus Credit Card Payoff Calculator

you can afford. The more the better. If you can afford $50 or $100, that's better still, but don't push it too hard. Then you focus on paying off that one account by using your extra payment amount. Meanwhile, you continue to pay on all your other accounts at their minimum monthly payment levels to keep them current.

When the account with the highest interest rate is finally paid off, you switch your focus to the account with the next highest interest rate, and so on, until all your accounts have been paid off. This strategy is extremely effective and can dramatically shorten the time it takes to retire your outstanding debts because it dramatically reduces the amount of interest you pay.

The trick is to pay more than the minimum on the targeted account, and continue that strategy every month until it's paid off. By utilizing this strategy, you can easily cut years off the time it would otherwise take you to retire the same debts if you made only the minimum payments. The table shown above is a dramatic example of what an extra monthly payment of just $20 can do to the length of time required to pay off a credit card account with a $2,000 balance at 20.9 percent APR and a $75 minimum monthly payment.

Just $20 a month extra slashes almost four and a half *years* off the time required to pay back the loan. This strategy works whether you're dealing with two accounts or a dozen or more. Just remember to keep focusing on the account with the highest interest rate, and each month always pay the extra amount above the minimum payment.

Using your savings

Using your savings is yet another debt reduction strategy that you might want to consider. This, of course, assumes that you have some savings to work with. Opinions differ within financial counseling circles about whether or not you should tap into your savings in order to pay down your debts faster. On the one hand, you can make a good case for having a financial cushion available for the inevitable emergency or unexpected expense. Regular savings is also a vital strategy to help you achieve your long-term financial goals. On the other hand, there are compelling reasons why you might want to use at least some of your savings to reduce your debt load in the short term. It's a legitimate payment strategy, but it is not without its dangers.

The most obvious peril of this approach is that if you completely drain your savings, you will be left in a precarious position if an unexpected expense pops up. Given Murphy's Law, one probably will. In that case, you may have to charge the unanticipated bill on one of your already overburdened credit cards, undoing much of your hard-won progress. Or, you may have to scramble to scrape up the money from some other source to cover the emergency. Neither option is very attractive. Consequently, I don't recommend emptying your savings.

However, if you use part of your savings to pay down some of your debts quickly, the financial advantages are considerable. For example, let's say you have $1,000 available in your savings account that is earning 3 percent interest (compounded monthly). In one year, your savings account will earn $30.42 in interest. If you're in the 28 percent tax bracket, you will net $21.90 after taxes on that savings account.

Now, for the purposes of the discussion, let's say that you are carrying an average $1,000 balance on a credit card at 19 percent interest. That account would cost you around $191 in interest for the year, assuming the balance remained more or less static. If you withdrew the $1,000 from your savings account and paid off the entire $1,000 credit card balance, you would, of course, lose the potential $21.90 in interest from the savings account; but you would not have to pay the $191 in interest charges on the credit card account. Your net savings would be $169.10 ($191 − $21.90 = $169.10).

That kind of savings is hard to ignore. Still, living without a financial cushion is a scary prospect for most people, so you really should have a modest amount of money set aside somewhere for emergencies. One alternative is to take your newly paid-off credit card and lock it away in a safe place, reserving it as a last-ditch source of money in an emergency. You decide.

The main thing to remember is that these are all temporary strategies until you can get your financial house in order again. If you can manage to squeak by for a year or so with reduced savings while you

Bright Idea
Restructuring and consolidating your debts can be powerful tools for reducing your interest charges and speeding up your repayment schedule.

are getting your debts under control, you can set up sounder, long-range savings and investment plans later on (see Chapter 16). That's something to look forward to.

Restructuring

We've examined repayment strategies to reduce your debt; now we'll look at other tools available to rebuild your finances and your credit rating. One of the most powerful is restructuring. In Chapter 10, we discussed a major aspect of restructuring—negotiating with your creditors to reduce your monthly payments. This strategy can temporarily give you the breathing space you need to get past an immediate credit crunch.

Restructuring has other aspects as well, ones that offer long-term advantages and also save you more money for paying off your debts. These strategies involve reorganizing your debts and consolidating them into more manageable loans with lower interest rates and lower monthly payments.

Your debt consolidation options

You may be able to downsize your debts dramatically by shifting or consolidating your loans. There are many different ways you can approach this strategy. Some make sense, and some don't. We'll look at all of them. One aspect that all of these strategies have in common, however, is that they involve some form of borrowing.

Borrowing money to get yourself out of debt can be a disastrous mistake for some people and a real moneysaver for others. Before you consider these consolidation strategies, you need to understand all the implications of what you are doing because if you get this wrong, you will end up in even worse shape than you were to begin with. Bankruptcy may then be your only remaining alternative.

In the next few pages, we'll be looking at a variety of ways to shift your high-interest loans to lower-interest loans. This strategy simplifies your payments, lowers your interest costs, and possibly lowers your monthly payments. However, if this strategy is not accompanied by real changes in your spending habits, you probably will end up with a whole new collection of high-interest bills on top of your low-interest loans. Double trouble.

You must be *absolutely* certain that you have the self-discipline to refrain from incurring any new debts until you have paid off your consolidated loans. If you blow the money you are "saving" with your consolidation on more spending, you will undo everything you've been trying to accomplish. The banks and other lenders who tout these consolidation plans in promotions almost never mention the potential dangers associated with such loans. But I will.

Illustrating my point is the fact that more than half of the $268 billion in home equity loans originated in 1997 were "subprime," meaning that they were obtained by consumers with less-than-perfect credit, according to the National Home Equity Mortgage Association. This means that these borrowers could have had anything from a few late payments to a bankruptcy on their credit reports. Nearly half of these loans were used to consolidate other debts. What's even more unsettling is that many of these same people are loading up their credit cards within a few months of erasing their previous debts, according to some economists. These folks are courting disaster.

You need to make a firm commitment to yourself, and perhaps to others as well, to repay your debt consolidation loans before you take on any new debts. If putting your promise in writing and signing it helps to make the point, do so. If you are unwilling to make a solid commitment or have serious doubts about your self-discipline, you would be better off not to pursue the debt consolidation strategies we're about to look at.

There are other ways you can get yourself into hot water with debt consolidation. One way is to take out the wrong kind of loan. Most of the consolidation loans you hear about on the radio or see in magazines, on TV, or the Internet from finance companies may sound like good deals with their low monthly payments. But if you carefully study all the fine print and calculate all of your real costs, you will probably discover that the loans carry excessively high interest rates and fees that in the long run will cost you far more than you should be paying. You can easily end up in worse shape than you were to begin with if you're not careful.

Another potential problem with debt consolidation loans is that, by lumping everything together, you may end up paying higher interest on debts that had low interest or no interest at all. Before you take out any kind of debt consolidation loan, be absolutely certain that it will actually save you money in the long run. Finally, at least one study has found that taking out a debt consolidation loan is often the last desperate step before some families are completely overwhelmed by financial disaster. Having forewarned you about the pitfalls, let's take a look at your options.

Watch Out!
Be careful about many debt consolidation loans that are widely advertised through commercial media and the mail. They can feature interest rates as steep as 30 percent and may have excessively long repayment terms that can boost your ultimate interest costs possibly two or three times higher than they should be.

Credit card surfing

One of the most popular strategies of debt shifting is to transfer the balance on your high-interest credit cards (like department store cards) to lower-interest cards. Also referred to as "credit card surfing," this strategy involves using the low-interest promotions offered by card issuers until they expire and then switching to another promotional come-on until it expires as well, and so on. The savings can be significant. If you're carrying, say, a $5,000 balance at 18.2 percent, lowering the rate to 5.9 percent by card surfing can save you $615 a year. It's not hard to see why this approach has been touted by financial counselors for years as a sure-fire way of saving hundreds of dollars annually on interest charges. It was.

All good things must come to an end, and I'm afraid that it's no longer possible to recommend this strategy without some significant caveats. Why is card surfing less attractive these days? The answer is simple. Card issuers are tired of losing money on the practice. Many are cutting back on their promotions, and some have dropped low introductory rates on card balance transfers altogether. At least one major card issuer has even started to charge fees on transfers in the 2 to 3 percent range.

In the third quarter of 1997, a whopping 77 percent of new card offers mailed to consumers had a low introductory rate. By contrast, just one year later, only 36 percent of new card offers included a teaser rate, according to a New York–based market research firm. Bad news for card surfers.

Some banks continue to offer low teaser rates—occasionally as low as 0 percent—but generally only on new purchases. Instead of low teaser rates for transfers, other banks are now issuing low, single-rate cards with percentage rates around 9.9 percent. The idea here is to attract you with relatively low rates and then keep you for more than a three-month introductory period.

This situation doesn't mean that card surfing is dead. It just means you have to be far more careful about where, when, and how you surf if you want to avoid a wipeout. And you'll have fewer choices. Here are some questions you need to ask before you decide to transfer a balance to a new card:

- Does that attractive 3.9 percent teaser rate cover transfers or just new purchases?

- What is the length of the introductory offer?

- Does the card have an annual fee? (Avoid cards with large annual fees.)

- Is there a charge for transfers? If so, how much is it?

Be sure to carefully read all the fine print on the back of the offer. Are the other terms as attractive as the ones on the card you are about to give up? Check everything—grace period, method of computing the balance, late payment fees, and so on. If you're not sure what some of it means, call the issuer to be certain you understand it correctly before you make a transfer. Here are some other things to watch out for before you transfer:

- The cash trap. Some teaser rates are for transferred balances and new purchases, but not for cash advances. Rates for cash advances can be much, much higher. You really shouldn't be taking advantage of cash advances with a debt consolidation loan in the first place, but if you do, and the rate is sky high, you're losing ground instead of gaining.

- Slow balance transfers. Read the fine print to see how long the balance transfer process takes. It can be up to eight weeks. This eliminates much of the benefit of making the transfer in the first place.

- Teaser rates that expire on a predetermined date. Some teaser rates expire a certain number of months, usually three or six, from the date you transfer your balance. Others expire at a predetermined date. If you sign up for an offer with a predetermined date that is only a month or two away, there isn't much point to signing up.

- Two-cycle billing. I warned you about this practice in Chapter 1, but it's worth repeating. If you pay your balance in one month but fail to do so in the next month, then the grace period you earned in the first month will be retroactively taken away from you and you will be charged interest for both months. In the case of a debt consolidation loan, you should not be missing any payments anyway, but if you do, and your new loan features one of these two-cycle billing terms, you stand to lose big time. And that interest could wipe out any benefits you might have gained from switching to the new account.

Another important thing to remember when you are card surfing is to make absolutely sure that you transfer your remaining balance before the rate jumps at the end of the promotional period. Then make sure that you close the account when you are done with it (see "Closed By Consumer Accounts" in Chapter 6). Remember what I said about leaving too many "open" accounts on your credit record?

Bright Idea
Before you surf to another credit card, see if your current card issuer will extend the low introductory offer. They probably won't, but it never hurts to ask.

Check out www.bankrate.com for listings of all the low-rate cards that are currently available. It's one of the easiest ways to make informed feature-by-feature comparisons.

Now, the news isn't all bad. Even though the number of your card surfing options has decreased dramatically, some teaser-rate offers are still available on transfers. The good news is that interest rates on the offers that remain have actually decreased. In the third quarter of 1998, the rate had drifted down to 4.14 percent from 5.33 percent in 1997. Rates began to head back up in 1999, however, consequently it's hard to predict where they will be by the time you read this. So, should you card surf? If you read all the details carefully before you jump on your new card, and the deal is clearly better, go for it. Just be careful.

Home equity loans

In Chapter 2, I explained the basic advantages and disadvantages of home equity loans (HEL). HELs are cheap and relatively easy to get, tend to have reasonably low interest rates, and generally offer substantial tax benefits. That's the good news. You may also recall that the major disadvantage of a HEL is that you can lose your home. That's the bad news. For most people, their home is their single largest asset. Putting that asset at risk doesn't make much sense. Yet millions of Americans do just that every year, and frequently for the wrong reasons. Okay, I'll try to stay off my soapbox for now and focus on the use of home equity loans as a debt consolidation tool. As such, a HEL can be an extremely useful strategy—as long as it's used carefully.

Most lenders will give you a home equity loan that equals anywhere from 50 to 80 percent of your home's value, minus the amount of your existing first mortgage. For example, if your home is worth $150,000 and you still owe $50,000 on your first mortgage, you would be able to get a home equity loan of between $25,000 and $70,000 ($150,000 × .50 = $75,000; $75,000 – $50,000 = $25,000 for the low end of the range; and $150,000 × .80 = $120,000; $120,000 – $50,000 = $70,000 for the high end). The so-called loan-to-value ratio (LTV) is lowest in New England, somewhat higher on the West Coast, and the highest in the Midwest, which largely accounts for the range between 50 and 80 percent.

Some lenders will even allow a 100 percent LTV, which is just plain scary in my opinion. When it comes to home equity loans, the maximum amount that you *can* borrow and the amount that you *should* borrow are not necessarily the same thing. In fact, it's a good idea to borrow less (assuming that you decide to borrow anything at all).

Before you decide to apply for a home equity loan, here are a few questions you should ask your lender:

- What is the actual interest rate on the loan? Is the advertised rate the real thing or just a teaser? Interest rates on HELs are normally less than on other consumer loans, but be sure you know what your rate is and whether it's fixed or variable. Except in a dire emergency, avoid the increasingly popular "interest only" payment option. This is a sure prescription for perma-debt and has no place in a debt consolidation scenario.

- What are the fees? Most HELs have a number of closing costs associated with them. These

Unofficially...
Almost half of
the home equity
loans taken out
in 1998 were
used to reduce
debt, according
to a Federal
Reserve study.

can include such items as an appraisal fee,
recording fee, title search and title insurance,
as well as a "loan origination fee." Get all the
facts.

- Is the interest going to be tax deductible? This
  is one of the main reasons for using a HEL in
  the first place. It might be wise to check with
  your tax advisor to be sure, since tax laws do
  change.

You may also recall from Chapter 2 that HELs
come in two basic varieties: a closed-end second
mortgage and an open-ended line of credit. Each
has its advantages and disadvantages. Let's start with
the second mortgage, which is the simpler of the
two.

Second mortgages

A second mortgage is for a predetermined amount
of money for a set term—normally between 5 and 15
years. The interest rate can be either fixed or variable, but most people opt for fixed.

Second mortgages offer several advantages. One
of the most important is that you know exactly
where you stand. Once you've signed the papers,
that's it. You have the amount of the loan to work
with, and you have a set number of payments to
make in a set number of years. Period. Because second mortgages have very clear limits, they are a
good choice for people who may not have the self-
discipline to handle a line of credit (more on that in
a moment).

Second mortgages do have some disadvantages,
however. The flip side of their predictability is their
lack of flexibility. If you find that you didn't borrow
enough, it's not easy to get more money without
going through a lot of hassle and paying a whole

new batch of fees. As a practical matter, this is rarely done.

Even more to the point is that this lack of flexibility may cause you serious problems if you should experience cash-flow difficulties in the future. If you start missing mortgage payments, you could lose your home. To avoid that, you could possibly refinance your mortgage, but that's a costly and time-consuming procedure. Nevertheless, even with its disadvantages, a second mortgage can be a pretty good choice for a one-time large payment scenario like a debt consolidation loan. Be absolutely certain, though, that you use it for its intended purpose and pay it off as quickly as possible.

Home equity line of credit

The other variety of home equity loan is the home equity line of credit (HELC). This is where things get more complicated—and far more dangerous. The main problems with HELCs are that they are so easy to obtain and the temptation to overuse them is substantial. Naturally, home equity lines of credit are extremely popular these days. Considering that they represent one of the last big remaining tax breaks for consumer debt, it's no wonder. A home equity line of credit has these advantages:

- They're flexible. You can use as little or as much as you want, when you want, up to your maximum "credit limit."

- They're easy to access. You can tap into a HELC simply by writing a check or sometimes by using an ATM or credit card (forget the plastic option; it's too similar to what got you into trouble in the first place).

- They tend to have lower, variable rates.

Of course, there are some disadvantages as well:

- Temptation. Unless you are self-disciplined, the temptation to repeatedly utilize your HELC to the maximum can be hard to resist. If lack of self-discipline got you into credit trouble in the first place, and you haven't totally mended your ways, a HELC is not a good choice.

- Low-pressure repayment terms. Once you've borrowed the money for a HELC, most lenders aren't in a big rush to have you pay it back. The longer it takes, the more you pay them in interest. This is counterproductive if you are trying to get rid of your debts quickly.

- Variable rates. The initially attractive lower variable rates won't look so attractive if they go up.

- Annual fees. This is one feature that second mortgages don't have. Unfortunately, lines of credit usually do.

When you are using a HELC for debt consolidation purposes, remember that the whole point of the exercise is to lower your interest costs, simplify your payment process, and get your debts paid off as quickly as possible. The leisurely repayment schedule that normally comes with a HELC (to say nothing of the "interest only" option) is not in line with those goals, so ignore the official schedule. Your new total monthly payment should be as large as your previous combined payments before consolidation if you want to really make progress on paying off your debts. If you can afford to pay more, that's better still. Be sure to check to see if your loan contains prepayment penalties. Get them removed, or try a different loan.

Tapping your retirement plan

In Chapter 2, I mentioned the possibility of tapping your retirement plan for a variety of loan purposes. Debt consolidation was one of them. Most employers allow loans from a 401(k), 403, or other retirement plans. Many municipal, county, state, and federal entities permit similar loans from their plans as well. Generally speaking, the same rules apply to everyone who borrows from these plans.

Normally, you may borrow up to 50 percent of your plan's assets, not to exceed a maximum of $50,000. Some plans have limits on the amount you can borrow based on a percentage of your salary. Most plans have limits on the number of loans you can have outstanding at any one time—usually one or two. Using your retirement plan as a source of money for a consolidation loan is not as attractive as a home equity loan because the interest is almost never tax deductible. But, on the other hand, you're paying interest to yourself, rather than to a bank, so it's not quite as bad as it sounds.

There are some drawbacks. If you borrow in order to consolidate your other debts (or for any other short-term purpose, excluding buying or renovating your home), you will have to pay your retirement plan back within five years. If you don't, the IRS will sock you with income taxes for the total amount of the loan, plus a 10 percent penalty if you are under the age of 59 and a half. If you leave your employer, you will probably have to pay back the loan promptly. If you can't, you may be subject to taxes and penalties again.

Probably the biggest disadvantage of this loan strategy is the loss of the potential earning power of your retirement money if it had been left in equities

Timesaver
The larger the amount of money that you can put toward your debt consolidation payments every month, the quicker you will retire your debts.

or other high-growth funds. Still, the interest rate is right—often prime rate plus 1 percent—and if you can consolidate your high-rate credit card loans with this strategy and manage to pay back the loan to your retirement plan within five years, this route may be worth considering. Check with your plan's administrator to find out the rules that apply to your plan.

Life insurance

I've already mentioned the advantages and disadvantages of borrowing against your life insurance policy in Chapter 2. When used for a debt consolidation loan, this strategy has the same general benefits as borrowing from your retirement plan, with the added bonus that there is no time limit for repayment. When it comes right down to it, you don't actually have to pay it back at all. Of course if you don't, the amount of your loan when you die will be deducted from the benefits paid to your heirs. If they don't need the money, then maybe repayment isn't an issue. But if they do, then make sure you repay the loan once you get back on your financial feet.

Turning to family or friends

Not everyone in the financial counseling sector agrees on this next strategy. Some say you should never borrow from friends or family. Never. Others suggest it as an option, as long as you treat the transaction as if it were an official loan from a regular lender.

The advantages are that you may be able to get a lower than usual interest rate and avoid having to fill out a loan application or pass muster with a credit check. The disadvantages are that you may be

Watch Out!
Borrowing money from family members can be a real disaster. Be careful if you decide to use this strategy.

tempted not to stick to your agreement and that you may end up estranging a friend (or even a family member) if you don't follow through with your payments as agreed. If you do decide to follow this route, be sure that you are up front about your financial situation and sign a contract that spells everything out in detail so everyone knows what they are getting into.

I'm inclined to lean toward those who feel that the potential for disaster is substantial when you mix money with either friendship or family. However, if you've got a rich relative who offers to help you get through a tight spot, maybe you should be gracious about it. Just be sure you pay them back.

What to avoid

Now we come to those other sources of money that folks who have their backs to the wall might be tempted to grasp at in a last-ditch attempt to stave off bankruptcy. I've already mentioned finance company loans that are widely advertised in the media. I don't recommend them, especially those that involve any kind of home equity feature. If a home equity loan with a reputable bank is potentially dangerous, then you can imagine the hazards involved with the finance company variety. Another good reason to avoid finance companies is that loans from these sources are viewed negatively by potential creditors who may see them on your credit report. Finance company loans frequently imply debt problems. Finally, I probably shouldn't have to mention this, but I will anyway. Pawnbrokers, loan sharks, and bill-paying services (or debt consolidation companies) are not good options either.

Stay on course

No matter what strategy you decide to follow, the process of climbing back up out of debt can be a long and tedious procedure. Try to enjoy the steady progress you make along the way and take satisfaction in retiring one debt after another. You almost certainly will be learning many lessons about financial responsibility (and irresponsibility) as you go. These lessons may have a profound, positive impact on your life. At the very least, if you stay on the path I've outlined, you will eventually reach the summit of the mountain. And the view from the top is grand.

Just the facts

- Being in debt isn't forever.

- Paying off your high-interest loans first is a good idea.

- Borrowing money to get yourself out of debt can be a disaster—but it can save you time and money if you do it right.

- Whatever strategy you use, stick with it.

Bankruptcy

GET THE SCOOP ON...
What bankruptcy really is ▪ The various types of
bankruptcy ▪ What events typically lead to
bankruptcy ▪ All of your choices

PART VI

Bankruptcy—Your Last Resort

Throughout this book, I have referred to bankruptcy as an unattractive option. Some people view bankruptcy as something far worse—right down there with anthrax and bubonic plague. That attitude may be a little extreme, since you can die from these diseases but you will certainly survive bankruptcy. Many people see the spread of the incidence of bankruptcy as a kind of modern plague on our society. Like the Black Death of medieval times, bankruptcy can infect almost anyone. Whether you live in a sumptuous castle on a hill or in a small apartment on a narrow street in a working class district, it really doesn't matter—bankruptcy stalks the land and walks among us all.

This pessimistic view is rather popular in the financial community, especially among banks, credit card issuers, and retailers who have lost billions of dollars because of consumer bankruptcies. And the trend is up. In 1998, a record 1.4 million Americans filed for bankruptcy, up 2.7 percent from 1997, and 1997 was up from the previous year. And so on.

Chapter 13

Approximately 1 in every 75 households in this country filed for bankruptcy in 1998. Now that's downright scary. The losses to our economy are staggering. Total annual costs for the country as a whole come to around $44 billion in fact.

"As Americans have taken on more and more credit-card debt, their capacity to weather the things that go wrong has declined," says Harvard Law School professor Elizabeth Warren, in a recent *Boston Globe* article. "Smaller and smaller bumps in the road cause them to trip and they can't get up." The dramatic increase in bankruptcies is one of the obvious manifestations of this trend.

I should point out that there is a completely different view of bankruptcy, notably among bankruptcy attorneys, some of whom seem to view bankruptcy as an inalienable right approaching divine absolution for all of our financial sins. Life, liberty—and the pursuit of bankruptcy. It's no wonder they hold this view. Lots of money is to be made by getting people to file for bankruptcy. I've read some of the literature that promotes bankruptcy, and frankly it leaves me cold. The main thrust seems to be to promote every conceivable (barely) legal way to avoid taking any financial responsibility for your actions and essentially walking away from your debts with nary a backward glance—after paying a hefty fee (frequently $500 or more) to your bankruptcy lawyer, of course.

This irresponsibility is not what I have been talking about for the last 12 chapters. Taking responsibility for your actions and facing your problems squarely has been the basic foundation of this book. It still is. I have repeatedly said that bankruptcy should be your last resort, and I again say it. However, I readily admit that in certain cases, such as being hopelessly in debt due perhaps to an accident, catastrophic illness, or divorce, then bankruptcy may be your only viable recourse. If, after trying (or at least carefully examining) every other option, you find that you have no alternative, so be it. Bankruptcy is there to help you out of your predicament.

In this chapter, we'll cut through the hype to get to the truth about bankruptcy. I'll explain what bankruptcy is and also give you the lowdown on the different types. We'll take a look at the usual causes of bankruptcies, and I'll spell out the difference between the voluntary and the involuntary varieties. Finally, we'll carefully examine all your options. In Chapter 14, "Bankruptcy—Chapter and Verse," we'll actually get into the nuts and bolts of filing for bankruptcy. For now, remember that although bankruptcy isn't the end of the world, it isn't very pretty either. If you're going to get involved in it, you need to have an objective view of what's in store for you.

Bankruptcy 101

If you are facing the prospect of bankruptcy, you probably have a bunch of questions you want to ask. Is bankruptcy a chance for a "fresh start" or a terrible mistake that will haunt you for years to come? How do you decide which type of bankruptcy to use: Chapter 7 bankruptcy or Chapter 13 bankruptcy? (More on them in a moment.) How do you file for them? What do you gain and what do you lose? How much does it cost? I'll answer all these questions and more in this and the following chapter.

I need to point out, however, that entire books have been written on the subject of bankruptcy (shelves-full, in fact), and I can't possibly cover everything in just two chapters of this book. So, one bit of advice I have for you right off is to visit your library or local bookstore and get a copy of the Nolo Press books *How to File for Bankruptcy* (which covers Chapter 7 bankruptcy) and *How to File Chapter 13 Bankruptcy*. These excellent consumer-oriented publications will explain the entire process in easy to understand terms without the promotional hype I complained about earlier. Even if you ultimately decide to work with a lawyer, you will already have a basic knowledge of the process, which should be very helpful.

[*A brief note to the reader:* In this chapter and the next, I will be discussing Chapter 13 bankruptcy. Unfortunately, I will be doing that partly in Chapter 13 of this book. Because there is potential for confusion, I'll try to make it clear which Chapter 13 I'm referring to as we go along.]

A brief history

First, a little historical background gleaned from Robin Leonard's excellent book *Money Troubles* (Nolo Press). U.S. bankruptcy law has its roots in England, where bankruptcy was initiated as an alternative to rotting in debtor's prison.

In the United States, the first bankruptcy law was passed by Congress in 1800. Voluntary bankruptcy became a part of U.S. law with the passage of the Bankruptcy Act of 1841. Unfortunately for consumers, the earliest U.S. laws were generally intended to protect the interests of creditors, rather than those of debtors.

Over the years, new laws were passed by Congress and then later repealed or amended as the pendulum swung back and forth between the interests of creditors and debtors—a process that has continued

Unofficially...
The first bankruptcy law was passed in England in 1542. Under the law, debtors were considered quasi-criminals.

unabated to the present time. The basic structure of modern bankruptcy law took shape with the Bankruptcy Act of 1898. This law included provisions for both voluntary and involuntary cases, allowed debtors to claim exemptions, and eliminated most barriers for discharging debts.

In more recent years, Congress continued to tinker with bankruptcy laws according to the prevailing sentiments of the day. The last major change took place with the passage of the Bankruptcy Reform Act of 1978. Since then, it's been a constant tug-of-war between the credit and banking industry on the one hand, and consumer advocates on the other, to make revisions to the law that favored their respective points of view.

Something's wrong

In recent years, the credit and banking industry has been faced with declining profits in its previously very lucrative credit card business (it's still lucrative—it's just not *as* lucrative as it once was). One of the reasons for that decline is the dramatic increase in personal bankruptcies. Sympathizing with the credit card issuers is difficult when they are complaining vigorously about consumers who resort to bankruptcy while at the same time the issuers are sending out 3.5 billion new solicitations for credit cards to almost anyone who might conceivably be talked into using one. The pressures on consumers to use credit in this country are enormous.

However, you don't have to hold a Ph.D. in economics to see that things have gotten somewhat out of hand with bankruptcy. At a time of low unemployment, strong economic growth, and low inflation, we should not be seeing record numbers of bankruptcies. And 1.4 million is a lot of bankruptcies a year.

When the economy turns sour, things could get ugly if these trends don't change significantly.

Clearly, something is seriously wrong with this picture. The credit and banking industry says the problem lies with consumers who are abusing the bankruptcy system, but consumer advocates point their fingers at what they view as a banking and credit industry that is out of control with its promotions. The truth, as usual, probably falls somewhere in between.

Studies funded by the credit industry in the past have claimed that up to 15 percent of people that file Chapter 7 bankruptcy could have paid off at least a portion of their debts. Recent studies, however, tend to indicate that a much smaller percentage of bankrupts may be abusing the system.

In fact, the American Bankruptcy Institute (ABI) in 1998 released a study showing that only about 3 percent of people who seek protection from their creditors can actually afford to repay their debts. The ABI (www.abiworld.org), whose members include more than 6,400 lawyers, bankers, judges, educators, and financial experts, takes no official position on bankruptcy issues.

The ABI study was the first of its kind that was not funded by the credit industry. The study indicates that the vast majority of people who file for bankruptcy have managed to accumulate overwhelming debts and truly need the protections that bankruptcy offers. Consequently, the high number of bankruptcies is not primarily a case of abuse of the law. So what's going on here?

There are undoubtedly many reasons for this trend. Rampant consumerism, an increasing tolerance of high debt levels, misplaced priorities, high divorce rates, continued corporate downsizing (with its accompanying sudden job losses), and the increasing acceptance of gambling come to mind. But lax bankruptcy laws, and the seductive inducements to take advantage of them, certainly have been a part of the mix. It should come as no great surprise that the credit industry and retailers have been pressuring Congress to change the laws.

In 1998, a bankruptcy reform bill was passed by the U.S. House of Representatives, but it died in the Senate. In May of 1999, a similar piece of legislation was passed by the House. Action by the Senate is possible late in the 1999 session, and if passed, it will probably be signed into law by President Clinton.

A key element of the proposed new legislation includes establishment of a so-called "needs-based" system that will force higher-income filers to pay back more than they have been under the previous law. This income or "means testing" will make it harder to file under Chapter 7 bankruptcy and is designed to increase the use of Chapter 13 bankruptcy.

The new proposed law also contains a financial education component and may make it easier to collect child support and alimony, among other things (some observers disagree). It is anticipated that the new law will rein in some of the worst bankruptcy abuses of recent years and may make it harder for some people to file. However, it probably won't have a major effect on the core of U.S. bankruptcy law, according to many observers (others disagree).

What is bankruptcy?

Of all the topics in this book, bankruptcy is probably the most controversial. The term itself is laden with all sorts of negative connotations. In addition to financial insolvency, bankrupt also conveys such meanings as destitute, impoverished, broken, ruined—in short, utter failure. Accuse someone of being morally bankrupt and—well—watch out.

Disadvantages

It should come as no surprise that bankruptcy has traditionally been viewed as a shameful situation to be avoided at all costs. To a certain extent, having to resort to bankruptcy is a shame, mainly because of what it does to your credit rating. It's the worst thing that you can possibly do to your credit. Bankruptcy will remain a blotch on your credit history for seven years in the case of a Chapter 13 bankruptcy and for ten long years in the case of a Chapter 7 bankruptcy. It can even prevent you from holding some jobs for the rest of your life. Some states prohibit people who have *ever* filed bankruptcy from certain fiduciary positions.

And, as I suggested earlier in the book, the bad odor of a bankruptcy will dog your steps for years afterward, making it difficult to rent a house or apartment, or to obtain any kind of personal or business credit. In addition, even if you can get a loan, you often end up having to pay higher interest rates because you are considered a poor credit risk. That can be a heavy burden to carry. In fact, it's not unusual for many people who have gone through bankruptcy to feel like total financial failures. The psychological costs can be extremely high as well. In fact, 76% of respondents in a recent survey said that bankruptcy was the most painful event in their lives.

What's worse is that some people have been talked into filing for bankruptcy without being properly warned about the inevitable downside associated with it. In some cases, they have actually been led to believe that their credit ratings would improve—because they wouldn't have any more debts after their bankruptcy had been discharged. Other people were led to believe that they were getting involved in a payment plan. That sort of misinformation is reprehensible, at the very least. Don't be fooled by this kind of garbage, regardless of where it comes from.

When is bankruptcy appropriate?

While resorting to bankruptcy is a shame, it's not shameful, as long as it's used in the right context. If you have explored every reasonable alternative to bankruptcy and just don't have any options left, try not to feel guilty. The bankruptcy laws are there to protect you and your interests in a real emergency. They can be very powerful and beneficial tools, indeed, when used under the right circumstances. On the other hand, if you are tempted to view bankruptcy as a "quick fix" for your financial indiscretions, it may be time to review your priorities.

How does bankruptcy work?

Put simply, bankruptcy is a legal process that allows you to tell your creditors that you are unable to pay your debts. That same process immediately stops your creditors from pursuing you to collect those debts. Then, depending on whether you choose Chapter 13 or Chapter 7 bankruptcy, you can either reorganize your debts and try to pay them off over a period of time under court supervision, or have most of them discharged (wiped out) altogether by the court.

A personal bankruptcy has three elements:

■ Your responsibility for repaying some of your debts is temporarily suspended while you and a

Unofficially... Unlike early U.S. bankruptcy laws, current bankruptcy procedures offer consumers considerable protections from their creditors.

bankruptcy trustee work out a plan for meeting part or all of your financial obligations.

- Your liability for certain debts may be limited to a smaller amount than the actual amount you owe, and you may be released from paying certain debts altogether.

- You repay all or a portion of your debts according to a repayment plan worked out by you, the court, and the trustee—either from the sale of your assets or from your income that exceeds your basic living expenses.

What this process does is give consumers who can't possibly pay their debts a chance to wipe the slate clean and start over fresh. Filing for bankruptcy also may provide a little extra time for someone who is facing repossession, disconnection of utilities, or eviction or foreclosure to work out a repayment schedule. That's it, in a nutshell. Of course the devil is in the details. And there are a few more details, to be sure. Quite a few. We'll be looking at many of them in the pages that follow.

Types of bankruptcy

Basically, there are four main types of bankruptcy that many people are familiar with: Chapter 7, Chapter 11, Chapter 12, and Chapter 13. The names come from the chapters of the federal statutes of the Bankruptcy Code that contain the bankruptcy law. Chapter 11 is mainly used by corporations (or extremely high-income individuals), so we won't be discussing it. Chapter 12 is primarily intended for family farms, so we'll pass on that one as well. The two forms of personal bankruptcy we'll be focusing on are Chapter 7 and Chapter 13.

Chapter 7 bankruptcy

The most popular form is Chapter 7 bankruptcy, usually referred to as "straight" or "liquidation" bankruptcy. In most cases, you can keep a small equity in your home, perhaps an inexpensive car, and a limited amount of personal property (especially the tools of your trade and clothing). These items are usually exempt from being liquidated under Chapter 7 bankruptcy.

Unfortunately, most of the rest of your property is taken and normally is sold under court order to raise cash to pay off your creditors. Secured debtholder claims—those with property as collateral—are paid first (your home mortgage lender or auto financing company are examples of secured lenders). If any money remains, unsecured debtholders (such as credit card issuers, gasoline companies, etc.) receive a proportionate amount of those remaining funds.

Once this has been accomplished, your bankruptcy is discharged and most creditors are barred from trying to collect any more money from you. The process sounds relatively simple, but it can be extremely painful. Especially if you have a lot of personal property with high sentimental or actual value that falls in the nonexempt category (more on that later in this and the next chapter), it is very difficult.

The Chapter 7 form of bankruptcy was traditionally used by people who did not have a steady income and who owned few assets. I should point out, however, that in recent years some very wealthy, high-profile individuals have also made use of Chapter 7 bankruptcy, with the assistance of well-paid bankruptcy lawyers who figured out "creative" ways of exempting almost every asset imaginable.

Unofficially...
A bankruptcy judge can dismiss a Chapter 7 bankruptcy if the judge decides that you have enough income or assets to repay most of your debts within a Chapter 13 bankruptcy, or outside of the bankruptcy system altogether.

Generally speaking, even people of modest means rarely lose much property in Chapter 7 bankruptcies. Given this reality, it's not surprising that Chapter 7 has been extremely popular with most "bankruptcy mills," which crank out bankruptcies like so many sausages. In recent years, around 80 percent of all personal bankruptcies filed have been Chapter 7. That figure is expected to decline as a result of the new Bankruptcy Reform Act.

The original intent of Chapter 7 bankruptcy was to give people who simply couldn't pay back all of their debts the chance to wipe them out and start over. It also was intended to prevent creditors from stripping you of all your assets when you couldn't pay what you owed. On the other hand, it wasn't intended that you would keep all your assets either.

Chapter 13 bankruptcy

Your other choice, Chapter 13 bankruptcy, is generally referred to as "wage earner" or "regular income plan" bankruptcy. In a Chapter 13 plan, you reorganize rather than liquidate your assets—and attempt to pay off as many of your debts as possible, normally within three (or sometimes up to five) years under the close supervision of a bankruptcy trustee. The trustee will require you to maintain a strict budget, and you will not be allowed to take on any new credit without the approval of the trustee.

You will make monthly payments on your debts from your disposable income after you have paid your basic living expenses. At the end of the repayment plan, assuming that you have made all of the agreed-upon monthly payments, any remaining debts are discharged (or forgiven), a provision that limits the total amount that you will have to pay under the plan.

One main advantage of a Chapter 13 bankruptcy is that the majority of your property is not liquidated—you get to keep it. The other advantage is that at least part of your debts will probably be discharged at the end of the repayment period.

This form of bankruptcy is generally used by people who own substantial assets (with the notable exceptions just mentioned) and who are regularly employed. Chapter 13 bankruptcy also gives people who are having a difficult time paying their bills a chance to work out a reasonable repayment schedule under court supervision.

That's a quick overview. We'll take a much closer look at these two varieties of personal bankruptcy in Chapter 14 of this book, where I'll show you how to file for and actually make use of them. Throughout the remainder of this discussion, I will describe how the system is supposed to work rather than the way it has sometimes worked in recent years, on the assumption that the proposed new Bankruptcy Reform Act will shift the balance back in that direction.

Watch Out!
You cannot file for Chapter 13 bankruptcy if your secured debts exceed $750,000 or your unsecured debts exceed $250,000.

Causes of bankruptcy

Now that you have an overview of bankruptcy, I'm going to put it into its proper context. What kinds of situations cause people to consider bankruptcy as an option? There are many reasons. Here are the main ones:

- Illness or injury
- Divorce or separation
- Loss of job
- Business failure
- Bad use of credit

If this list sounds familiar, you're right. It's virtually identical to the list of frequent causes of money problems we looked at in Chapter 7; at this stage, though, the problems have become so severe that normal remedies are no longer effective. I'm not going to repeat what I've already said about the individual categories, but I would like to make a few observations about how these problems relate to bankruptcy.

The first four categories, illness or injury, divorce or separation, loss of job, and business failure, are events that generally involve a measure of bad luck or chance. True, bad choices can lead to some of these problems, but by and large these things just happen. And there you are, suddenly facing a huge debt.

The last category, bad use of credit, is avoidable, yet millions of people stumble into this trap. The point I want to make is that there are some circumstances that may force you to file for bankruptcy that are almost totally beyond your control. On the other hand, you may have dug yourself into a deep financial hole, possibly over a long period of time. Nonetheless, the end result is the same: crushing debt.

To my way of thinking, resorting to bankruptcy is a lot easier to justify if you are basically not to blame for your debts and you really don't see any other way out of your dilemma. Now, if you got yourself into financial trouble on your own, then you should exhaust every other option before you file for bankruptcy. If you don't, you may simply be setting yourself up to repeat your mistakes in the future. Avoiding that scenario is one of the main goals of this book.

What triggers bankruptcy?

There are two ways that a bankruptcy can be triggered: voluntarily or involuntarily. A *voluntary bankruptcy* is initiated when you file a bankruptcy petition on your own behalf. An *involuntary bankruptcy*, on the other hand, can be filed by your creditors, and this action forces you into bankruptcy. Involuntary bankruptcy is rarely initiated, and can be accomplished only through the use of Chapter 7 (or Chapter 11) filings. You can't be forced into a Chapter 13 bankruptcy. Voluntary bankruptcies make up the vast majority of personal bankruptcies, and that's what we will focus on.

Your choices

Should you file for bankruptcy? That's a good question that does not have a simple answer. You have a number of options and many different factors to consider. Since bankruptcy has so many negative consequences, it's a decision that should not be taken lightly. Obviously the answer to this question varies somewhat depending on whom you ask, but most credit counselors generally agree that you should not file for bankruptcy unless:

- All your attempts to get your spending and credit use under control have failed, even with the help of a credit counselor or debt consolidation plan.

- You are unable to meet your debts with your current income.

- Your honest efforts to set up a repayment plan with your creditors have failed.

- Your debt-to-income ratio is 40 to 50 percent or more.

- You really have no other viable alternative.

If all or most of these circumstances apply to your situation, then bankruptcy is probably your best option. But not always. You might be surprised to know that one of your options may be to do absolutely nothing.

Do nothing

Do nothing? I know this sounds nuts, but bear with me. This strategy is not for everyone; under certain circumstances, though, it might be a viable course of action—or inaction. In this scenario, the amount of debt is not as important as your lifestyle and your assets. If you live simply on little income, have accumulated little property, and have no plans to drastically alter your lifestyle in the future, you may be what is known in the financial industry as "judgment proof."

This means that if your creditors were to bring suit and obtain a court judgment against you, the suit would be pointless because you essentially have nothing for them to take. You can't be thrown in jail for refusing to pay your debts (tax protestors and child support scofflaws excepted), and your creditors can't take your basic necessities of life, such as food, clothing, regular household furnishings, and so on. Consequently, there is very little that your creditors can do to you in this situation. That's the theory.

In actual fact, there are a number of serious drawbacks to this strategy. You need to know that your creditors may file suit anyway, in the hope that you will *eventually* have something they can get their hands on. You also need to be aware of the fact that a court judgement against you may remain in force for as long as 20 years in some states. In addition, the "do nothing" approach runs counter to most of

Bright Idea
In certain situations, especially where you are facing huge bills that were caused by circumstances beyond your control, filing for bankruptcy may be the only reasonable course of action. However, in most cases there are other alternatives that may make more sense.

the advice I've been giving so far. Frankly, I'm not thrilled about this idea, and I don't personally recommend it, but I would be remiss if I didn't mention it.

Negotiate with your creditors

Another possible option that we have already covered extensively in Chapters 10 and 12 is to restructure and consolidate your bills and pay off your creditors. As I've said, if you can manage to arrange it, restructuring is a far better alternative than bankruptcy. Restructuring will allow you to gradually restore your financial stability and your credit rating at the same time. You'll also be avoiding the stigma attached to bankruptcy and help to instill better discipline in the handling of your financial affairs. This can be done either with or without the help of a credit counseling agency.

Trying to determine where the cutoff point is between choosing restructuring over bankruptcy can be a tricky proposition. Financial counselors are not in agreement on when you can avoid bankruptcy by restructuring your debts. One rule of thumb is that if your total debt is under $10,000, restructuring may be your best choice. Obviously, there are so many variables that this can be only the roughest of guides. Sometimes, people with $100,000 or more in debts successfully restructure, so you really should get competent, unbiased advice before you decide which way to go.

Get outside help

If you are seriously considering bankruptcy, I strongly urge you to get some outside help in making that decision, preferably from a nonprofit group or service that isn't trying to sell you on bankruptcy.

Bright Idea
If you are thinking about filing for bankruptcy in order to stop collection agencies from hassling you, remember that you can usually do that simply by writing a letter telling them to stop. Bankruptcy is not necessary to accomplish this.

If you go to a bankruptcy attorney first, guess what kind of advice you'll get? In fact, 7 out of 10 bankruptcy filers in a recent survey were unaware that they had alternatives before filing. A trusted family lawyer might be a good resource, however. Don't wait until it's too late; that's a common mistake that many people make. By the time they finally get around to asking for help, bankruptcy is their only remaining alternative.

At some point in the bankruptcy process, you should seek sound legal advice, especially if there are issues that you are not sure about, or if your particular circumstances don't seem to fit the standard strategies. This is especially important if you are not sure how to deal with your house in a bankruptcy situation because there is considerable danger that you may lose it (see Chapter 14 of this book for more issues related to your home).

As I mentioned in Chapter 11, one organization in particular, Debt Counselors of America®, will work tenaciously with you to try to figure out a viable way to avoid bankruptcy. If there's a way, they'll find it (this unique Crisis Relief service does cost $425, however). There are other nonprofits where you can go for advice, as well (see Chapter 11). If you don't have the necessary negotiating skills to deal with your creditors, many of these nonprofits can act as your intermediary for little or no money. You don't need a bankruptcy lawyer for that.

I do need to add one caveat. If you go to a Consumer Credit Counseling Service (CCCS), or similar organization, for advice, remember that a good deal of their funding comes from credit grantors. And it's not in those creditors' best interest if you file for bankruptcy.

Filing for bankruptcy does offer some legal protections that a CCCS-type plan does not offer. For example, if you miss a payment, Chapter 13 bankruptcy protects you from your creditors, but a CCCS-type plan does not. Also, a CCCS-type plan generally calls for full repayment of your debts, whereas a Chapter 13 bankruptcy normally calls for repayment of less than the full amount. On the other hand, a bankruptcy can cost more in fees, especially if you hire a bankruptcy attorney. Those fees vary widely, but can easily come to $500 or more, depending on your particular situation. You decide.

Does bankruptcy make sense?

Last, but by no means least, is the question of whether it makes financial sense to file for bankruptcy. To determine that, you need to ask yourself several questions. The first one is, "Will bankruptcy discharge (wipe out) enough of my debts to make it worth all the trouble and expense?" Here's a list of dischargeable debts to help you answer that question:

- Back rent
- Utility bills
- Credit card bills
- Department store and gasoline company bills
- Newspaper and magazine subscriptions
- Legal, medical, and accounting bills
- Deficiency balances
- Court judgments
- Loans from friends or relatives
- Other unsecured loans

If the majority of your debts fall in these categories, then filing for bankruptcy may make sense for you, since all of these debts are usually eliminated in a bankruptcy.

On the other hand, some debts are nondischargeable in both Chapter 7 and Chapter 13 bankruptcies. Here's a list:

- Court-ordered alimony or child support
- Student loans (unless the court determines that the payment of the loans will cause an undue hardship on you or your family)
- Most federal, state, or local taxes
- Automobile accident claims in which you were intoxicated or reckless
- Court-ordered fines or restitution payments in a criminal case
- Debts you forgot to list

You need to know that other debts may be ruled nondischargeable by a bankruptcy judge. These frequently are related to some type of fraud. We'll look at some of them in the next chapter. The rule of thumb to remember for now is that if more than 50 percent of your debts are nondischargeable, bankruptcy may not be your best choice.

The second question you have to ask yourself in order to decide whether bankruptcy makes financial sense is, "Will I be forced to give up property that I don't want to lose?" If you own a lot of the following items and don't want to give them up, a Chapter 7 bankruptcy probably doesn't make sense:

- Cash, bank accounts, stocks, bonds, and other investments
- Second car or truck

- Second or vacation home
- Expensive musical instruments (unless you are a professional musician)
- Stamp, coin, or other collections
- Family heirlooms

This gets into the rather complex realm of "exempt" versus "nonexempt" property, which we will look at in greater detail in the next chapter. The point to remember here is that the questions about having to give up this property relate only to a Chapter 7 bankruptcy. In a Chapter 13 bankruptcy, you get to keep your property. So, the rule of thumb is: If you have mostly nonexempt property, then your best option is to consider filing a Chapter 13 bankruptcy. Or, you might want to consider negotiating with your creditors to restructure your debts, and skip bankruptcy altogether.

Just the facts

- Bankruptcy should always be your last resort.
- If you really need to file for bankruptcy, don't feel guilty.
- Beware of anyone who tells you that bankruptcy will improve your credit rating. It won't.
- Get unbiased advice from a nonprofit credit counseling agency before you decide to file for bankruptcy.
- Before you file for bankruptcy, be sure that you will gain more than you will lose.

GET THE SCOOP ON...
How to choose the right type of bankruptcy ▪
How to file for bankruptcy ▪
Your court appearance ▪ What you can keep—
and what you will lose ▪ Bankruptcy and
your home

Bankruptcy—Chapter and Verse

Your financial ship ran into an iceberg in the North Atlantic and has been taking on water ever since. Despite the best efforts of you and your crew to keep her afloat, it's clear that your vessel is hopelessly damaged and is about to sink. The bow, weighed down by your debts, is already underwater, and you don't have much time left.

You've given it your best shot, so there's no need to go down with the ship. It's time to lower the lifeboats. And your lifeboat actually has a name on it: "bankruptcy." I think the lifeboat analogy is appropriate. Few people would decide to use a lifeboat unless there was a real danger of sinking. However, as a last-resort measure, a lifeboat (and bankruptcy) can be lifesavers in a genuine emergency.

In the previous chapter, we covered most of the basics about bankruptcy. In this chapter, we'll look at additional factors that you need to consider when trying to decide which type of bankruptcy to choose, or whether to file at all. Then, we'll go through the

335

Chapter 14

process of how to actually file for both Chapter 7 and Chapter 13 bankruptcies—one step at a time. Along the way, I'll explain such issues as automatic stays, exempt and nonexempt property, trustees, and secured and unsecured debts. We'll also examine the many factors involved in whether or not you will lose your home in a bankruptcy. Finally, we'll take a brief look at life after bankruptcy.

You may not be thrilled about climbing into a crowded, little lifeboat on a cold, dark night in the middle of a very big ocean, but it sure beats the alternative. The same goes for bankruptcy.

How to decide which way to go

As I said in the last chapter, you need to make sure that you will actually be coming out ahead financially before you file for bankruptcy. This involves comparing your dischargeable debts with your nondischargeable debts. If the latter exceeds the former, it's probably not a good idea to file. We also looked briefly at exempt and nonexempt property as they relate to a Chapter 7 bankruptcy. We'll examine that in more depth shortly. First we need to look at a few other issues that should help you decide which kind of bankruptcy to pursue—or whether to pursue it at all. There are some situations where filing for bankruptcy may not be wise or even possible.

Previous bankruptcy discharge

If you have obtained a discharge of your debts under a Chapter 7 or Chapter 13 bankruptcy in a case begun within the last six years, you are not allowed to file for Chapter 7 bankruptcy. However, this restriction does not apply to a Chapter 13 bankruptcy; you are permitted to file as often as you wish as long as you have sufficient income for a repayment plan.

> "
> Bankrupt debtors are a cross section of America. There are some important subgroups in bankruptcy, but the data generally show that bankrupt debtors are not an identifiable class.
> —Teresa A. Sullivan, Elizabeth Warren, Jay Lawrence Westbrook, *As We Forgive Our Debtors: Bankruptcy and Consumer Credit in America*
> "

This does not mean that filing Chapter 13 bankruptcies on a recurring basis is a good idea. It's not. However, it is possible to do so, and unusual circumstances might actually make it necessary.

You don't want to hurt a cosigner

If someone has cosigned or guaranteed a loan for you or has a joint account with you, that person can be held entirely responsible for repayment if you fail to do so. If you file for Chapter 7 bankruptcy, as soon as your liability is discharged by the court, the creditor can, and almost certainly will, go after your cosigner for repayment. If that individual happens to be a friend or relative, the situation can become particularly sticky and unpleasant. You may end up with a former friend, to say nothing about what this might do to your familial relationship.

It gets worse. In addition to paying the outstanding amount you owe, your cosigner may also have to declare any money that you paid to them (within a year of filing for bankruptcy) and hand it over to the bankruptcy court. This is because such payments to relatives or close business associates are considered "preferences," which are not allowed under bankruptcy law (see Chapter 1 for more on the many perils of cosigning loans).

There are ways to avoid this scenario. You can pay off the creditor, or you could "reaffirm" the loan, if the creditor agrees, by signing a reaffirmation agreement that spells out the amount you owe and the terms you agree to for repayment. Another alternative would be to file for Chapter 13 bankruptcy instead, and include your cosigned debt as part of your repayment plan.

If you've tried to beat the system

The bankruptcy court takes a dim view of people who try to beat the system. If there is evidence of fraud, your creditors or the court may challenge your bankruptcy. Whether or not your intent was to defraud your creditors, if you have been involved in any of the following activities, you should probably not file for bankruptcy:

- Charging large bills for nonessentials just before filing
- Recent transfer of ownership in real estate, cash, or other assets to family or friends
- Hiding money or property from your spouse during a divorce
- Attempting to hide assets from the court
- Taking out large cash advances prior to filing
- Lying about income or debts on credit applications
- Running up big debts for vacations or entertainment just before filing

Any or all of these activities will act as large red flags to bankruptcy judges, trustees, and your creditors. Visa and some banks are getting very aggressive about challenging large, last-minute debts. Don't play matador with those red flags.

"Liquidation bankruptcy" Chapter 7

As I've said, Chapter 7 bankruptcy has been the most popular form of personal bankruptcy in recent years, accounting for around 80 percent of filings. If most of your debts fall in the dischargeable category, and you don't have a lot of nonexempt property, Chapter 7 probably makes sense for you. Let's look at Chapter 7 in detail.

Watch Out!
If you decide to fill out your own bankruptcy forms, be extremely careful that you don't inadvertently forget to list a creditor. If you do, you will have to pay that debt back even after all of your other debts have been discharged.

The front page of a Voluntary Petition for Bankruptcy. Source: *How to File for Bankruptcy*. Nolo Press.

Filing the petition

Here's how it works. A Chapter 7 bankruptcy generally takes about three to six months. The first step is to file for bankruptcy. There is normally a $130 filing fee and about $30 in administrative fees (in extenuating circumstances, these fees may be waived). You will need to fill out a two-page bankruptcy petition and a number of other forms. The forms will ask you to describe your property and income, as well as your debts and monthly living expenses. In addition, you will be asked to list the

The back page of a Voluntary Petition for Bankruptcy. Source: *How to File for Bankruptcy*. Nolo Press.

Name of Debtor	
Case No.	
	(Court use only)

FILING OF PLAN

For Chapter 9, 11, 12 and 13 cases only. Check appropriate box.

☐ A copy of debtor's proposed plan dated _____ is attached.　　☐ Debtor intends to file a plan within the time allowed by statute, rule, or order of the court.

PRIOR BANKRUPTCY CASE FILED WITHIN LAST 6 YEARS (If more than one, attach additional sheet)

Location Where Filed	Case Number	Dated Filed

PENDING BANKRUPTCY CASE FILED BY ANY SPOUSE, PARTNER, OR AFFILIATE OF THIS DEBTOR (If more than one, attach additional sheet)

Name of Debtor	Case Number	Date
Relationship	District	Judge

REQUEST FOR RELIEF

Debtor requests relief in accordance with the chapter of title 11, United States Code, specified in this petition.

SIGNATURES

ATTORNEY

X _____　　　　_____
　Signature　　　　　　　　　　　　　　　　　　Date

INDIVIDUAL/JOINT DEBTOR(S)	**CORPORATE OR PARTNERSHIP DEBTOR**
I declare under penalty of perjury that the information provided in this petition is true and correct.	I declare under penalty of perjury that the information provided in this petition is true and correct, and that the filing of this petition on behalf of the debtor has been authorized.
X _____ Signature of Debtor	X _____ Signature of Authorized Individual
Date _____	Print or Type Name of Authorized Individual
X _____ Signature of Joint Debtor	Title of Individual Authorized by Debtor to File This Petition
Date _____	Date _____ If debtor is a corporation filing under chapter 11, Exhibit "A" is attached and made part of this petition.

TO BE COMPLETED BY INDIVIDUAL CHAPTER 7 DEBTOR WITH PRIMARILY CONSUMER DEBTS (See P.L. 96-353 § 322)	**CERTIFICATION AND SIGNATURE OF NON-ATTORNEY BANKRUPTCY PETITION PREPARER (See 11 U.S.C. § 110)**
I am aware that I may proceed under Chapter 7, 11, or 12, or 13 of title 11, United States Code, understand the relief available under each chapter, and choose to proceed under Chapter 7 of such title. If I am represented by an attorney, Exhibit "B" has been completed.	I certify that I am a bankruptcy petition preparer as defined in 11 U.S.C. § 110, that I prepared this document for compensation, and that I have provided the debtor with a copy of this document.
	Printed or Typed Name of Bankruptcy Petition Preparer
X _____ Signature of Debtor　　　　　　　Date	Social Security Number
X _____ Signature of Joint Debtor　　　　Date	Address　　　　　　　　　　　　　　Tel. No. Names and Social Security numbers of all other individuals who prepared or assisted in preparing this document:
EXHIBIT "B" (To be completed by attorney for individual Chapter 7 debtor(s) with primarily consumer debts.) I, the attorney for the debtor(s) named in the foregoing petition, declare that I have informed the debtor(s) that (he, she, or they) may proceed under Chapter 7, 11, 12, or 13 of title 11, United States Code, and have explained the relief available under each such chapter.	If more than one person prepared this document, attach additional signed sheets conforming to the appropriate Official Form for each person.
	X _____ Signature of Bankruptcy Petition Preparer
X _____ Signature of Attorney　　　　　　Date	A bankruptcy petition preparer's failure to comply with the provisions of title 11 and the Federal Rules of Bankruptcy Procedure may result in fines or imprisonment or both. 11 U.S.C. § 110; 18 U.S.C. § 156.

property that you feel is exempt and your property transactions during the previous two years.

The automatic stay

After you file, you will be given a court date and your creditors will be notified that you have filed. The act of filing for bankruptcy initiates a so-called automatic stay, which immediately stops your creditors from attempting to collect what you owe. This should provide you almost instant relief from being hassled. If creditors continue to call you after you have filed for bankruptcy, informing them that you have filed should get them off your back promptly.

In addition, an automatic stay immediately stops any lawsuit against you and can provide temporary but immediate protection from utility disconnects, eviction from your house or apartment, foreclosure on your home, and wage garnishments. The stay remains in effect until the bankruptcy case is discharged or dismissed.

The bankruptcy trustee

The next step in the process is your court appearance with your court-appointed bankruptcy trustee. You must attend this meeting. This appearance is incongruously called the "creditors' meeting," although your creditors are unlikely to put in an appearance unless they are planning to challenge your petition. As a practical matter, a challenge rarely happens unless you've recently been involved in dubious activities with your accounts. At the meeting, the trustee goes over your papers and will ask you a few questions, most likely about your property lists.

The trustee's main duty is to see that your unsecured creditors are paid as much as possible on what you owe them. The trustee, incidentally, is paid a percentage of the money that is recovered for your creditors. As a consequence, the trustee will take a close look at the property you claim as exempt.

After this meeting, you are generally required to surrender most of your nonexempt private property to the trustee, who sells it to pay your creditors. You don't necessarily have to give up a particular item of nonexempt property if you can pay the trustee its value in cash. The trustee may also be willing to take exempt property of the same value instead; there is usually some room for negotiations.

If you have second thoughts about going through with the process, you can ask the court to

Watch Out!
If you change your mind and decide to ask the court to dismiss your bankruptcy case, be aware that the fact that you filed for bankruptcy will still appear on your credit history for up to 10 years.

dismiss your case. Generally speaking, the court will dismiss a Chapter 7 bankruptcy as long as this action will not adversely affect your creditors.

Discharge of debt

The final part of the process occurs when most of your debts are discharged by the court, which frees you from the debts that you owed to your creditors. Although a hearing will be scheduled for this, you probably won't have to attend in person and will instead receive notification of the court's action through the mail. You have to wait six years from the date you filed for Chapter 7 bankruptcy before you can file again—not that you will be in any great hurry to do so.

What's exempt?

Now that we've gone through the Chapter 7 bankruptcy process, it's time to look at some of the details. What exactly is this "exempt" personal property that you get to keep under a Chapter 7 bankruptcy? This is not an easy question to answer because there are so many variables. To begin with, there are two sets of rules: state and federal. If you live in Arkansas, Connecticut, Hawaii, Massachusetts, Michigan, Minnesota, New Jersey, New Mexico, Pennsylvania, Rhode Island, South Carolina, Texas, Vermont, Washington, Wisconsin, or the District of Columbia, you may choose either the federal or your state's exemptions. If you live in California, you have two lists to choose from. In the states not mentioned above, you can use only the state exemption list.

Although the variations between states are wide, you almost always can keep exempt property. I mentioned a few of them previously:

- Part of the equity in your home
- Motor vehicles, up to a certain value
- Necessary clothing
- Necessary household furnishings
- Household appliances
- Jewelry, up to a certain value
- Personal effects
- Tools of your trade, to a certain value
- Life insurance, to a certain value
- Pensions
- Public benefits

There may be some difference of opinion over what is "necessary" and what isn't, but it's safe to say that a mink coat would not qualify. The same common sense guidelines generally apply to everything else. In addition, the federal list and many of state exemption lists include what is called a "wild card" exemption that you can apply to any item or even split between several items. For example, if your vehicle is exempt up to $2,000 and you have a wild card amount of $1,000, you can add the wild card to your vehicle exemption to bring it up to $3,000. Or you could split the wild card to cover two nonexempt items valued at $500 each.

I suggest you look in the Nolo Press book *How to File for Bankruptcy* for extensive state-by-state listings of exempt property. The items on some of the state personal property lists are intriguing. Bibles, burial plots, and church pews are exempt in some states, while in others it's pianos, leased organs, or a cow. In still others, rifles, muskets, or shotguns are exempt. I'll leave the fun (or agony) of matching which items go with which states to you.

If you have a choice of using either the federal or your state's exemption lists, carefully examine which would be more advantageous in your particular circumstances before you decide which way to go. It may not be an obvious decision.

If your largest asset is the equity in your home, your choice of exemption lists may be entirely dictated by your "homestead exemption." In some states, that may come to $100,000 or more, and in others it may be as little as $5,000. The federal exemption is $15,000 (see "Keep Your Home—Maybe," at the end of this chapter for important additional considerations relating to your home).

If you have little or no equity in a home, you need to identify the most valuable property that you own and compare how you would make out with the federal or state exemptions. The exemption list that lets you keep the most is the one to choose.

If you still can't make up your mind, try comparing even small differences in relatively less expensive items. The federal list limits most personal property exemptions to $400 per item, with an $8,000 total. However, some states have no limit at all. On the other hand, the federal exemptions offer an $8,300 wild card that you can use on anything, so this may be your best deal if you don't have a house.

If you are married and filing for bankruptcy jointly, you generally can double your exemptions unless your state does not allow this strategy. The federal list lets you double all of your exemptions. This alone can be a strong incentive to use the federal exemptions if they are available to you.

What's not exempt

Naturally there is a downside to this equation. Here's a list of the items that you typically will have

Bright Idea
If you are trying to decide whether to use the federal or the state exemption list in a Chapter 7 bankruptcy, start with your large assets (your home or car) and work your way down to items of lesser value to help speed the comparison process.

to give up (nonexempt property) in a Chapter 7 bankruptcy:

- Cash, bank accounts, stocks, bonds, and other investments
- Second car or truck
- Second or vacation home
- Expensive musical instruments (unless you are a professional musician)
- Stamp, coin, or other collections
- Family heirlooms

Giving up any or all of these items can be a terribly painful experience, especially if you have spent years collecting valuable stamps, coins, or whatever.

In addition, even though you will be able to erase most of your debts with a Chapter 7 bankruptcy, you will still be responsible for paying your nondischargeable debts such as: alimony or child support; student loans; most federal, state, and local taxes; accident claims; court-imposed fines; etc. (see the previous chapter).

"Wage earner bankruptcy" Chapter 13

Now let's look at your other option, Chapter 13 bankruptcy. To qualify for Chapter 13, you must have a regular income from wages or other sources such as alimony, a pension, or perhaps government benefits.

In some ways a Chapter 13 bankruptcy is similar to Chapter 7, but in other ways it's quite different. To begin with, a Chapter 13 bankruptcy immediately stops your creditors from taking any further action against you. The cost for filing is the same as a Chapter 7—about $160 in various fees, although they cannot be waived under extenuating circumstances, as they can with the Chapter 7 fees. You get

Bright Idea
If you have a lot of nonexempt property that you would lose in a Chapter 7 bankruptcy anyway, it might be better to sell some of it and pay off your creditors, perhaps allowing you to avoid bankruptcy altogether.

to keep your property in a Chapter 13 bankruptcy, which is a real advantage if you have a lot to keep.

However, in exchange for hanging onto your property, you have to pay off your creditors (sometimes in part, and sometimes in full) over a three-year period in a repayment procedure not unlike what you would follow if you were working with a credit counseling agency. In some circumstances, the repayment period may be extended for as long as five years by the court.

In general, here's how it works. For your unsecured debts (credit card bills, department store charges, and so on), you will pay back at least as much to your creditors as they would have received had you filed a Chapter 7 bankruptcy. For your secured obligations (car loan, home mortgage, major appliances, etc., which act as collateral for the loan), you must pay at least the amount that the creditor agrees to accept, or you may have to return the collateral to the creditor. You need to be particularly careful about filing for Chapter 13 bankruptcy to avoid foreclosure on your home. Even in a Chapter 13 bankruptcy, you must continue to make at least your regular mortgage payment in order to keep your loan current. If not, you may end up in bankruptcy *and* lose your home as well.

As in a Chapter 7 bankruptcy, you are required to pay back your nondischargeable debts such as: alimony or child support; student loans; most federal, state, or local taxes; accident claims; court-imposed fines; and so on.

Filing the petition

To actually file for Chapter 13 bankruptcy, you fill out a number of forms similar to those used for a Chapter 7 bankruptcy. The forms ask you to list your income, assets, expenses, and debts. You also must file a plan for repaying your debts over three (or possibly five) years, taking your income and expenses into account. You will be required to use your "disposable income" (what's left after paying your monthly expenses) to pay off your debts every month until the repayment plan is completed.

Court appearances

Shortly after filing, you will be notified by the court of the "creditors' meeting," where you will meet with the court-appointed trustee and any creditors who want to attend. Although both unsecured and secured creditors can attend, normally only secured creditors (who don't agree with your valuation of the secured property in question) actually come to the meeting. The trustee will go over your papers and ask you a few questions about them and your proposed repayment plan.

The next step is a "confirmation hearing," where the bankruptcy judge makes a decision whether to accept your plan. If the decision is in the affirmative, the court "rules on confirmation." Once this technical step has been taken, you begin to pay the trustee, who in turn begins making payments to your creditors (again, not unlike a debt repayment plan with a credit counseling agency).

Discharge of debt

During the time that your repayment plan is in effect, as long as you make your court-approved payments to the trustee, you are more or less free to manage the rest of your finances. However, you must obtain the trustee's approval before you take on any additional debt. Getting further into debt would, of course, not be productive. If you follow through with your repayment plan to its conclusion,

Unofficially...
If your repayment plan in a Chapter 13 bankruptcy is denied by the judge, you can modify it to answer the objections of the court, and try refiling it.

your Chapter 13 bankruptcy will be discharged by the court and the case will be closed.

Extenuating circumstances

In the event that for some reason you cannot complete your Chapter 13 repayment plan—perhaps you suddenly lose your job in a company downsizing—the bankruptcy trustee can modify the plan. If your problems are temporary, the trustee can give you a grace period, reduce the amount of your monthly payments, or extend the length of the repayment period. If it becomes clear that you will not be able to complete the remainder of the plan because of circumstances beyond your control, say, serious illness or injury, the court may allow you to discharge your remaining debts on a hardship basis. If the court is not sympathetic to your plight, you still have several options:

- You can convert your Chapter 13 case to a Chapter 7 bankruptcy (as long as you haven't filed a Chapter 7 bankruptcy within six years).

- You can dismiss your Chapter 13 bankruptcy, in which case you will be back where you started from before filing, minus the payments that you have made, plus the interest that was halted by your Chapter 13 filing.

Most bankruptcy trustees are willing to help you get through a difficult period as long as it appears to be a temporary situation and that you are making an honest effort to live up to your part of the agreement.

Keep your home—maybe

A few cautionary words before we get too far into this subject. Entire books are written on the subject of bankruptcy, so I can't do more than skim the surface of this subject. I'll explain the basics of what's involved, but this is a situation in which you could easily lose your home because you didn't completely understand a minor but vital legal technicality. It's especially problematic because state exemption rules vary so widely and because so many other factors are involved. If, after reading this section, as well as *How to File for Bankruptcy* (Nolo Press), there is any doubt in your mind about Chapter 7 bankruptcy as it relates to your home, you should get sound legal advice.

With that caveat in mind, if you are a homeowner and are facing the possibility of bankruptcy, there are several important points you need to be aware of before you file. Most important is the fact that a Chapter 7 bankruptcy won't stop a foreclosure on your mortgage by the lender. To keep your home, you must continue to make regular mortgage payments before, during, and after bankruptcy (this also applies to a Chapter 13 bankruptcy).

The other crucial point is that if you have any nonexempt equity in your home, you will almost certainly lose your home, because the bankruptcy court will take your house and sell it to pay off your creditors. What's more, bankruptcy won't eliminate most liens on your home either. A home equity loan is considered a lien, as is an IRS tax lien. Most lienholders can foreclose on your home if you don't pay back the loan within a certain amount of time. It stinks, but that's what it says in the fine print of the loan agreements that you signed.

Keeping your home in a Chapter 7 bankruptcy is possible, but it is dependent on a number of factors. Here's how it works. The difference between what you owe your mortgage lender (and all other lienholders) and what your house is worth is your

Watch Out!
An automatic stay in a Chapter 7 bankruptcy won't prevent foreclosure on your home if you fall behind on your mortgage payments. At best, it may delay foreclosure for a month or so.

equity. If you were to sell your home on the open market without filing for bankruptcy, the proceeds of the sale would first go to pay off the mortgage and then to any lienholders to pay off the liens. You would get any money that was left over.

But under Chapter 7 bankruptcy, there is a key difference. If the bankruptcy trustee sells your home to pay your creditors, your mortgage and lien-holders get paid in the same order as I just mentioned, but your unsecured creditors end up getting what's left over—instead of you.

The homestead exemption

Here is where the "homestead exemption" I mentioned earlier comes into play. If your homestead exemption covers the amount that would otherwise go to your unsecured creditors, *you* get the money instead of them. What's more important, in almost all cases, if there isn't going to be anything left over for your unsecured creditors, the bankruptcy trustee won't even bother to sell your home in the first place.

For example, you have a home worth $120,000 and you have a homestead exemption of $40,000. If your mortgage(s) and lien(s) total $80,000, you won't lose your home because there isn't any nonexempt equity ($120,000 − $80,000 = $40,000). On the other hand, if your mortgage(s) and lien(s) come to only $60,000, your home will be sold by the bankruptcy trustee to recover the nonexempt $20,000 ($120,000 − $60,000 = $60,000; $60,000 − $40,000 = $20,000).

Consequently, the amount of your homestead exemption and how it relates to the amount of equity you have in your home frequently determine whether you will lose your home in bankruptcy.

But it gets more complicated. Some states base your homestead exemption on lot size, some use a combination of lot size and equity, and the majority base it on equity alone. Check the Nolo Press books I mentioned earlier or your state's bankruptcy exemption lists to see what rules apply in your state.

Foreclosure

Assuming that your debt problems are severe and you have already missed a number of payments on your mortgage, your lender will probably begin to take steps toward foreclosure. This usually entails having the lender "accelerate" your debt or "call the loan." This action requires the immediate payment of the entire balance. If you fail to do so, the lender will foreclose.

The foreclosure process usually takes from 3 to 18 months, depending on where you live and what kind of loan you have. While this process is underway, you still have some options:

- You can sell your home.

- You can obtain another loan from a different lender (perhaps with better terms, or at least lower monthly payments) and pay off your delinquent mortgage.

- You can file for Chapter 13 bankruptcy, which will allow you to make up your missed payments and resume your normal payment schedule.

In addition, if you can somehow come up with enough cash to make up your late mortgage payments before the foreclosure sale actually takes place, most states require your lender to reinstate your mortgage.

Bright Idea
If it looks like you will lose your home in a Chapter 7 bankruptcy, you may be able to substitute cash for the amount of the nonexempt equity—if it's not too much. Finding the cash may be problematic, but it's worth a try if it saves your home.

Finally, if foreclosure is inevitable, the good news (if I can call it that) is that losing your home in a bankruptcy is generally a somewhat better deal than losing it in a foreclosure sale. The reason is that the more money the bankruptcy trustee sells your home for, the more you get toward your homestead exemption after the secured creditors have been paid. And you get it in cash. If your home is sold through foreclosure, however, you rarely are entitled to a homestead exemption. So, if you are going to lose your home anyway, a Chapter 7 bankruptcy is the lesser of two evils. The tax consequences of all of this can become fairly complicated. Seek competent tax and legal advice if you are unsure about how to proceed.

Is there life after bankruptcy?

Yes, there really is life after bankruptcy. Although going through a Chapter 7 or Chapter 13 bankruptcy is traumatic, once it's over with, most people experience an enormous sense of relief. Unfortunately, they also experience an enormous number of hassles getting credit, renting apartments, and buying cars, among other things. We'll look at a variety of strategies to ease the pain and help you get back on your financial feet in Chapter 15, and how to avoid future problems in Chapter 16.

After you climb out of your financial lifeboat and set foot on dry land again, your life will begin to return to normal. You certainly won't forget your ordeal, but you probably won't forget the lessons that you've learned about yourself and your spending habits either.

Just the facts

- Don't file for bankruptcy if you've tried to "beat the system."
- A Chapter 7 bankruptcy takes from three to six months.
- You can lose your home in a Chapter 7 bankruptcy.
- A Chapter 13 bankruptcy takes from three to five years.
- You get to keep your home—and much more—in a Chapter 13 bankruptcy.
- There is life after bankruptcy.

GET THE SCOOP ON...
Dealing with bad credit ▪ Building good credit
▪ Secured credit cards ▪ What to avoid

Chapter 15

Reestablishing Your Credit

So you ran into a little financial trouble, and now your credit rating looks like it's gone through a meat grinder. It must smell as bad as rotten hamburger to your prospective lenders too, because they keep holding their noses and running the other way once they've seen your report.

Regardless of how you ended up with bad credit, you can take some comfort in knowing that you're not alone. Millions of your fellow citizens are experiencing the same problem. Some folks have managed to trash their credit ratings because of overspending and poor money management, but others have justifiable (or at least understandable) reasons for their predicament—everything from business failure and medical bills, to unemployment and divorce. Still, having bad credit isn't much fun.

Getting a regular major credit card is difficult, if not impossible, when you're saddled with a bad credit rating. As I've mentioned before, without a credit card, simple tasks such as renting a car, reserving a hotel or motel room, buying plane tickets, or even writing or cashing a check become a hassle. You probably will find it difficult to rent a house or an apartment, and you may be required to pay a deposit on your new utility services before the company will hook you up. You can even be turned down for a new job because of negative information in your credit report. It's not a pretty picture.

But don't despair. Fortunately, you have the option of making a fresh start. In this chapter we'll look at the problems most people run into when they are trying to rebuild their credit, and I'll offer strategies to help you deal with them. I'll explain how long the process will take and how long the bad marks on your credit report will continue to haunt you. I'll also warn you about what to watch out for while you're getting back on your financial feet. Then, we'll explore some of the best ways to rebuild your credit. Also, because secured credit cards are so important in this process, we'll take a close look at them—and how to shop for them. By the time you finish this chapter, you will have all the basic information you need for a fresh start on the road to a good credit rating.

Up from the ashes

There's good news and bad news about having bad credit. First the bad news. The effects of bad credit unfortunately tend to hang around long after the problems that caused the bad credit have been resolved. Now the good news. Bad credit doesn't last forever. So if you are sitting unhappily amidst the ashes of your former good credit history, it's time to get up and do something positive about rebuilding your finances and your credit report. The sooner you get started, the quicker your recovery.

> ❝
> I am so changed that my oldest creditors would hardly know me.
> —Henry Stephen Fox, 1791-1846
> ❞

Catch-22 again

However, you almost certainly will have one big initial hurdle to contend with. It's the old Catch-22 situation I mentioned in Chapter 1 all over again. Instead of being unable to get a loan because you don't have a credit history, this time you won't be able to get loans or credit cards (or much of anything else) because you have a *bad* credit history.

The problem, of course, is that lenders don't want to loan you anything unless you can demonstrate that you already have good credit. You can't demonstrate that unless someone will give you the benefit of the doubt and loan you some money so you can show your other potential lenders that you're going to pay it all back on time. Around and around you go, getting nowhere fast. What are you supposed to do?

Check your credit report

Actually, you can do quite a lot, and we're going to cover all of it in the pages that follow. One of your first actions (if you have not done so already) should be to get a copy of your credit report so you will know exactly how bad things are (see Chapter 5 for details on how to request a copy). How can you reestablish your credit if you don't know where you stand in the first place?

Once you get your report, check it over carefully to see what kind of information it contains. Here are some of the key things to look for that will cause you problems with your creditors:

- **Late payments.** A history of late payments is one of the first red flags that your creditors will pay attention to. Some may not be too concerned about the late payments if your recent payment history has been good, but others may reject your application immediately for just a few late payments somewhere in the distant past. Ironically, the size of the late payment is not as important as how late you were in making it.

- **Charged-off or collection accounts.** Any of your accounts that were "charged off" by your creditors or that were turned over to a collection agency will cause you problems. Most lenders view these notations on your credit history very negatively. If you have not already paid off these accounts, do so. The less outstanding debt you are carrying, the better. You may still be able to negotiate for a smaller amount than what you actually owe (see Chapter 10 for more details).

- **Judgments, tax liens, or lawsuits.** Any of these items that show up on your report are viewed very negatively, especially if they are still outstanding, because they indicate your unwillingness to deal with your situation. If at all possible, pay these off in order to present as clean a record as you can to prospective lenders in the future.

- **Bankruptcy.** As I've said repeatedly, this is about the worst item to have on your credit report. Most lenders won't even consider approving your application for credit if you've had a bankruptcy within the past few years.

- **Delinquent child support.** As I mentioned previously, lenders increasingly view this situation as a strong indication of financial irresponsibility. The fact that child-support payments take precedence in bankruptcy court over other consumer loans makes anyone with these delinquent payments on their credit report particularly unattractive to a lender.

See Chapters 5 and 6 for detailed explanations of what's in your credit report and how to interpret it. Keep in mind one key point: Only time and an accumulation of positive credit information will cure most of these ills. And speaking of time, I'm going to put this whole process in perspective for you.

How long will this take?

One of the questions that many people ask when they begin to realize how seriously their credit problems can affect the rest of their lives is, How long is this going to last? Good question. The answer depends partly on how you managed to get into financial trouble in the first place.

If your financial problems were due to circumstances essentially beyond your control—accident, illness, or job loss, for example—your explanation of the situation may go a long way toward speeding up your credit restoration efforts. Some lenders are willing to take these kinds of extenuating circumstances into account and may offer you credit more quickly once they understand the context of your difficulties. If your problems were due to overspending and bad financial management, they may not be as sympathetic, and your task may be more difficult.

The duration of your credit problems also depends on the length of time that derogatory information is listed on your credit report. There are specific rules governing these records. Let's look at each of the credit report problems I just

Watch Out!
There is nothing you can do to erase negative information such as a bankruptcy from your credit report. Only time and an accumulation of positive credit data will counterbalance bad credit information.

mentioned to see how long they will actually remain on your report:

- **Late payments.** A record of these transgressions will remain on your report for seven years from the date the payment was supposed to have been made. Even a $10 balance that was 90 or 120 days late can theoretically cause you problems many years later.

- **Charged-off or collection accounts.** These blotches on your credit report will last for seven years from the date they were written off or placed for collection.

- **Lawsuits.** Records of lawsuits can remain on your report for seven years from the date they were initiated. In the case of *unpaid* lawsuits, the statute of limitations may also apply (whichever is longer) and can cause these black marks to hang around for 20 years (or longer)—all the more incentive to pay off these obligations as quickly as possible. Check with a lawyer or your state attorney general's office to find out what the statute of limitations is in your state.

- **Judgments.** These can be listed for seven years from the date the judgment was rendered. Again, unpaid judgments may be reported longer, depending upon the statute of limitations in your state.

- **Tax liens.** Tax liens may remain on your credit report for seven years after they are paid, or theoretically longer if they are unpaid. However, as a practical matter, the major credit bureaus will normally remove this information after seven years.

■ **Bankruptcy.** Technically, both Chapter 7 and Chapter 13 bankruptcies can be reported for ten years from the date they were filed with the bankruptcy court. However, all the major credit bureaus have agreed to remove the negative information associated with a Chapter 13 bankruptcy (where you've paid back some of your debts under court supervision) seven years after you filed. You need to know that the individual debts that were discharged in a bankruptcy can, and probably will, remain on your report for seven years. That's a lot of negative information to overcome. Difficult, but not impossible.

The limitations mentioned above do not apply if your credit report is being furnished for a loan application for $150,000 or more or a life insurance policy of $150,000 or more, or if you are applying for a job with a salary of $75,000 or more. Theoretically, under these circumstances the negative information could remain on your report indefinitely, although in reality it usually won't.

The main point to remember about rebuilding your credit is that you probably didn't get yourself into trouble overnight, and you won't get out of trouble overnight either. Although there are a lot of different factors that might affect your particular situation, many people who patiently and persistently work at rebuilding their credit by bringing their spending under control, making timely payments, and so on, usually accomplish their goal within a couple of years.

What to avoid

Now that you know how long this derogatory information remains in your report, you can clearly see

Bright Idea
The Consumer Credit Counseling Service (CCCS) offers their former clients a Credit Recovery Program. If you have been a CCCS client, this may be just what you need to help reestablish lines of credit with major credit grantors.

that rebuilding your damaged credit is a slow and painful process. Consequently, after being repeatedly turned down for all types of credit, many people in this situation become desperate to find a quick solution. There is a huge and growing industry in this country that feeds on that desperation, and, unfortunately, this problem has no quick solution.

Credit repair

The perils of credit repair clinics are not obvious to people who are desperate to restore their credit. These places are such a threat that I want to make a few more observations (see "Other Fraud and Theft" in Chapter 3 and "Credit Repair Services" in Chapter 6). After you have been through a serious financial crisis, and especially if you have gone through bankruptcy, it may seem like no one is willing to give you a break—or even the benefit of the doubt. Enter the credit repair crew. "We'll fix everything," they claim in their slick, ubiquitous ads. It sounds too good to be true. And it usually is.

These folks may suggest that you engage in all sorts of questionable activities to try to confuse, delay, or otherwise overload the system in an attempt to clean up your bad credit. Ironically, most of their tactics do anything *but* clean up your report. They only complicate an already bad situation—and cost you big bucks to boot.

These services may also instruct you to dispute everything in your credit report. This strategy supposedly will cause your report to essentially disappear off the credit bureau radar screen because of the confusion caused by conflicting information. It won't. All the major credit bureaus now use sophisticated new computer programs that sift out most of the common credit repair clinic strategies, so you're just wasting your time (and money) following this kind of questionable advice.

As noted in Chapter 3, some of these slick operators have sold expensive "legal secrets" about how to create a new credit identity so that you can evade the problems associated with your real identity. It's a felony to do this. Don't even think about following this sort of advice. Instead of spending years trying to repair your bad credit rating, you could end up spending years trying to repair your bad legal record as well. Of course, you might have lots of time to research the subject while you're cooling your heels in jail.

Other things to avoid

Here are a few other things that you might be tempted to try if you are struggling under the burden of a bad credit rating—but I don't recommend them:

- **Catalog cards.** These so-called credit cards are tied directly to the merchandise offered by one company and cannot be used anywhere else. They are frequently described as "gold cards" but have no other similarity to real gold credit cards beyond the name. These plans are usually targeted at people with credit problems. The people are told that, by signing up and using the cards, they will improve their credit rating and be eligible for a Visa or MasterCard. Such results almost never happen. A secured credit card is a far better alternative (more on them shortly).

- **Rent-to-own agreements.** This alternative to buying various kinds of merchandise, such as furniture, appliances, televisions, VCRs, etc.,

Moneysaver
There is nothing that the many incarnations of credit repair clinics can do for you for a fee that you can't do for yourself for little or nothing. Why bother with them?

allows people to rent these items over a period of time and then at some point gain ownership of the item. These arrangements are especially popular with people who don't have the cash to buy the item or who have bad credit and can't obtain regular financing. Although you could make a case that rent-to-own plans offer these folks an option that might otherwise be unavailable, overall they are a bad deal if you look carefully at the numbers. The cost of most items obtained through this strategy is often twice as high (or more) than an identical item purchased through normal retail channels— even when the normal method involves financing. In a rent-to-own deal, you'll end up paying far too much in interest; and since these transactions rarely appear on your credit report, they won't help rebuild your credit rating either. Try something else. Better yet, be patient, save for the item, and pay cash.

- **One-time references.** A number of companies will offer to provide credit bureaus with "one-time" positive reports about your credit or to otherwise provide positive credit references for you. Since the major credit bureaus don't routinely get information about you from these sources, they probably won't pay much attention to them. The credit bureaus are interested only in their regular credit reference providers, so you are probably wasting your time and money on this strategy.

- **Finance companies.** As I've mentioned before, finance companies have not traditionally been viewed very favorably by the credit bureaus because they tend to loan money to people with bad credit. If you're trying to rebuild your credit, generally speaking you'll be better off going elsewhere for a loan.

The bottom line here is that you are trying to repair your credit, not damage it further. Even if these various options don't hurt you outright, they will probably cost you extra money that you could put to better use elsewhere. There are more effective ways to improve your credit.

Pay off your debts

One of the best ways to get your credit rating headed in the right direction is to reorganize your resources, set up a financial plan, and begin paying off your debts (see Chapter 9). Start with any liens or judgments against you. Taking care of tax liens is especially important because they will remain on your credit record for seven years *after they have been discharged.*

Next, work on paying off your merchant and credit card debts. A series of formerly delinquent accounts that have been returned to current status is proof positive that you are turning things around. As I've mentioned previously, you may be able to negotiate lower payments in exchange for taking care of these accounts.

Your potential creditors are going to be leery of lending you anything as long as the possibility exists that some of your other creditors may take you to court over unpaid accounts. Thus, do everything you can to clean up these old bills, even if they have been sent to a collection agency. I understand that you probably won't be able to eliminate all of your bills right away, and that's not even necessary. The main thing to strive for now is to get all your accounts current as quickly as possible.

Watch Out!
Some creditors don't care if a judgment, collection account, or write-off has been paid—they will automatically reject your application if it contains this kind of information.

Even though your credit report will remain filled with negative information for many years, the more positive *current* information you can accumulate, the greater the likelihood that some lender will give you a chance to prove yourself. This may take a while.

The credit restoration process is not the instantaneous miracle many credit repair clinics tout. It's more accurately likened to a set of scales that is initially weighed down with many pieces of negative information on one side and only a few pieces of positive information on the other side. Over time, as you gradually add more and more positive information, the positive data begins to tip the balance in your favor. The old negative listings are still there, but the more recent positive information now outweighs it. Eventually, the negative information is removed altogether, and the balance at that point is firmly in your favor.

Remember that different lenders have different thresholds of tolerance for bad credit information. If you are turned down by one lender, it's possible that another may offer you credit, so don't be discouraged too quickly. Patience, persistence, and a philosophical attitude will be useful as you gradually work at improving your financial situation—and your credit rating.

Credit rating builders

Repaying your old debts is only one part of the picture for reestablishing your credit. At the same time you are repaying your debts, you can make other efforts on different fronts. In fact, the more efforts you undertake the better. Remember, it's a question of seeing how quickly you can generate a large quantity of positive information on your credit report to counterbalance the bad stuff.

Take out a new loan—really!

One strategy is to take out a small loan at your local bank or credit union and then use the money to pay off the loan over time. This strategy is almost foolproof—as long as you don't blow the money on something else. You may have to open a small savings account in order to get the loan, but it's one way of establishing a new record of regular payments. Before you try this option, make sure that your payments will be reported to the credit bureaus. Not all credit counselors are in agreement on this strategy, but it is viable when used in conjunction with a larger credit rehabilitation plan. If you have very little cash to work with, a secured credit card is probably a more cost-effective approach.

Be creative

You may have to resort to some creative strategies if most lenders are stonewalling you. You might be able to talk a merchant into letting you buy something on credit if you make a large down payment and agree to pay slightly higher than normal interest rates. If you're a good negotiator, you might be able to wrangle an acceptable deal. Make sure that your purchase is for a necessity and that your payments will be reported to the credit bureaus, or your efforts are for naught.

Perhaps a friend or relative would be willing to add you to their major credit card as a cosigner or joint applicant. If so, the joint account will be listed on your credit report, and it will help you rebuild your credit rating.

I'm not a big fan of this next strategy unless all else fails. You might be able to find someone who would be willing to cosign or guarantee the amount of a loan for you (see "Cosigning a Loan" in Chapter 1). In this case, however, the dangers inherent with the cosigning strategy are not resting on your shoulders, but rather on the cosigner's. As long as you pay back the loan, there's no problem (except in the unlikely event that the cosigner is declared insolvent and the loan is called).

Getting new plastic

Having at least one major credit card is almost a necessity these days. Now if the imprudent use of credit cards was the main reason for your financial downfall, you may be reluctant to resume their use. That's understandable. Even laudable. However, having a credit card is more than an essential convenience; it's also one of the best ways to rebuild a tattered credit rating—especially a major credit card like Visa, MasterCard, or Discover. One of these cards paid on time every month over a period of time will quickly result in your financial redemption, and your mailbox will soon be bulging with enough promotional credit card offers to wallpaper your entire house.

If you had a major credit card that was revoked by the issuer because of your credit problems, you might try to get it back after you have the account paid up, especially if you regularly paid your bills on time before you got into financial trouble. In an increasingly competitive market, card issuers are eager to retain their good customers—even those who have temporarily run into difficulties. You may be pleasantly surprised to find that the issuer will give you your card back. On the other hand, if your credit rating has been seriously damaged, you may not be able to get a major credit card. At least not yet. You may have to try other alternatives.

Department store

One alternative is a department store or other retail credit card (not to be confused with the fake "gold cards" associated with catalogs mentioned earlier in the chapter). These are generally somewhat easier to obtain than a MasterCard or Visa, so this is a good strategy to follow if you can't get a major card. The downside is that these cards generally carry higher interest rates and don't wield as much clout on your credit report. Still, they're better than no card and no positive report at all.

Gasoline cards

Gasoline credit cards are perhaps the easiest of all cards to obtain. Unfortunately, they almost never are listed on your credit report (unless they're overdue), so they're not going to help you restore your credit rating very much. I suppose you could use the card as a reference when applying for another card, if nothing else. If you buy a lot of gas, and the credit card offers a rebate of some sort, it won't hurt you to get one.

Regardless of the type of credit card you use, your main focus is using credit cards that will help you rebuild your credit rating as wisely, quickly, and efficiently as possible.

Secured credit cards

If you can't get the issuers of Visa or MasterCard to give you a regular credit card, you have one other option, and it's actually a pretty good one: a secured credit card. A secured card is an excellent way for someone with a damaged credit history—or no credit history—to quickly build a good rating. Here's how it works.

Timesaver
One of the fastest ways to rebuild a damaged credit rating is to get and use a secured credit card.

What you should know

First, you will have to fill out an application for a
secured card just as you would for any other credit
card. Although approval is not automatic, it's easier
than it is for an unsecured card. Next, if you are
approved, you will be required to make a deposit of
between $200 and $500 (on average) into a savings
account or possibly a certificate of deposit. Your
deposit then becomes the security guaranteeing that
the card issuer will get paid—even if you default on
your bills.

The amount of the deposit is roughly equivalent to the credit limit of the card. Generally speaking, the larger the amount of the deposit, the lower
the amount of the interest rate, so it's a trade-off.
The money remains on deposit until you close the
account or until you eventually graduate to a regular credit card. In either case, you won't get your
deposit back until a waiting period of up to 90 days
has expired. This waiting period is an insurance for
the lender that no last minute purchases are floating
around.

The best deals

There are lots of secured cards to choose from.
Consumer Action, a California-based consumer advocacy and educational group (www.consumeraction.
org), puts together an annual survey of secured
credit cards. Their 1998 survey of cards offered by
20 banks, including Bank of America, Chase
Manhattan, Key Bank, and others, listed interest
rates ranging from 9.72 percent to 20.05 percent,
and annual fees from $18 to $39. Minimum deposits
ranged from $100 to $500, while the interest paid on
savings ranged from zero to 4.60 percent. The
Consumer Action survey also revealed that 8 out of

the 20 banks would consider applicants who had major credit problems, including bankruptcy on their credit histories.

I did a little research of my own at bankrate.com (www.bankrate.com) and found a list of the top 10 national secured cards that offered interest rates ranging from an incredibly attractive 5.9 percent on up to 18 percent, and with annual fees that started at $20 and went up to $50. Clearly, if you can't qualify for a major credit card and you're willing to shop around for a secured card, some good deals are available.

Important factors

Although secured credit cards tend to have higher interest rates and higher annual fees than regular cards, they do provide a valuable steppingstone for first-time borrowers or people with damaged credit. Of course, if you pay the balance in full every month (and that's what you should be doing in this scenario anyway), the interest rate doesn't matter. When applying for a secured credit card, you need to be aware of several important factors. Here are some questions put together by Consumer Action that you should ask the issuer before you apply for a secured credit card:

- Do you accept people with bad credit, or just those with no credit?

- Can I qualify for your card if I have declared bankruptcy in the past?

- Will you report my payment history to all three major credit bureaus?

- Will potential creditors who inspect my report be able to tell that this is a secured card?

- What interest rate is paid on my deposit?

- How long must I leave funds on deposit in order to earn that interest rate?

- Will my line of credit be equal to, less than, or more than my deposit?

- How long will it take me to become eligible for an unsecured card?

The question about whether your prospective creditors will be able to tell if your card is secured is especially important. Some issuers identify secured cards as such in their reports. Some don't. Avoid the cards that are flagged because this defeats the whole purpose of getting a secured card. An account that is identified as being secured will not be viewed as favorably by your creditors.

If you pay your bills on time every month, some banks will convert your secured card into an unsecured card in about 18 months or maybe sooner. Having an assured conversion date is a nice feature to look for. Other issuers may gradually increase your credit limit, sometimes actually exceeding the amount of your security deposit by as much as 100 percent. Shop around to see what deals you can find. This can almost be fun.

Bright Idea
Try to find a secured credit card that pays you interest on your deposit. Even a few dollars a year is better than nothing.

What to avoid

Naturally, there are some things to watch out for when you apply for a secured credit card. In the past, secured credit cards had a fairly wretched reputation—and for good reason. For years, many secured credit card offers were simply scams in which consumers paid a fee, say $50, for a "guaranteed credit card." For their money, the unfortunate individuals received an application form in the mail for a secured card. The consumer, of course, could have obtained an application form directly from the bank for free. Many other secured cards carried large application and processing fees, to say nothing of hefty annual fees.

The Federal Trade Commission offers the following list of things to look out for with deceptive credit card advertising:

- Offers of easy credit. No one can guarantee to get you credit. Before deciding whether to give you a credit card, legitimate credit providers examine your credit report.

- A call to a 900 number for a credit card. You pay for calls with a 900 prefix—and you may never receive a credit card.

- Credit cards offered by "credit repair" companies or "credit clinics."

Although scams are still plentiful, secured cards have begun to acquire a better reputation because so many banks have jumped into the fray with attractive offers. Not all those offers are as great as they sound at first blush, though. Read the fine print. As always, caveat emptor!

"There are plenty of good secured cards out there," says Linda Sherry, spokesperson for Consumer Action in San Francisco. "But there are some things that people need to look out for that aren't so good," she adds. Things like up-front processing or application fees, for instance.

Some high-profile lenders have recently introduced "secured" cards that don't require a security deposit. It sounds great, but be careful. These cards come with high application or processing fees and even higher interest rates. "Those interest rates can be out of this world—like 23 or 24 percent," says Linda Sherry. "This is something that people need to be aware of; they may think they are saving by not having to put down a deposit, but those other charges add up quickly." Sometimes as much as $200 or more on your first bill, according to Sherry. That's a lot of expense for a credit card that you will probably be carrying only for a year or two at the longest. With all the good deals available, there simply is no reason for paying an application fee. Look before you leap.

Admittedly, you may have to settle for reduced credit limits or slightly higher interest rates when you are getting a secured credit card, but that just goes with the territory. One thing you might want to consider is using your new card more frequently than you otherwise would as a strategy to help you accomplish your goal. I'm not suggesting going on a spending spree, just use your card for buying necessities, rather than using cash. And be sure to pay your bill on time every month. Once your credit rating is restored, you may decide that you would rather live without credit cards altogether. That's fine. But for now, they are a valuable tool. Use them often, but use them wisely.

Just the facts

- Bad credit doesn't last forever.
- Most negative credit listings will be removed from your report in seven years.
- Rebuilding your credit is a gradual process that takes time, patience, and persistence.
- A secured credit card can be an effective tool to help you rebuild your credit.

GET THE SCOOP ON...
Your new financial goals ▪ Using your credit
wisely ▪ Investing in your future ▪ Prepaying
your loans ▪ Automatic deposits and payments

Avoiding Future Problems

Have a seat. We're going to look into the future. My crystal ball is beginning to clear...ah...I see the Internet profoundly changing our lives in ways we can barely imagine. Some people are going to win big time in cyberspace. Some are going to lose. I see more corporate mega-mergers and related downsizing. I see the stock market going up—and I see it going down. I see striking new developments in medicine—and new drug-resistant disease organisms outsmarting those developments a short time later. I'm afraid I also see fires, windstorms, earthquakes, and other natural disasters too. And I see the next winner of the Kentucky Derby is going to be...oh, oh...the crystal ball just went all cloudy. Funny how that happens just when things start to get interesting.

The point is that dealing with the results of your past financial problems is one thing. Trying to anticipate or avoid future problems is another matter altogether. Too many variables and uncertainties are involved. It's as problematic as trying to predict your future with a crystal ball.

Happily, your future isn't completely left to chance. It is possible to at least avoid repeating your past mistakes. Even though you can't see clearly into your future, you can do your best to prepare for whatever may come. By following a prudent, forward-looking financial strategy, you should be able to protect yourself from some of life's many unpleasant surprises. And that same strategy can allow you to take advantage of some of life's wonderful opportunities as well.

In this chapter, we'll look at a variety of ways to help you prepare for the inevitable uncertainties of the future. I'll explain the importance of developing new financial goals and establishing sound savings habits. Now that you're well on your way to straightening out your past debts, it's time to start thinking seriously about avoiding them in the future.

With that thought in mind, we'll look specifically at investing in your future, and I'll offer some ideas to get you started in the right direction. Also, since you're now familiar with budgets and other financial calculations, we'll work up a few figures to see how much money you can save by prepaying your loans. We'll look at the many advantages of prepayment. Lastly, I'll go over some ways to fine-tune other parts of your finances for greater efficiency and savings. When we finish, you should be well positioned to face the future with confidence and enthusiasm. And you don't need a crystal ball for that.

Develop new financial goals

As you have worked your way through this book—and hopefully through your financial redemption as well—you have undoubtedly learned some useful skills and adopted helpful strategies along the way. Out of necessity, most of these efforts have been designed to deal with your existing problems. Now it's time to shift your focus from the past and the present to the future. This is an exciting transition that will open up a whole new range of possibilities.

You may recall that Chapter 12 suggested thinking about where you would like to be once you were debt free. Although you may not be debt free yet, you are ready to take that idea off the back burner, turn up the heat, and start stirring things up. You need to develop some new, long-range financial strategies that rest firmly on what you've already learned and that will help you get from where you are to where you would like to be. Where that is, of course, is up to you. Everyone will have a slightly different vision of what it would look like, but the financial means to get there are much the same for everybody. You figure out where you want to go—I'll describe the vehicle.

In general, these strategies for the future have three main elements:

- Avoiding or minimizing your use of credit
- Living primarily on cash
- Establishing regular savings habits

The idea is to shift your focus from patterns of behavior that cost you money to patterns that save or actually earn you money, while building a happy, productive, and fulfilling lifestyle at the same time. Let's examine each of these elements.

Limit your use of credit

A key element of this strategy is to limit your use of credit. If your financial difficulties were primarily due to overuse of credit in the past, you probably

Bright Idea
The secret to surviving unexpected hard times is to have a sound financial plan and a three- to six-month "safety cushion" of savings outside of your retirement plan.

don't need any additional incentive to mend your ways. You already know first-hand how destructive the misuse of credit can be. Regardless of how you got into trouble, it's a good idea to limit your use of credit to not more than 10 percent of your annual take-home pay. Less than that is better still. Of course, be scrupulous about making the payments on time.

Keep a constant, watchful eye on all of your credit and spending practices, and be alert for the first signs of credit distress. If you spot a problem, act promptly to head it off at the pass before it becomes serious. Having worked so hard up to now, you do not want to fall back into those old spending habits and patterns. It truly would be awful to end up in debt again. If you limit your use of credit and follow the other two guidelines—living on cash and saving regularly—you should not have any future problems with your consumer credit.

Wise use of credit

Credit in itself is neither good nor bad. It just depends on how you use or misuse it. Let's look at some examples. The use of credit definitely makes sense in certain situations, such as taking out a mortgage to buy a home that you would not otherwise be able to afford to pay for. Over time, not only will you build equity, but also your house will likely increase in value. The fact that the interest on your home mortgage or home equity loan is tax deductible is an added bonus.

Your car

Borrowing money to buy a car is another matter. The problem is that instead of building equity with your loan, you are actually losing money, because your new car depreciates as soon as you drive it off the dealer's lot. And it's downhill from there, even if you live in Kansas. This doesn't mean you shouldn't finance a car. In many parts of the country, having a car is a necessity. Nevertheless, it doesn't make financial sense to get a loan for a fancy, expensive car that is going to take you many years to pay off. You're paying interest on top of depreciation. It's a lose-lose situation. Now, if you happen to like fancy, expensive cars and can afford to pay cash, that's an entirely different situation. But if you have to finance a vehicle, keep it simple, and pay off the loan as quickly as possible. You might also want to consider buying a three- to four-year-old car in good mechanical shape instead of buying a new one. With the availability of extended warranties, a used car like this can be a very smart purchase.

Borrowing money to have your car fixed does make sense, however. Use your credit card to pay for auto repairs—especially if you have a breakdown and don't know anything about the repair shop you are dealing with. In most situations, the Truth in Lending Act allows you to withhold payment if there are problems with the repair work or the billing. The same strategy goes for almost any product or service that might give rise to questions or problems later on (see "How to Stop Payment with Your Credit Card" in Chapter 3).

The Internet

Shopping on the Internet or by mail is another area where using your credit card makes sense. This is particularly true when you are dealing with a merchant for the first time. If there's a problem with the merchandise or service, the Fair Credit Billing Act offers you some protections (see Chapter 3 again) that you won't be able to take advantage of if you pay by check, money order, or debit card.

The float

Last, but not least, using your credit card to take advantage of the float (the time between when you make your purchase and when the payment is actually due) is a smart use of credit that amounts to an interest-free loan during the term of the float. Of course, you have to pay the bill in full for this to work. Be sure to make your payment on time, or any benefit from this strategy will be gobbled up by late payment fees.

Cool cash

Directly related to limiting your use of credit is the strategy of increasing the use of cash for your purchases. Using cash wisely isn't rocket science. Mainly it means reining in over stimulated desires for immediate consumption and then planning ahead for as many of your big-ticket purchases as possible. Is your car nearing the end of its career? Start putting money aside on a regular basis so that you will not have to finance too much of the cost of a replacement when Old Faithful finally succumbs (having an emergency fund can help with this sort of situation—more on that in a moment). Here's an interesting variation on this strategy. If you are currently making car payments, when the loan is paid off, keep making the monthly payments to yourself. Deposit the money into an account so that in a few years you can pay cash for your next car.

The same goes for other consumer goods—or just about anything else, for that matter. Do you really need that new audio system? Fine. Start saving for it. It doesn't matter what the item is. If you can't

Watch Out!
Using your credit card to take advantage of items that are on sale can backfire if you can't pay off your account promptly. You may end up paying as much as you would have if the item had not been on sale. This is not wise use of credit.

pay cash, you can't afford it. I realize this runs counter to the prevailing message promoted virtually everywhere these days, which practically screams: "Buy, buy, buy! And buy it now!" That's probably how you got into trouble in the first place. There's no point in repeating the same mistakes. The main thing is to begin changing your basic way of thinking about how and when you spend your money. This is a vital part of your new financial strategy.

Establish sound savings habits

Another key element of your new long-range financial strategy is to establish sound, regular savings habits. Previous chapters have mentioned a number of times the importance of savings; now it's time for the details. Establishing a successful savings plan is somewhat similar to a weight-reduction program— getting into the habit and making progress is really more important than the specific numbers.

You are probably used to making regular monthly payments on your debts by this time. When you have eventually paid off those debts (or even sooner, if you are very disciplined and determined), that same strategy can be used to improve your bottom line, instead of some bank's. Regular saving is a great habit to get into. The sooner you begin, the better.

Being a consumer on auto-pilot and changing to being a conscious consumer and saver may represent a major shift in your financial thinking. It's an important shift that should help to free you from the tyranny of just scraping by (or slowly falling behind), which so many people struggle with these days. Regular saving also begins to make investing for your future possible as well (more on that in a moment), and that's where things begin to get really interesting.

First, some basic points. When people save money, they are normally interested in three main goals: protection, growth, and availability (or stated another way, safety, yield, and liquidity). Unfortunately, no one savings vehicle will simultaneously meet those three goals. Regardless of where you put your money, you have to balance your desire for growth (yield) against your need for availability (liquidity). Your desire for protection (safety) for your money also runs counter to your desire for growth, since the lower the risk, the lower the return on your money—and vice versa. This is true for almost any investment.

Given these facts, you have to arrive at a balance between your competing desires. The nature of that balance depends largely on what you want to do with your savings—and what your tolerance is for risk. If your time horizon is short-term, then you need to lean toward liquidity. If your time horizon is long-term, you can tilt toward greater growth. We'll revisit these issues as we go through the different aspects of your new financial strategy.

Incidentally, entire books are written on these subjects, so my comments in the next few pages can only skim the surface. I highly recommend *The Unofficial Guide™ to Investing* by Lynn O'Shaughnessy for lots of additional ideas on how to make your money work more efficiently for you.

Create an emergency fund

One of the most important parts of a savings strategy is an emergency fund. Most financial counselors recommend that you sock away a nest egg that equals at least three months of your average take-home pay

Bright Idea
An emergency "rainy day" fund that will help you get through some of life's many surprises is the most important part of your new financial strategy to avoid future debt problems.

(six months-worth is even better) to help you deal with those inevitable, unexpected surprises that arrive at irregular intervals in our lives. I'm not sure you need to slavishly adhere to these recommendations, but you absolutely should have some sort of rainy day fund. And the larger the fund, the better off you will be. You decide what is enough for your particular situation.

Your unpleasant financial surprise could be anything from emergency home repairs, to job loss from downsizing or a recession. Perhaps the sudden death of a family member or the untimely demise of your car precipitates the crisis. Whatever the reason, if you have a financial cushion to fall back on, you probably won't have to resort to going into debt to weather the crisis. Having one of these unfortunate events take place is bad enough. Being forced into debt because you have no financial contingency plan in place makes a bad situation even worse. It doesn't have to be this way. Be prepared. And start now.

First, figure out how much money you would immediately need for emergencies. It may not be as much as you would think in all cases. Now, I'm still talking about the three-month (or so) cushion here, but you don't necessarily have to put all of it in a low-interest savings account. The reason is that some of these emergency situations, such as damage to your car in an accident, or bills for hospitalization due to injury or disease, may be covered, at least partly, by insurance.

Even a major disaster such as losing your job doesn't normally require you to immediately withdraw all your savings next week. Job loss is a problem that may last for several months or more, but you can draw on your emergency cushion over a number of months as well. The point is, for most emergencies you probably won't need access to all your money right away. Consequently, you might consider having some of your rainy day fund in a savings or money market bank account (for easy availability) and the balance in a three-month certificate of deposit (for slightly higher yield).

If not having access to your CD funds for 90 days makes you nervous, you can set up a series of three-month CDs, one every month for three consecutive months, thereby giving yourself access to one-third of the total amount every month. If you don't need the CDs, keep rolling them over until you do. It's a reasonably effective strategy for squeezing a little extra interest out of your deposits while retaining fairly good access. Many CDs, however, require a minimum deposit that may be beyond your reach at the present time. But if you can afford it, you might want to give it a try.

At the very least, shop around for a savings or money market account that pays the best interest you can get (some of the new Internet banks are offering highly competitive rates), while still allowing you quick access, and start depositing a regular amount with every paycheck. Initially, the amount is not as important as establishing the routine. You can always adjust the deposit figure once you get into the habit (preferably increasing it, but also decreasing it a bit if you discover that you were overly optimistic).

If you can arrange an automatic deduction from your paycheck or your checking account, better still. That way, you won't be tempted to blow the money on other things. I've set up this sort of strategy myself, and I hardly ever notice the pain of the deduction, but I do notice the steady increase in my savings. This really is the only way to go for most people. Out of sight, out of mind—and especially out of temptation's reach.

General savings

Once you've set up your emergency fund, you are ready to expand on the savings theme even further. Hopefully, you now are in the habit of salting money away for a rainy day. Keep the momentum (and the habit) going and look for more-productive places to put your money. A regular savings account is not a good location for any money that is over and above your emergency fund. There are far better options for your investment money. Since we're not talking about saving for an emergency any more, your time horizon expands considerably (and so do your possibilities for greater yields).

We have already looked at one option—certificates of deposit. Because you won't need quick access to this investment money, you can think about the possibility of longer-term CDs, say, for a year or more, which offer somewhat higher interest rates. The main advantage of CDs, beyond their interest rates, is that they are protected by the FDIC, just like your other bank deposits. The downside is that if you change your mind and withdraw your funds before the term of the CD ends, you will be hit with a stiff penalty. You should not be investing in a CD if this is a likely scenario.

An even better place to put your money is into a money market mutual fund (as opposed to a money market bank account mentioned above). Money market mutual funds have been quite popular, and for good reason. They usually have better returns than savings accounts offered by banks and thrifts,

Unofficially...
In general, with most savings accounts and other investments, the higher the safety, the lower the yield—and the higher the yield, the lower the liquidity.

and in recent years they have even exceeded returns on some CDs. Although they are not insured by the FDIC, they are considered to be both safe and dependable (if not spectacular) performers. There are hundreds of money market funds to choose from.

Although there are differences between funds, generally you can write a reasonable number of checks every month, usually with a minimum amount—around $100 to $500—per check. Most funds have initial minimum investment amounts of $1,000 or more, but others will let you start with as little as a $25 monthly automatic deduction from your bank account. Shop around and see what kinds of deals you can find. A good place to start your search is at Morningstar, Inc., an independent service that rates mutual funds and variable annuities; call (800) 735-0700. They also have a Web site at www.morningstar.net.

There is yet another rock-solid option for investing your money at a pretty good return: U.S. Treasury securities. Investing in Treasury securities can get fairly involved, so I'll just cover the highlights. There are three main varieties: bills, notes, and bonds. The minimum investment for all three versions is $1,000, and they can be purchased in multiples of $1,000. Many savvy investors use T-bills as a temporary parking place for their money between longer-term investments. Treasury bills come in 13-week, 26-week, and 52-week varieties—the length of the term of the bill.

Treasury notes (as opposed to bills), on the other hand, have a longer time horizon and are available in 2-, 5-, and 10-year varieties. The final option, a 30-year bond, has the longest time horizon of all—30 years, as its name implies. The general auction schedule for Treasury securities ranges from weekly for 13-week bills to three times a year for the 30-year bonds. In the past, actual paper documents were issued for these securities, but today it is all done electronically. The best way to buy Treasury securities is from Treasury Direct (www.publicdebt.treas.gov). I've used the program myself, and after you learn the basics, it's really easy.

Begin retirement savings

As I've mentioned previously in the book, gone are the days when people had a guaranteed job (and a company pension) for life. And, as the questions about the long-term viability of Social Security multiply, more and more people are coming to the realization that if they don't make some additional preparations for their retirement, no one else is going to do it for them.

If you're not particularly market-savvy, one of the best places to start preparing for your own retirement fund is at work. If a 401(k), 403(b), or similar retirement plan is available at your place of employment, start putting money into it on a regular basis. The more money the better, since most plans call for your employer to make additional payments on your behalf (typically 50 cents on every dollar you put in). The total amount your employer will pay into your account is usually based on your contribution up to a certain percentage of your pay (often around 6 percent). That's free money. It's a great deal that's hard to beat.

If you don't have access to an employer-sponsored 401(k) or 403(b) plan, don't worry; you can always invest in one of the vast number of mutual funds that are available. To say that mutual

Bright Idea
One of the simplest ways to establish regular savings is to instruct your bank, employer, or mutual fund to withdraw a set amount automatically from your bank account or paycheck to be deposited into a savings, investment, or retirement account.

funds are popular these days is an understatement. Over $4.3 *trillion* dollars are currently invested in some 7,000-odd mutual funds. There are so many options I can't begin to do them justice here. Here are a few facts about mutual funds that you should know:

- You don't need to be a financial genius to invest in them. Let somebody else worry about which stocks and bonds to pick.

- They're affordable. Most no-load funds typically have low operating expenses, and they offer an easy way to enter the market with an initial investment of as little as $250 (or $25 or $50, if you set up a monthly automatic savings plan).

- Mutual fund companies are solid institutions. Although your investments are not guaranteed to increase in value (they're subject to market fluctuations and can go up or down along with the market), mutual fund companies in general are sound organizations with good track records.

A good place to start looking for information on mutual funds is *The Unofficial Guide™ to Investing in Mutual Funds*, by Stacie Zoe Berg. Also check out Morningstar's Web site at www.morningstar.net, or *Mutual Funds Magazine's* Web site at www.mfmag.com.

Another retirement savings option is an IRA (Individual Retirement Account). Over the years, IRAs have had their ups and downs—usually in response to congressional tinkering—but, since 1997, IRAs have made a strong comeback. There are probably almost as many IRAs to choose from these days as there are mutual funds. IRAs allow you to invest up to $2,000 per year in what amounts to a self-funded mini-pension plan that grows tax-free until you start to draw on it at retirement. And the new Roth IRAs, authorized by Congress in 1997, offer tax-free withdrawals at retirement, and consequently are even more attractive for most people.

Other investments

If you enjoy seeing your savings and retirement accounts grow, and you want them to grow even more, you may decide to take investing to the next level. We've already looked briefly at Treasury securities and mutual funds, which are a part of the larger financial market picture. However, a vast number of other investment opportunities are available, ranging from every conceivable type of stock to all manner of bonds, and other possibilities as well. This investment level is beyond the scope of this book, so I once again direct your attention to *The Unofficial Guide*™ *to Investing;* it has tons of additional information and advice on your many, many investment opportunities. Now, isn't this more interesting than getting a nasty phone call about an overdue bill?

The wonders of prepayment

What would you say if I told you that you can save $25,000 or more by regularly putting your pocket change in a jar. "It's going to have to be a pretty big jar," you might reply in disbelief. You might also be forgiven if you thought it might take several lifetimes to accomplish. Saving this kind of money may take years, but you can save huge amounts of money by prepaying your loans—especially your home mortgage. And you won't need a big jar either, because you'll be emptying it every month and using the money to pay down your mortgage.

> 66
> Money is better than poverty, if only for financial reasons.
> —Woody Allen
> 99

Which debts should you prepay?

In recent years, numerous magazine and newspaper articles have explored the subject of prepayment. Most of them have focused on prepaying your home mortgage. That's understandable because the results can be so spectacular. However, don't overlook your other loans, because the same strategy works with them too. It's actually a better idea to prepay your other loans first, because they're probably carrying higher interest rates than your home mortgage.

In Chapter 12, we looked at the savings you can enjoy by prepaying your credit accounts (see "Pay Off Your High-Rate Debts First"). The same strategy works for almost any type of loan. You may recall that the best approach is to focus on the loan with the highest interest rate first; once it has been paid off, work your way down your list of loans in descending order of interest rate. I'm assuming at this point that you have your other debts more or less under control, so we'll focus here on your home mortgage.

Strategies to use

One of the best parts of home mortgage prepayment is that almost any strategy will work. You can be organized and methodical or haphazard and sporadic. Even spontaneous, if that suits your personality. It really doesn't matter what strategy you use as long as you keep it up, although the more methodical approach may get you to your goal a bit sooner.

Here's how it works. The original amount of your loan is known as the "principal balance." Generally, your lender calculates interest on your outstanding balance, rather than the original amount of your loan. Thus, by reducing the size of your outstanding balance, you reduce the amount of interest you end up paying. Simply write a separate check for whatever amount you can afford, say, $25, $30 or whatever, and include a note to your lender stating that the extra money is to be applied to your principal balance. Include the extra check and explanatory note along with your regular monthly mortgage payment. That's all there is to it. Virtually all mortgage lenders will allow you to do this.

Almost anyone who is a homeowner can make this idea work. It doesn't require huge amounts of extra money, it just requires patience and persistence. One of the best books on this subject is Marc Eisenson's *The Banker's Secret*. Eisenson is a firm believer in the money jar approach. Even just $5 a month in pocket change used to prepay on your $50,000, 30-year, 8 percent fixed-rate mortgage will save you $5,217 in interest. The idea is to use money that you basically won't miss. In his book, Eisenson notes that an extra $50 payment per month on a $100,000 loan at 8 percent will save $39,906 in interest payments and shave six years off the term of the loan. Now, that's not small change.

After you have paid off your other debts, you may find that you have quite a bit more than $25 or $50 extra a month to put toward mortgage prepayment. If so, your savings in terms of interest and years eliminated from the duration of your loan can be truly breathtaking. Depending on the size of your loan and the interest rate involved, you could conceivably save $50,000, $75,000 or more in interest and chop 10 or 15 or more years off the term of your mortgage. Sound like a good idea? Absolutely.

When you prepay your mortgage, in addition to building up equity in your home, you are basically making a guaranteed, risk-free investment that will give you an annual pretax return exactly equal to the interest rate of your loan, compounded for the life of your mortgage. It's an investment opportunity that is hard to ignore. Once your mortgage is paid off, you'll be freed from an enormous financial albatross. You'll suddenly discover that you have *a lot* of extra money to use for other things. And that's really exciting.

What about prepayment penalties?

Before you start any prepayment plan, check your loan agreement for prepayment penalties. Most loans don't have them these days. But if yours does, you may find that the prepayment penalty applies only to the first few years of the loan. If your loan contains a prepayment penalty, check with your lender to see if it can be waived.

Streamline your finances

Fine-tuning and simplifying your money management are essential parts of carrying out a successful financial plan. The strategies discussed next will save you time and money, and insure that your routine finances are taken care of automatically.

Direct deposits

Direct deposits are increasingly common. A direct deposit means that your paycheck, Social Security check, or other regular sources of income are directly deposited electronically into your checking or savings accounts. This strategy offers a number of advantages:

- Direct deposits are automatic. If you are sick, incapacitated, or simply out of town, you will get paid on time without any intervention on your part.

Watch Out!
Don't completely prepay your low-cost mortgage if you will need to borrow money in the near future for such things as college or home improvement. Your home mortgage is usually the least expensive financing you can get, with the least amount of hassle.

- Sometimes you will have quicker access to your funds than you would with a normal paycheck.

- You can avoid long lines at the bank.

- Direct deposit may mean lower bank charges in some cases.

- It eliminates the problems associated with the theft of paper checks from the mail.

Although this strategy is especially attractive to people who use financial management software packages like Quicken or Money, it's a great idea for almost anyone. You don't need a computer for direct deposits. If you have the option to get direct deposit, try it. You'll probably never again want to go back to standing in line at the bank on Friday afternoon.

Automatic bill payments

The flip side of automatic direct deposits are automatic withdrawals. These are handy for routine monthly obligations such as mortgage payments, utility bills, car payments, and so on. Again, although this strategy is popular with people who use computer software to manage their finances, it will work for anyone, whether you are online or not. Consider the advantages:

- Paying bills is simplified. No checks to write, no stamps to lick, no envelopes to stuff, and no trip to the mailbox or post office.

- These bills will always be paid on time. No more late payment penalties or interest charges.

- Automatic payment may qualify you for a lower interest rate on a new loan at your bank or credit union.

Bright Idea
Automatic bill payments are a great way to ensure loan-repayment discipline, especially for home-equity lines of credit.

The one caution about automatic bill payment is that you must always have enough money in your account to cover the payments. If that may be a problem, then this is not the best strategy for you. Automatic deposits, coupled with automatic payments, are a winning combination for many people, however.

Building on your success

The fact that you have succeeded in turning your finances around should be extremely satisfying, regardless of whether you did it by yourself or with the assistance of others. Your success proves that you can tackle a difficult task (that may have even seemed hopeless) and come out on top. Just as important is that along the way you have almost certainly learned much about your motivations, strengths, and weaknesses—invaluable information that you can apply not only to future financial challenges but to other parts of your life as well (more on that in Chapter 17). If you're facing additional problems, why stop with just fixing your credit?

What's more, you now have experiences under your belt and some hard-won insights that you could share with others who are struggling with credit problems of their own. Especially if you worked with some kind of support group, such as Debtors Anonymous, you probably will want to give something back to the group that helped you. Even if you didn't work with a group, you have a lot to offer others. Think about it.

Just the facts

- Developing a new financial plan will help you attain your goals.

- Everyone should have an emergency fund.

- Regular savings lead to numerous money-making options.

- Mutual funds and IRAs are great investments for your future.

- Direct deposits and automatic bill payments are a winning combination.

GET THE SCOOP ON...
The American Dream ▪ More money-saving ideas
▪ The cure for "Affluenza" ▪ Living more on less
▪ The New American Dream

One More Step

I n most books written about conquering your debts, the authors offer their congratulations at this point on your success, pat you on the back, and wish you a good life. I'm not going to do that yet because I'm going to take you one step further.

Anyone who has gone through the traumatic experience of heavy debt invariably emerges with keen, new insights about what's important—and what's not. I hope that has been the case for you too. I rather suspect that some of those insights are about aspects of your life that really don't have much to do with money.

In this chapter, I'll help you explore some of those insights that you have picked up along the way, and I'll share some that have been gained by others who have struggled through the same process you've been through. Next, we'll look at some sobering statistics about consumption habits and what they mean for us and the rest of the world. With those statistics in mind, we'll investigate additional ways to consume less, save money, and live better—all at the same time.

Then, I'll introduce you to the increasingly popular concepts of downshifting and voluntary simplicity, and I'll profile some people and organizations who have intriguing ideas about building a new, sustainable economy and, by extension, a sustainable world. If you and your family can live a happier, healthier life by reducing or eliminating your debt load and part of the excessive consumption that goes with it, imagine how our entire society—and the planet—could benefit from adopting the same general strategy.

What have you learned?

At the very least, I hope you have learned how to get, maintain, and use credit wisely. If you were drowning in debt, I also hope you've learned how to keep yourself from going under and how to get your finances back on a firm foundation. And of course I hope you will avoid repeating your previous financial mistakes in the future. If you have managed to learn all of this, I'm pleased.

But there's another issue. You may have noticed a secondary theme woven throughout some of the chapters, one only loosely related to finances. On a deeper level, I have been talking about more than money problems. I've been alluding to the fundamental causes of those problems—overconsumption, misplaced priorities, compulsive and addictive behaviors, and so on. As we've seen, you can't effectively come to grips with your consumer debt problems until you've dealt with these other issues.

Having gone through this process, you might well ask, "Why are these misplaced priorities and other problems so common in our society?" Excellent question. We've already taken a hard look at individual financial motivations and habits. Now we'll do the same for our society as a whole. To answer the question, we need to look beneath the symptoms for the cause of the problem. The root of these issues is that, as a nation, we are pursuing a myth—a myth based on a dream. The American Dream.

Waking up from the American Dream

Ever since this nation's founding, the idea of unlimited potential, unlimited resources, and unlimited consumption has been central to the American Dream. The image of the rugged, individualistic cowboy riding off into the sunset to carve out a chunk of that dream for himself has become so firmly entrenched in the national psyche that it has been virtually unassailable—right into the twentieth century and long after the West was "won" (or lost, depending on your point of view). Unfor-tunately for us, and especially for the rest of the world, that old dream is inexorably turning into a nightmare.

One of the main problems is that this vision, which may have been appropriate for the Industrial Revolution, has become increasingly out of synch with current reality. For the most part, our basic physical needs have been met—a long time ago in most cases. Yet we continue to pursue the old American Dream in a futile attempt to buy happiness, accumulating more and more stuff along the way, to the point of spawning an entire industry devoted to helping us store the excess stuff that we don't know what to do with.

This trend has only accelerated in the past decade. Luxuries once viewed as unattainable are now commonly accepted as necessities, and the more we have, the more we want.

> 66
> The lust for comfort, that stealthy thing that enters the house a guest, and then becomes a host, and then a master.
> —Kahlil Gibran
> 99

Our insatiable consumption of goods and resources, driven by the American Dream and an economy that is founded on (and that continues to perpetuate) this dream, is leading us toward disaster. Moreover, in the process we're stealing resources and potential options from our children and grandchildren.

Worse yet, most of the developing nations around the world are blindly following our unfortunate lead. The long-term consequences of this trend are troubling, to say the least. They do not auger well for the future, especially when you consider nations with huge numbers of relatively impoverished citizens like China or Indonesia, for example. This dream of spending and consuming our collective way to happiness and contentment based on the American model is not only unrealistic on a global level but also unsustainable.

Some folks, however, are beginning to wake up from the dream. In the cold light of day, they don't like what they see, and they're actually doing something about it. You may recall Jef and Lorraine Murray, from Georgia, whom I left teetering on the brink of financial disaster back in Chapter 7. It's finally time to see how they made out. It was 1992, 10 years after their marriage, and the Murrays, actively pursuing the American Dream, had managed to acquire two houses, a boat, and around $140,000 worth of indebtedness. But no savings. Then, in January of 1993, their lives took a dramatic and unexpected turn. A friend gave Lorraine a copy of *Your Money or Your Life: Transforming Your Relationship with Money and Achieving Financial Independence*, by Joe Dominguez and Vicki Robin.

"It was a rude awakening," says Jef. "The book had an enormous impact on me because when I ran the numbers I was horrified—absolutely shocked at what I saw. When I checked with Social Security to see how much money I had made in prior years, it turned out to be a pretty staggering amount, and yet the only things we really had to show for it were two houses that we were deeply in debt for."

Rich in things—poor in spirit

Like many people in this country today, the Murrays had all the material trappings of a successful life, yet there was something fundamentally wrong with it. Reading *Your Money or Your Life* was a major catalyst in helping them understand their problem. A major part of that problem was that, like millions of other Americans, they had been operating largely on autopilot, blindly pursuing the American Dream for many, many years. In the process, they had been trading a future part of their lives to pay for the debts caused by their excessive current consumption.

With this wake-up call, the Murrays decided to do something about their situation. They started by cutting back on their consumption and spending. Eventually they turned their attention to one of their biggest problems—their second home in Florida. "We finally recognized that having two households was insane," admits Jef. "We realized we could be debt-free if we sold one of the houses." They did. Then they paid off the mortgage on their remaining home in Georgia.

Over a four-year period while the Murrays were eliminating their debts, they saved thousands and thousands of dollars in interest charges. Recently they have been able to accumulate enough savings to allow Lorraine to quit her regular day job so she can focus on other, more satisfying activities. Jef hopes to be able to do the same in a few more years.

Unofficially...
The median size of a new house built in the United States in 1949 was 1,100 square feet. In 1970, the figure had risen to 1,385 square feet. By 1997, it was up to 1,975 square feet.

The Murrays are now pursuing a new American Dream that has a very different focus from the old one.

The dramatic turnaround in the Murrays' financial situation was a reflection of an equally dramatic shift in their thinking about their money and their work, and how those things affected their lives—a major theme of *Your Money or Your Life.* Getting out of debt was a crucial part of the picture, but it was only the first step in a larger process that included greater involvement in community activities and a rediscovery of their spiritual sides.

"When we started getting involved with the local community, all of a sudden we recognized that you can have a lot of fun without spending money—friends don't cost money," Jef says. "We started doing things like hosting potluck parties at our house where everybody would bring food—instead of expensive dinner parties which we had done previously."

The Murrays also became involved in a church-sponsored house renovation project for women who were suffering from AIDS. "It was a big undertaking, but it remains one of the highlights of our lives," Jef maintains. "Recognizing that we needed to connect spiritually with other people, or at least on the human level rather than on the credit card level, was a major insight for us. We found that we enjoyed helping people that needed it more than we enjoyed going out on shopping binges." Almost everything that the Murrays have done since then has been based on that insight. Jef and Lorraine have created an entirely new life for themselves, one that now focuses on nurturing their spiritual needs, strengthening ties to friends and community, and giving much of their time and energy to helping others in a variety of ways.

You can't buy happiness

The Murrays aren't the only ones who have discovered that "money doesn't buy happiness." In fact, there is a mounting body of evidence gathered by psychological researchers that strongly reinforces that old view. Dr. Richard Ryan, professor of psychology at the University of Rochester, and Dr. Tim Kasser, his former student who is now an assistant professor of psychology at Knox College in Illinois, have focused a lot of their research on people who value so-called "extrinsic goals" like money, fame, and beauty. Their findings are not encouraging for those individuals.

In a recent *New York Times* article, Ryan and Kasser said that their studies offered a look at the "dark side of the American Dream," and that our culture in some ways appeared to be built on qualities that turned out to be detrimental to mental health. Americans are encouraged to try to strike it rich, but "the more we seek satisfactions in material goods, the less we find them there," Ryan said. "The satisfaction has a short half-life; it's very fleeting." The negative effects of these goals seem to be true for people regardless of their age or level of income. The problem isn't just an American one. Similar results came from studies done in various countries around the globe.

Sobering statistics

The dark side of the American Dream is also graphically illustrated by the thousands of homeless persons who live in the streets and back alleys of almost every major U.S. city. Yet, at the same time, 10 million

Watch Out!

Recent research has shown that people who have a preoccupation with money tend to suffer from unusual amounts of anxiety and depression and tend to experience lower overall levels of well-being.

Americans own two or more homes, according to statistics gathered by the New Road Map Foundation, an all-volunteer, nonprofit organization located in Seattle, Washington. The group, founded by Joe Dominguez and Vicki Robin, authors of *Your Money or Your Life*, promotes a humane, sustainable future for the world. Here is some food for thought compiled by the foundation (some of the statistics are a little out of date, but they show interesting trends nevertheless):

- The percentage of 18- to 29-year-olds who think they have a very good chance of achieving "the good life": in 1978, 41 percent; in 1993, 21 percent

- The rise in per capita consumption in the U.S. in the last 20 years: 45 percent.

- The decrease in the quality of life in the U.S. since 1970, as measured by the Index of Social Health: 51 percent.

- The percentage of Americans who feel the American Dream is very much alive: in 1986, 32 percent; in 1990, 23 percent.

- Compared with their parents in 1950, people in the U.S., on average, own twice as many cars and drive two times as far.

- American parents spend 40 percent less time with their children today than they did in 1965.

- Employed Americans spend 163 hours more per year on the job than they did in 1969.

- The percentage of college freshmen who reported thinking that it is essential to be well off financially: in 1967, 44 percent; in 1987, 76 percent.

- The percentage of college freshmen who reported thinking that it is essential to develop a philosophy of life: in 1967, 83 percent; in 1987, 39 percent.

- The average time spent shopping per week: 6 hours.

- The average time spent playing with children per week: 40 minutes.

- The waste generated each year in the United States would fill a convoy of 10-ton garbage trucks 145,000 miles long—over halfway to the moon.

- The percentage of Americans who would like to "slow down and live a more relaxed life": 69 percent.

The list goes on and on. If you want to see more of it, check out the Living Lightly on the Earth page (www.scn.org/earth/lightly) on the Seattle Community Network Web site, where you'll find many more ideas and related links.

Taken together, statistics like these paint a disturbing picture that stands in stark contrast to the promise of the traditional American Dream. This picture also does not square with glowing U.S. economic reports of recent years. Business has been good. In fact, it doesn't get much better. Yet, a lot of people are feeling bad. Something is clearly wrong here. In addition to the fact that a disproportionate amount of the gains are benefiting a small number of people at the top of the economic spectrum, too many people are spending too much time working too many hours in order to buy too much stuff—resulting in too little real happiness. If, like many other people, you've reached a similar conclusion, you may have been wondering what you can do about this.

Same money-saving ideas, new perspective

Actually, there's a lot you can do to reduce consumption and spending and make your life reflect the values that are important to you. We've already covered many of these strategies earlier in this book. Any steps that you can take to reduce or eliminate your debts will head you in the right direction. Reducing your spending in general is another useful strategy we've already explored (see "Tips for Reducing Expenses" in Chapter 9).

Cutting back on debts and spending is only part of a larger strategy that you might want to consider. For most of this book, I've focused primarily on debt and how it affects your life from a financial standpoint. The idea now is to look at these same issues to see how they affect the rest of your life. This is where the insights you gained about yourself during the debt management process can be applied to those other parts of your life. This is also where things can get interesting.

Look at your lifestyle

If you take a long, hard look at your lifestyle, you may decide that what you have been spending some (or much) of your money on isn't in line with your core beliefs. If this is the case, you may decide to redirect your spending (and other aspects of your life) in ways that may allow you to reduce your expenses substantially. If your expenses are less, you suddenly have some intriguing options.

You can spend your new-found money on things that are more reflective of your real values. Or, you might want to put your excess funds into savings or investments, which is a perfectly sound strategy. Alternatively, you may decide that your income (and consequently your work schedule) can be reduced, since you no longer have to support your previous expensive spending habits. This decision can give you more time to devote to other, more satisfying pursuits. At least you have the option of exploring these issues.

Now, I admit that some of these ideas run counter to currently accepted norms—especially in much of corporate America. But the majority is frequently wrong anyway, so paddling against the prevailing tide may make sense in the long run if it meets your needs. As we've already seen, you aren't alone in questioning the traditional American Dream—you've got a lot of company.

Where else can you save?

In a moment, we'll take a look at some of the strategies that other people are using in their attempts to create a new American Dream for themselves. Before we do, I'd like to offer a few more quick suggestions for possible ways to live better on less (or just live better, period):

- Use your legs not your car to take care of local errands if stores are within walking distance (saves gas, good exercise).

- Work where you live, or live where you work (eliminates commuting expenses and gives you more time and money for more interesting things).

- If you must drive, hang onto that old car. Keep repairing it until it's totally worn out, rather than buying a new one (and then you can brag about it on Car Talk).

- Find a reliable and reasonable auto mechanic before you actually need one (be prepared; you'll spend less).

- Move to a less-expensive part of the country, especially if your line of work is not location-specific.

- Barter goods and services with your neighbors.

- Recycle wherever possible.

- Plant a garden and grow some of your own vegetables or fruits (or grow some herbs in a window box, if that's your only option).

- Network with your friends or family for things that you need (they may have just what you're looking for sitting around gathering dust).

- Consider renting things that you use only occasionally.

- Turn off the TV (one of the simplest and best suggestions).

The idea here is to look at these strategies from a new perspective that allows you to improve other parts of your life in addition to your credit. Viewed separately, these suggestions may seem relatively minor, but taken together and multiplied by millions of Americans, the effects could be profound.

Escape from affluenza

Let's say you're convinced that you have a problem. But what about everybody else? Actually, there is a growing realization among many people in this country that we are pursuing a lifestyle that is both unhealthy and unsustainable in the long run. The Seattle-based KCTS television program "Affluenza," which has been shown on most Public Television stations a number of times in recent years, has brought

Bright Idea
Try a progressive dinner party. Start at one person's house with appetizers, go on to the next person's house for soup, and keep on going for each successive course. It's a great way to socialize with friends, and no one gets stuck with all the cleanup.

that message to a wider audience. "Affluenza" was defined in the program as:

1. The bloated, sluggish, and unfulfilled feeling that results from efforts to keep up with the Joneses.
2. An epidemic of stress, overwork, waste, and indebtedness caused by dogged pursuit of the American Dream.
3. An unsustainable addiction to economic growth.

The program starkly portrays the destructive nature of that addiction. In recent years, Americans, who make up only 5 percent of the world's population, used nearly two-thirds of its resources and produced almost half of its hazardous waste, according to promotional material about the program. Add overwork, personal stress, the erosion of family and community, skyrocketing debt, and the growing gap between rich and poor, and it's no wonder that increasing numbers of people are viewing the American Dream as a nightmare.

Although the picture may look grim, happily, there is a cure for Affluenza. For most people the cure costs nothing, except changing their attitudes about money and their spending and consuming habits. In fact, if you take the cure, it may end up saving you money and making your life better at the same time. And that's a combination hard to beat. Here are a few simple suggestions gleaned from the Affluenza Web site (www.pbs.org/kcts/affluenza):

▪ Before you buy, ask yourself: Do I need it? Do I want to dust (dry-clean or otherwise maintain) it? Could I borrow it from a friend, neighbor, or family member? Is there anything I already own that I could substitute for it? Are the resources that went into it renewable, or non-renewable? How many hours will I have to work to pay for it?

- Avoid the mall. Go hiking or play ball with the kids instead.

- Figure out what public transportation can save you (time, money for gas and parking, peace of mind).

- Become an advertising critic. Don't be sucked in by efforts to make you feel inadequate so you'll buy more stuff you don't need.

- Volunteer for a school or community group.

- Splurge consciously. A few luxuries can be delightful, and they don't have to be expensive.

- Stay in—have a potluck, play a game, bake bread, write a letter, cuddle a loved one.

- Make a budget—know how much you are earning and spending. Each dollar represents precious time in your life that you worked. Are you spending money in ways that fulfill you?

If some of these ideas sound familiar, you're right. They're similar to those that I have offered in previous chapters. This again highlights the relationship between overconsumption, our current economic system, and the dangers of excessive indebtedness that I've been talking about throughout this book. You can't talk about one aspect of the problem without looking at the other aspects as well.

You've probably noticed that there are as many ideas for saving money and simplifying your life as there are for spending money and complicating your life. So, it's mainly a question of becoming aware of these issues and then deciding for yourself which direction you want to head in. Once you decide, you will find that many options open up for you.

Where do you go from here?

We've identified the problem, and we've seen some potential solutions. But, exactly how do you disentangle yourself from the old American Dream and start on the path to a new one? There are probably as many answers to that question as there are people working on it. Most people are following two main strategies these days: downshifting and voluntary simplicity. We'll examine each.

Downshifting

The growing dissatisfaction of many Americans with their overworked and overstressed lives has prompted an increase in the number of people who are voluntarily cutting back on their workloads, or opting out of the corporate rat race altogether. This action is generally referred to as *voluntary downshifting* (not to be confused with involuntary downsizing, which is an entirely different phenomenon resulting from corporate mergers).

This voluntary downshifting, which wasn't even on the radar screen a decade ago, is becoming increasingly popular, especially among two-income couples employed as managers, professionals, and technology workers. In fact, about one-half of women and about 20 percent of men in that grouping would like to work part-time, according to a recent Cornell University study. Of course, not everyone who wants to downshift actually does. Many people fear that they will be viewed unfavorably by their employers or coworkers if they try to cut back on their work schedules.

The single most important contribution any of us can make to the planet is a return to frugality.
—Robert Muller, Retired Assistant Secretary-General of the United Nations

Nevertheless, for those who do pursue it, downshifting allows people to realign their lifestyle with their core values, according to Juliet Schor, author of *The Overspent American*. "...Downshifting is happening because millions of Americans are recognizing that in fact their lives are no longer in synch with their values, either because they have no time for what they care about most (their children, their families, their communities, or their personal development), because they can't believe in the work they are doing, or because the money and the consumption-identity link has started to seem meaningless," she says in her book.

Not surprisingly, downshifting often involves a good deal of soul-searching, especially for people who have been drifting through their lives on automatic pilot. Nevertheless, the problems faced by people who decide to downshift (related to lower incomes) seem to be balanced by the advantages offered by the strategy (more time, less stress, and a more balanced life).

Between 1990 and 1996, about 19 percent of all adult Americans made a voluntary lifestyle change that involved earning less money, according to Schor. And 85 percent of them reported being happy about the change they had made. It's interesting to note that an almost equal number of men and women were in this group, dispelling popular perceptions that women are more likely to be downshifting candidates.

In addition to looking for more free time, less stress, and a more balanced life, a number of downshifters want to spend more time with their children or other family members. Regardless of their motivations, most downshifters tend to be solidly middle class.

Obviously, anyone who is deeply in debt is not going to be in a position to consider downshifting—yet. However, if your debts are under control, and you really would like to spend more quality time at home (or anywhere), you might consider downshifting—as long as you're willing to accept the trade-offs.

Voluntary simplicity

In recent years, another strategy for developing a new American Dream has been gaining in popularity: *voluntary simplicity*, or simple living. This idea is nothing new. In fact, the concept goes back thousands of years in various religious traditions. In his 1981 book, *Voluntary Simplicity: Toward a Way of Life That Is Outwardly Simple, Inwardly Rich,* Duane Elgin popularized the term that is now generally used to describe the current secular movement.

"There is no special virtue to the phrase 'voluntary simplicity'—it is merely a label and a somewhat awkward label at that," Elgin says in his book. "Still, it does acknowledge explicitly that simpler living integrates both inner and outer aspects of life into an organic and purposeful whole. To live more voluntarily is to live more deliberately, intentionally, and purposefully—in short, it is to live more consciously."

Voluntary simplicity essentially begins where downshifting leaves off. It takes the money-saving ideas we've looked at one or more steps further. In the case of downshifting, most people would like to have more money but are willing to forego it in exchange for a better quality of life. The voluntary simplicity adherent, on the other hand, moves beyond these issues and settles at a low level of income beyond which spending is no longer viewed as positive. In fact, more spending is viewed by many

Unofficially...
Unlike many groups who have opted for simpler living in the past, today's "downshifters" are remaining firmly within the confines of the American mainstream—they're just swimming against the prevailing tide.

in this group as actually being negative because of various environmental concerns or because it results in too much external "clutter," which gets in the way of a simple but internally satisfying lifestyle.

"Simple-livers," as they are also called, tend to be highly motivated by a variety of ethical, moral, and spiritual concerns that extend far beyond monetary issues. Yet they put a good deal of emphasis on careful, intentional spending, and they tend to buy products that are durable, easy to repair, energy-efficient, functional, aesthetic, and nonpolluting in their manufacture and use. They also tend to use their consumption politically by boycotting goods and services of companies whose actions or policies they believe to be unethical or environmentally unsound.

Accurately characterizing all simple-livers is hard, but many who follow the voluntary simplicity model tend to be single (some are divorced or widowed), well-educated, middle-class whites with grown children no longer living at home. Many of them formerly held jobs as corporate managers, administrators, or computer professionals, and as a result they tend to enter their new lifestyle in reasonably good financial shape (some are financially independent).

Simple-livers follow many different strategies, but as a rule most of them live in downsized housing, drive older cars (if they drive at all), spend much of their limited shopping time in thrift shops or secondhand markets, and tend to wear what they find there. They generally avoid expensive entertainment—first-run movies, theater performances, and restaurants—and opt instead for home-cooked meals, potluck gatherings, and other low-cost but high-quality-of-life activities.

Although simple-livers can be found almost anywhere in the country these days, the Pacific Northwest seems to have attracted relatively large numbers of enthusiastic adherents. Seattle, Washington in particular, has a fairly large and active simple-living community. A good place to start looking for additional information on voluntary simplicity is at www.awakeningearth.org/simplicity.html. Also see "Voluntary Simplicity and Downshifting" in the Resource Guide, Appendix B, for other organizations that can help you learn more.

A new American Dream

In addition to the New Road Map Foundation, another group that has been actively trying to do something about charting a new course for this country is the Center for a New American Dream in Takoma Park, Maryland. Founded in 1997, the Center is a not-for-profit membership-based organization dedicated to reducing and shifting North American consumption while promoting opportunities for people to lead more secure and fulfilling lives.

The organization helps individuals, communities, and businesses establish sustainable practices that are intended to ensure a healthy planet for future generations. In addition, the Center distributes educational materials and conducts campaigns to help people make constructive changes within their homes, schools, workplaces, and communities. The group has an extensive and informative Web site at www.newdream.org.

"The challenges are immense," the Center notes on its Web site. "Consumers need to recognize the link between their collective choices and the survival

> 66
> Half the confusion in the world comes from not knowing how little we need.... I live more simply now, and with more peace.
> —Admiral Richard E. Byrd, (1888-1957)
> 99

of the planet. Governments must establish incentives for individuals and corporations to do the right thing. Private businesses must radically change the design and production of many consumer and industrial products. Children must be taught the importance of thrift and stewardship of nature. Families must rediscover the simple pleasure of old-fashioned play and community service as non-material sources of joy. Perhaps most important, individuals need to be encouraged to examine their deepest values, reflect on their life priorities, and take steps toward a more fulfilling, less materialistic path."

If some of these sentiments sound slightly familiar, you're right. A few of them are part of the debt management strategy described earlier in this book. And some were among the insights gained by the people we've met who managed to get themselves out of debt. There is unquestionably a direct relationship between our individual overspending and overconsumption problems and the same problems we see on a national and international level.

Many people tend to view overconsumption as a problem caused by others—but not themselves. Unfortunately, we *are* the problem, or at least part of it. We're definitely not talking about only individuals teetering on the edge of financial bankruptcy. We're talking about an entire nation racing, lemming-like, toward the precipice. As you know, persuading politicians and governments to look beyond the next election and make the politically unpopular decisions needed to avoid catastrophe is extremely difficult.

So, where does this situation leave us? In the end, it all comes back to you. Obviously, the government isn't going to solve your personal debt problems for you. You have to do that for yourself (and I hope you have). And just as obviously, the government isn't going to lead the way in promoting the kind of fundamental changes that are required to transform our economy into a saner, more sustainable model.

But why wait for somebody else? Create your own new American Dream. If you change your spending and saving patterns, and vote with your dollars as well as your ballots, you can directly affect the direction our economy will take in the years ahead. If millions of other Americans do the same, those changes *will* take place—even if we have to drag our elected officials along by the scruffs of their necks. The challenges are immense, but as the ancient Chinese proverb says, "A journey of a thousand miles begins with a single step."

It's only money

Out of necessity, money has been the main topic of this book. However, money should not dominate your life. Money, saving, and investing are means to an end, not ends in themselves. If you find that you are spending most of your time fretting over money, it might be time to step back and take a hard look at your priorities.

I realize that when you are up to your ears in debt, it's hard not to obsess about money. But once your finances are back on a firm footing, you might want to explore some of the deeper issues I've raised in this chapter. Wise, conscious use of your financial resources can open up a whole new world of possibilities for personal fulfillment. What you choose do with those possibilities is entirely up to you, but I hope you do something wonderful.

Oh, I almost forgot. Now I can pat you on the back, offer my congratulations on getting your debts under control, and wish you a happy and fulfilling life.

Just the facts

- The old American Dream is unsustainable.
- A change in how you think about money can dramatically affect your life.
- It's possible to live better on less.
- You can create your own American Dream.

Glossary

annual percentage rate (APR)   The cost of credit as a yearly rate.

appraisal fee   The charge for estimating the value of property offered as security for a loan.

asset   Anything you own that has a monetary value, such as stocks, bonds, a car, or house.

ATM card   *See* debit card.

ATMs   *See* automated teller machines.

automated teller machines (ATMs)   Electronic terminals located at banks or elsewhere, through which you can make deposits, withdrawals, or other transactions as you would through a bank teller.

automatic investment plan   An arrangement with a mutual fund to make a regular investment through payroll deductions or automatic transfers from a checking account.

automatic stay   In a bankruptcy, this ruling immediately stops your creditors from attempting to collect what you owe and also halts lawsuits.

balloon payment   A large, final principal payment that may be charged at the end of a loan or lease.

419

bankruptcy When a person is unable to pay their debts, they may file for bankruptcy through a federal bankruptcy court. The debts may be reorganized or even erased by court order. Chapter 7 or chapter 13 bankruptcies are the two main options for individuals.

billing error Any mistake in your monthly statement as defined by the Fair Credit Billing Act.

bond A debt security that generally pays interest at regular intervals for a set period of time and repays your principal at maturity.

certificate of deposit (CD) Debt securities issued by banks. CDs pay a stated amount of interest and mature on a specific date.

charge accounts These open-end charge or revolving-credit accounts permit you to make repeated purchases until you reach your pre-arranged credit limit.

charged-off (collection) account A credit account that has remained unpaid for at least 90 days, and sometimes as long as 180 days, at which point the creditor "charges it off" as a bad debt.

collateral property Property offered to support a loan and subject to seizure if you default. In a car loan or home mortgage, the collateral is typically the car or home.

collection agency A company or agency that specializes in recovering money from "charged-off" accounts.

commingling The accidental mixing of information for more than one person on a credit report by a credit bureau.

cookies Electronic notations used to identify Internet users; they help a Web site send a customized page or specific account information.

cosigner   Another person who signs your loan and assumes equal responsibility for it.

credit   The right granted by a creditor that allows the applicant to pay in the future in order to buy or borrow in the present; a sum of money due a person or business.

credit agency   *See* credit bureau.

credit bureau   An agency that maintains your credit record.

credit card   Any card that can be used repeatedly to borrow money or buy goods or services on credit.

credit card surfing   The practice of applying for a new credit card to take advantage of a low introductory interest rate, and then switching to another card when the introductory rate expires.

credit history   The record of how you've borrowed and repaid your debts over time.

creditor   A person or business from whom you borrow or to whom you owe money.

credit repair services   Any number of for-profit companies or organizations that claim to be able to "repair" your credit—for a fee.

credit scoring system   A statistical system used to rate credit applicants according to various characteristics related to their creditworthiness, for example a recent bankruptcy or income below a certain minimum.

credit union   A not-for-profit financial service cooperative owned and operated by its members.

creditworthiness   Past and future ability to repay debts.

debit card (ATM card)   A plastic card, similar to a credit card, that you may use to make purchases, withdrawals, or other types of electronic fund transfers.

debt consolidation The process of combining many different debts into one loan, resulting in one monthly payment instead of many.

debt management plan An organized debt reduction program offered by a credit counseling service. Such plans typically require regular monthly payments that are applied toward paying off your debts.

debtor A person who owes money.

default Failure to repay a loan or otherwise meet the terms of your credit agreement.

discharge of debt The final stage in a bankruptcy, where most of your debts are discharged (eliminated) by the court.

disclosures Information that must be given to consumers about their financial dealings.

downshifting The deliberate reduction of work hours to gain more time for other activities.

early withdrawal penalty A penalty charged by a bank for early withdrawal of funds from a certificate of deposit.

electronic fund transfer (EFT) card *See* debit card.

electronic fund transfer (EFT) systems A variety of systems and technologies for transferring funds electronically rather than by check.

equity The value of something you own after deducting all liabilities.

FDIC *See* Federal Deposit Insurance Corporation.

Federal Deposit Insurance Corporation (FDIC) A federal agency that guarantees that your money in a bank will be protected—up to a certain amount—if the institution fails financially.

Federal Reserve banks The 12 banks, along with their branches, that make up the Federal Reserve System.

Federal Reserve Board The governing board of the Federal Reserve System.

Federal Reserve System A centralized system established in 1913 to regulate the country's monetary and banking system.

Federal Trade Commission (FTC) The agency that enforces a variety of federal antitrust and consumer protection laws.

finance charge The total dollar amount that credit will cost.

float *See* grace period.

foreclosure Proceedings instituted by a bank or lender to collect the amount due on a mortgage loan for a home when the loan payments are delinquent.

401(k) An employer-sponsored retirement plan named after a section of the Internal Revenue Code. Workers contribute pretax dollars, which grow tax-deferred until withdrawn.

FTC *See* Federal Trade Commission.

grace period The time between when a purchase is made with a credit card and when the account must be paid.

home-equity line of credit A form of open-end credit in which the home serves as collateral.

home equity loan A traditional second mortgage granted for a set number of years and a fixed (or sometimes variable) interest rate, repaid in monthly installments.

identity theft The illegal use of someone else's personal information to make fraudulent purchases.

Individual Retirement Account (IRA) A retirement savings vehicle, allowing you to save $2,000 every year if you have earned income.

installment loans Also referred to as closed-end credit plans, this type of loan involves a predetermined number of monthly payments for a set amount of money.

IRA   *See* Individual Retirement Account.

joint account   A credit account held by two or more people, all of whom can use the account and assume the responsibility to repay.

judgment   A court decision about a lawsuit, frequently relating to delinquent bills.

late payment   A payment made later than agreed upon in a credit contract and on which additional charges may be imposed.

lessee   A person who signs a lease to get temporary use of property.

lessor   A company or person that provides temporary use of property, usually in return for periodic payment.

liability on an account   Legal responsibility to repay debt.

lien   A court-ordered legal ownership or interest in your property that must be satisfied before the property (or the proceeds of the sale of your property) can be used for other purposes.

money market fund   A mutual fund that invests in safe, liquid short-term securities.

mortgage loan   A type of closed-end credit plan that is generally used to finance the purchase of a home.

mutual fund   A company that pools the money of thousands of shareholders and invests the money in stocks, bonds, or cash.

no-load fund   A mutual fund that does not impose a sales charge.

online credit card   An Internet-based electronic credit card.

open-end credit   A line of credit that may be used over and over again, including credit cards, overdraft credit accounts, and home equity lines.

open-end lease   A lease that may involve a balloon payment based on the value of the property when it is returned.

origination fee   A fee that covers the lender's work in preparing your mortgage loan.

overdraft checking   A line of credit that allows you to write checks or draw funds, by means of an EFT card, for more than your actual balance, with an interest charge on the overdraft.

pension plan   A qualified retirement plan established by an employer for its employees.

points   Finance charges paid at the beginning of a mortgage in addition to monthly interest. One point equals 1 percent of the loan amount.

prepayment   A strategy to save on interest charges and shorten the duration of a loan by paying off the principal sooner than called for by the terms of the loan.

prescreening   The compiling or editing of lists of consumers who meet specific credit criteria. Such information is frequently used to solicit specific consumers for credit products (usually credit cards).

prime rate   The interest rate that banks charge their most creditworthy customers.

principal   The amount of money you originally put into an investment or, in the case of a loan, the amount remaining on the debt.

punitive damages   Damages awarded by a court above actual damages as punishment for a violation of law.

rollover   A tax-free transfer of assets from one retirement plan to another.

Roth IRA   Named after a senator from Delaware, this is a fairly new type of IRA. You can invest up to $2,000 a year in a Roth IRA if you have earned income, and you don't have to pay taxes at withdrawal.

Secure Electronic Transaction (SET) An Internet security protocol that uses digital signatures to ensure that merchants and Internet credit card users are actually who they say they are.

Secure Socket Layer (SSL) An Internet security protocol that uses encryption to keep your credit card (and other) data safe while it's in transit.

secured credit card A credit card normally offered to people with troubled credit histories (or no credit history) by banks who, in turn, require a security deposit as collateral.

secured loan A type of loan that requires some sort of collateral (security) to back the loan.

security Property pledged to the creditor in case of a default on a loan; *see* collateral.

security interest The creditor's right to take property or a portion of property offered as security.

service charge Any number of miscellaneous charges made by credit card issuers for certain transactions.

smart card A new multiple-purpose card with an embedded microchip that has the capability of storing a wide range of information.

term life insurance Life insurance that provides a cash benefit to your survivors if you die during the period or term covered.

Treasury bill Also called a T-bill, this is a short-term security issued by the federal government, with a maturity that doesn't exceed one year.

Treasury bond A federal government obligation that matures 30 years after it's issued.

Treasury note A federal government obligation that matures from 2 to 10 years after it's issued.

uniform resource locator (URL) A Web site's address.

unsecured loan A personal loan that does not require the use of security or collateral. The amount of the loan is generally based upon your income and ability to repay the lender.

voluntary simplicity A deliberately simple lifestyle characterized by low levels of consumption and spending and by high levels of awareness about those decisions.

wage garnishment (or "wage attachment") A method of satisfying a debt in which your employer deducts from your paycheck a certain amount of money, which is then applied toward the debt. A creditor or collection agency must go to court and obtain a judgment in order to garnish your wages.

Web site The location of a business or other entity on the Internet. The opening screen that you see at a Web site is known as its *home page*.

Resource Guide

Bankruptcy
Cornell Law School
Legal Information Institute
www.law.cornell.edu
Search for "bankruptcy" to get good, unbiased legal
background information at this Web site.

Children and money
Jump Start Coalition for Personal Financial Literacy
919 Eighteenth Street, NW
Washington, D.C. 20006
(888) 400-2233
National Center for Financial Education
P.O. Box 34070
San Diego, CA 92163-4070
(619) 232-8811
www.ncfe.org

Consumer organizations
Consumer Action
717 Market Street, Suite 310
San Francisco, CA 94103
(415) 777-9648
www.consumer-action.org

This Web site offers a vast array of multilingual information related to consumer protection topics.

Consumer Federation of America
1424 Sixteenth Street, NW, Suite 604
Washington, D.C. 20036
(202) 387-6121
www.consumerfed.org

Consumers Union
101 Truman Avenue
Yonkers, NY 10703-1057
(914) 378-2000
www.consunion.org

This consumer advocacy group provides information on health care, financial services, food product safety, and more. Consumers Union is the publisher of *Consumer Reports*.

National Center for Financial Education
P.O. Box 34070
San Diego, CA 92163-4070
(619) 232-8811
www.ncfe.org

National Consumers League
1701 K Street, NW, Suite 1201
Washington, D.C. 20006
(202) 835-3323
www.nclnet.org

National Institute for Consumer Education
Eastern Michigan University
559 Gary M. Owen Building
300 West Michigan Ave
Ypsilanti, MI 48197
(734) 487-2292
www.emich.edu/public/coe/nice

Money 2000
www.human.cornell.edu/extension/money2000/nys

This site offers a self-directed home-study course of financial education.

Credit bureaus

If you live in Colorado, Georgia, Massachusetts, Maryland, New Jersey, or Vermont, you're entitled to a free report (two in Georgia) every year, but you must place your order by phone or in writing to get it.

Equifax

P.O. Box 740241

Atlanta, GA 30374

To order a credit report, call: (800) 685-1111.

To talk to a customer service representative about your report, call: (888) 909-7304.

www.equifax.com

Experian (formerly TRW)

P.O. Box 8030

Layton, UT 84041-8030

To order a credit report, call: (800) 682-7654.

To talk to a customer service representative about your report, call: (888) 397-3742.

www.experian.com

TransUnion

Customer Relations Dept.

P.O. Box 390

Springfield, PA 19064-0390

To order a credit report, call: (800) 645-1938.

To talk to a customer service representative about your report, call: (800) 916-8800.

www.tuc.com

Associated Credit Bureaus, Inc.

1090 Vermont Avenue, NW, Suite 200

Washington, D.C. 20005-4905

(202) 371-0910

This international trade association represents over 1,450 consumer credit, mortgage reporting, and collection service companies.

Credit card companies

American Express

For emergency card services in the United States, call: (800) 554-AMEX.

www.americanexpress.com

MasterCard

For emergency card services in the United States, call: (800) 307-7309.

www.mastercard.com

Visa

For emergency card services in the United States, call: (800) 847-2911.

www.visa.com

Credit card information

Bank Rate Monitor

P.O. Box 088888

11811 U.S. Highway One, Suite 200

North Palm Beach, FL 33408

www.bankrate.com

CardTrak

P.O. Box 1700

Frederick, MD 21702

www.cardtrak.com

This company publishes lists of the best credit cards.

Credit unions

Credit Union National Association

www.cuna.org

Counseling services

Consumer Credit Counseling Services

(*see* National Foundation for Consumer Credit)

Debt Counselors of America®
(800) 680-3328
www.getoutofdebt.org
This is a nonprofit online resource.

Debtors Anonymous
General Services Board
P.O. Box 920888
Needham, MA 02492-0009
(781) 453-2743
www.debtorsanonymous.org

Genus Credit Management
5950 Symphony Woods, Suite 600
Columbia, MD 21044
(800) 210-4455
www.genus.org

National Foundation for Consumer Credit
8611 Second Avenue, Suite 100
Silver Spring, MD 20910
(800) 388-2227
www.nfcc.org

Debt collectors

American Collectors Association
P.O. Box 39106
Minneapolis, MN 55439-0106
(612) 926-6547
www.collector.com

Divorce and remarriage

These excellent Web sites maintain numerous articles about common divorce issues and family law information, and also include bulletin boards, recommended reading lists, and links to other sites:

Divorce Central
www.divorcecentral.com

Divorce Helpline
www.divorcehelp.com
Divorce Online
www.divorce-online.com
DivorceNet
www.divorcenet.com

Federal agencies

National Banks
Compliance Management
Office of the Comptroller of the Currency
250 E Street, SW
Mail Stop 7-5
Washington, D.C. 20219
(202) 874-4820

State Member Banks of the Federal Reserve System
Division of Consumer and Community Affairs
Federal Reserve Board
Washington, D.C. 20551
(202) 452-3693

Nonmember Federally Insured State Banks
Office of Consumer Programs
Federal Deposit Insurance Corp.
Washington, D.C. 20456
(202) 898-3536 or (800) 934-FDIC

Savings and Loan Associations
Division of Consumer and Civil Rights
Office of Community Investment
Office of Thrift Supervision
1700 G Street, NW
Washington, D.C. 20552
(202) 906-6237

Federal Credit Unions
Office of Public and Congressional Affairs
Office of Consumer Programs
National Credit Union Administration
1776 G Street, NW
Washington, D.C. 20456
(202) 682-9640

Other Lenders
Division of Credit Practices
Bureau of Consumer Protection
Federal Trade Commission
Washington, D.C. 20580
(202) 326-3233
www.ftc.gov
Department of Justice
Civil Division
Office of Consumer Litigation
550 Eleventh St., NW
The Todd Building
Room 6114
Washington, D.C. 20530
(202) 514-6786

Federal Reserve Banks
Board of Governors of the Federal Reserve System
Publication Services MS-138
Washington, D.C. 20551
(202) 452-3000
Atlanta, Georgia
Public Affairs Department
104 Marietta Street, NW
Zip 30303-2713
(404) 521-8500

Boston, Massachusetts
Public Services Department
P.O. Box 2076
Zip 02106-2076
(617) 973-3000
Chicago, Illinois
Public Information Center
230 South LaSalle Street
P.O. Box 834
Zip 60690-0834
(312) 322-5322
Cleveland, Ohio
Public Affairs Department
P.O. Box 6387
Zip 44101-1387
(216) 579-2000
Dallas, Texas
Public Affairs Department
2200 North Pearl Street
Zip 75201
(214) 922-6000
Kansas City, Missouri
Public Affairs Department
925 Grand Avenue
Zip 64198-0001
(816) 881-2000
Minneapolis, Minnesota
Public Affairs Department
250 Marquette Avenue
Zip 55401-0291
(612) 340-2345
New York, New York
Public Information Department
33 Liberty Street
Zip 10045
(212) 720-5000

Philadelphia, Pennsylvania
Public Information Department
P.O. Box 66
Zip 19105
(215) 574-6000
Richmond, Virginia
Public Services Department
P.O. Box 27622
Zip 23261
(804) 697-8000
St. Louis, Missouri
Public Information Office
P.O. Box 442
Zip 63166
(314) 444-8444
San Francisco, California
Public Information Department
P.O. Box 7702
Zip 94120
(415) 974-2000

Other Federal agencies
Department of Housing and Urban Development (HUD)
451 Seventh Street, SW
Washington, D.C. 20410
www.hud.gov
Federal Trade Commission
Bureau of Consumer Protection
Washington, D.C. 20580
(202) 326-3233
www.ftc.gov
FTC Consumer Response Center
(202) FTC-HELP

Identity theft

www.identitytheft.org

California attorney Mari Frank's site offers her "Identity Theft Survival Kit" as well as free form letters.

www.idfraud.com

Bob Hartle's Web page offers tips and information about his book, which is a personal account of his ID theft experiences.

www.pirg.org

This is the Web portal for the 20-plus state Public Interest Research Group organizations. Most offer consumer credit and privacy protection information and tips.

www.pirg.org/calpirg/consumer/privacy

This Consumer Privacy Rights Program site from the California Public Interest Research Group site has lots of useful information and links for additional help.

www.privacyrights.org

Privacy Rights Clearinghouse site.

www.gao.gov

U.S. General Accounting Office; Report number GGD-98-100BR.

Internal Revenue Service

Guide to Free Tax Services and Other Publications

(800) 829-3676

www.irs.ustreas.gov

Legal information

Nolo Press

www.nolo.com

Offers a wealth of legal information on dozens of topics.

Online security and ethics
Better Business Bureau Online
www.bbbonline.org

Social Security
Social Security Administration
Call your local office or (800) 772-1213
www.ssa.gov

Telemarketing and online fraud
Federal Trade Commission
Bureau of Consumer Protection
Washington, D.C. 20580
(202) 326-3233
www.ftc.gov
FTC Consumer Response Center
(202) FTC-HELP
National Fraud Information Center
Consumer Assistance Service
(800) 876-7060
Monday–Friday 8:30 A.M. to 5:30 P.M.
www.fraud.org
Securities and Exchange Commission (SEC)
450 Fifth Street, NW
Mail Stop 11-2
Washington, D.C. 20549
(202) 942-4108
www.sec.gov

Voluntary simplicity and downshifting
Center for a New American Dream
6930 Carroll Avenue, Suite 900
Takoma Park, MD 20912
(301) 891-3683
www.newdream.org

The Media Foundation
1243 West 7th Avenue
Vancouver, BC V6H 1B7
Canada
(604) 736-9401
www.adbusters.org
Check out the information on "Buy Nothing Day."
New Road Map Foundation
P.O. Box 15981
Seattle, WA 98115
(206) 527-5114

Recommended Reading List

Appendix C

Addiction

Schaef, Anne Wilson. *When Society Becomes an Addict.*
San Francisco: HarperCollins, 1987.

Bankruptcy

Elias, Stephen, Albin Renauer, and Robin Leonard.
How to File for Bankruptcy. Berkeley: Nolo
Press, 1998.

Elias, Stephen, Albin Renauer, Robin Leonard, and
Lisa Goldoftas. *Nolo's Law Form Kit: Personal
Bankruptcy.* Berkeley: Nolo Press.

Leonard, Robin. *Chapter 13 Bankruptcy; Repay Your
Debts.* Berkeley: Nolo Press, 1999.

Sullivan, Teresa A., Elizabeth Warren, and Jay
Lawrence Westbrook. *As We Forgive Our
Debtors: Bankruptcy and Consumer Credit in
America.* New York: Oxford University Press,
1989.

Car buying

Howell, Donna. *The Unofficial Guide™ to Buying or Leasing a Car.* New York: Macmillan Publishing, 1998.

Children and money

Godfrey, Neal S., and Carolina Edwards. *Money Doesn't Grow on Trees: A Parent's Guide to Raising Financially Responsible Children.* New York: Simon & Schuster, 1994.

Zillions (children's magazine from Consumer Reports), P.O. Box 54861, Boulder, CO 80322-4861; (800) 234-2078.

Credit cards

Strong, Howard. *What Every Credit Card User Needs to Know.* New York: Owl Books, 1999.

Debt management

Detweiler, Gerri. *Debt Consolidation 101: Strategies for Saving Money & Paying Off Your Debts Faster.* Good Advice Press. Booklet can be obtained by calling (800) 255-0899.

———. *The Ultimate Credit Handbook.* New York: Plume Books, 1997.

Feinberg, Andrew. *Downsize Your Debt.* New York: Penguin Books, 1993.

Leonard, Robin. *Credit Repair: Clean Up Your Credit Report.* Berkeley: Nolo Press, 1999.

———. *Money Troubles: Legal Strategies to Cope with Your Debts.* Berkeley: Nolo Press, 1999.

Leonard, Robin, and Shae Irving. *Take Control of Your Student Loans.* Berkeley: Nolo Press, 1997.

Mundis, Jerrold. *How to Get Out of Debt, Stay Out of Debt, and Live Prosperously*. New York: Bantam Books, 1988.

Divorce, remarriage, and finances

Naylor, Sharon. *The Unofficial Guide™ to Divorce*. New York: Macmillan Publishing, 1998.

Schiff Estess, Patricia. *Money Advice for Your Successful Remarriage*. Cincinnati: F&W Publications, 1996.

Woodhouse, Violet, and Victoria F. Collins, with M.C. Blakeman. *Divorce and Money: How to Make the Best Financial Decisions During Divorce*. Berkeley: Nolo Press, 1998.

Downshifting and voluntary simplicity

Elgin, Duane. *Voluntary Simplicity: Toward a Way of Life That Is Outwardly Simple, Inwardly Rich*. New York: William Morrow, 1981.

Saltzman, Amy. *Down-shifting, Reinventing Success on a Slower Track*. San Francisco: HarperCollins, 1991.

Home buying

Perlis, Alan D., with Beth Bradley. *The Unofficial Guide™ to Buying a Home*. New York: Macmillan Publishing, 1999.

Investment

Berg, Stacie Zoe. *The Unofficial Guide™ to Investing in Mutual Funds*. New York: Macmillan Publishing, 1999.

Eisenson, Marc, Gerri Detweiler, and Nancy Castleman. *Invest in Yourself: Six Secrets to a Rich Life*. New York: John Wiley & Sons, 1998.

O'Shaughnessy, Lynn. *The Unofficial Guide™ to Investing*. New York: Macmillan Publishing, 1999.

Legal assistance
Warner, Ralph. *Everybody's Guide to Small Claims Court*. Berkeley: Nolo Press, 1993.

Money
Savage, Terry. *Terry Savage's New Money Strategies for the '90s: Simple Steps to Creating Wealth and Building Financial Security*. New York: HarperBusiness, 1993.

Personal finance
Dominguez, Joe, and Vicki Robin. *Your Money or Your Life: Transforming Your Relationship with Money and Achieving Financial Independence*. New York: Viking Penguin, 1992.

Prepayment
Eisenson, Marc. *The Banker's Secret*. New York: Villard Books, 1990.

Psychology of debt
Goldberg, Herb, and Robert T. Lewis. *Money Madness: The Psychology of Saving, Spending, Loving, and Hating Money*. New York: William Morrow and Company, 1978.

Schor, Juliet. *The Overspent American*. New York: Basic Books, 1998.

Saving and thrift
Dacyczyn, Amy. *The Tightwad Gazette: Promoting Thrift as a Viable Alternative Lifestyle*. New York: Villard Books, 1993.

Important Documents

Here are some documents that might come in handy:

SUMMARY OF TERMS FOR A CREDIT CARD

Annual Percentage Rate (APR)	2.99% introductory rate for first six months, a 17.99% fixed rate thereafter.
Grace Period for Repayment of Balances for Purchases	Not less than 25 days (no grace period for balance transfers)
Annual Fee	None
Minimum Finance Charge	$.50 (if a finance charge is imposed)
Method of Computing Balance for Purchases	Average Daily Balance (including new purchases)
Miscellaneous Fees	Cash advance fee: 2.5% of amount of the cash advance, but not less than $2.50
	Late payment fee: $25
	Over-the-credit-limit fee: $25

A typical summary of terms for a credit card, usually referred to as the Schumer Box.

WORKSHEET FOR COMPARING CREDIT CARD BENEFITS

Card Company Name and Telephone Number				
Annual Percentage Rate (APR)				
Grace Period				
Annual Fee				
Minimum Finance Charge				
Method of Computing Balance				
Cash Advance Fee				
Overlimit Fee				
Late Fee				
Bounced Check Fee				

NATIONAL BANK OF MIDDLEBURY
P.O. BOX 189
MIDDLEBURY, VERMONT 05753
(802) 388-4982

CREDIT APPLICATION

TYPE OF CREDIT REQUESTED	FOR CREDITOR USE
IMPORTANT: Check (√) the appropriate boxes below and complete the applicable sections.	DATE _____ CLASS NO. _____
☐ SECURED ☐ INDIVIDUAL CREDIT - relying solely on my income or assets	ACCOUNT NO. _____
☐ UNSECURED ☐ INDIVIDUAL CREDIT - relying on my income or assets as well as income or assets from other sources	APPROVED ☐ BY _____
☐ JOINT CREDIT	DECLINED ☐ BY _____

AMOUNT REQUESTED	FOR HOW LONG	PAYMENT DATE DESIRED	WANT TO REPAY ☐ MONTHLY ☐	PROCEEDS OF LOAN TO BE USED FOR:
$				

SECTION A - INDIVIDUAL APPLICANT INFORMATION

NAME (Last, First, Middle)

BIRTHDATE / /	TELEPHONE NO.	DRIVER'S LICENSE NO.	SOCIAL SECURITY NO.	NO. DEPENDENTS	AGES OF DEPENDENTS

ADDRESS (Street, City, State & Zip)	COUNTY	Do you ☐ own or ☐ rent?	HOW LONG

PREVIOUS ADDRESS (Street, City, State & Zip) (Complete if less than 3 years at present address)	COUNTY	Did you ☐ own or ☐ rent?	HOW LONG

EMPLOYER (Company Name & Address) — HOW LONG

BUSINESS PHONE	Ext.	POSITION OR TITLE	GROSS: $	SALARY PER MONTH NET: $

PREVIOUS EMPLOYER (Company Name & Address) — HOW LONG

NAME & ADDRESS OF NEAREST RELATIVE NOT LIVING WITH YOU	RELATIONSHIP	TELEPHONE NO. (Include Area Code)

Alimony, child support, or separate maintenance income need not be revealed if you do not wish to have it considered as a basis for repaying this obligation.

Alimony, child support, separate maintenance received under: ☐ Court Order ☐ Written Agreement ☐ Oral Understanding

SOURCES OF OTHER INCOME	AMOUNT PER MONTH $

Is any income listed in this Section likely to be reduced before the credit request is paid off? ☐ No ☐ Yes (Explain)	Have you previously received credit from us? ☐ No ☐ Yes - When?

SECTION B - JOINT APPLICANT OR OTHER PARTY INFORMATION

Complete only if: for joint credit, for individual credit relying on income or assets from other sources, or applicant is married and resides in a community property state.

NAME (Last, First, Middle)

BIRTHDATE / /	TELEPHONE NO.	DRIVER'S LICENSE NO.	SOCIAL SECURITY NO.	NO. DEPENDENTS	AGES OF DEPENDENTS

RELATIONSHIP TO APPLICANT (if Any)	PRESENT ADDRESS (Street, City, State & Zip)	HOW LONG

EMPLOYER (Company Name & Address) — HOW LONG

BUSINESS PHONE	Ext.	POSITION OR TITLE	GROSS: $	SALARY PER MONTH NET: $

PREVIOUS EMPLOYER (Company Name & Address) — HOW LONG

Alimony, child support, or separate maintenance income need not be revealed if you do not wish to have it considered as a basis for repaying this obligation.

Alimony, child support, separate maintenance received under: ☐ Court Order ☐ Written Agreement ☐ Oral Understanding

SOURCES OF OTHER INCOME	AMOUNT PER MONTH $

Is any income listed in this Section likely to be reduced before the credit requested is paid off? ☐ No ☐ Yes (Explain)	Has Joint Applicant or Other Party ever received credit from us? ☐ No ☐ Yes - When?

SECTION C - MARITAL STATUS

Complete only if: for joint or secured credit, or applicant resides in a community property state or is relying on property located in such a state as a basis for repayment of the credit requested.

APPLICANT	☐ Married	☐ Separated	☐ Unmarried (including single, divorced, and widowed)
OTHER PARTY	☐ Married	☐ Separated	☐ Unmarried (including single, divorced, and widowed)

© 1986 Bankers Systems, Inc., St. Cloud, MN Form UCA 5/28/92

(page 1 of 2)

The front page of a sample credit application.
Source: Middlebury National Bank

The back page of a sample credit application. Source: Middlebury National Bank

SECTION D - ASSET & DEBT INFORMATION

If Section B has been completed, this Section should be completed giving information about both the Applicant and Joint Applicant or Other Person. Please mark Applicant-related information with an "A". If Section B was not completed, only give information about the Applicant in this Section.

ASSETS OWNED (Use separate sheet if necessary.)

DESCRIPTION OF ASSETS	NAME IN WHICH THE ACCOUNT IS CARRIED	SUBJECT TO DEBT?	VALUE
CHECKING ACCOUNT NUMBER(S) (where)			$
SAVINGS ACCOUNT NUMBER(S) (where)			
CERTIFICATE OF DEPOSIT(S) (where)			
MARKETABLE SECURITIES (issuer, type, no. of shares)			
REAL ESTATE (location, date acquired)			
LIFE INSURANCE (issuer, face value)			
AUTOMOBILES (make, model, year)			
OTHER (list)			
TOTAL ASSETS			$

OUTSTANDING DEBTS (Include charge accounts, installment contracts, credit cards, rent, mortgages and other obligations. Use separate sheet if necessary.)

CREDITOR	ACCOUNT NUMBER	NAME IN WHICH THE ACCOUNT IS CARRIED	ORIGINAL AMOUNT	PRESENT BALANCE	MONTHLY PAYMENTS
LANDLORD OR MORTGAGE HOLDER	☐ Rent Payment ☐ Mortgage		(OMIT RENT) $	(OMIT RENT) $	$
AUTOMOBILES (describe)					
TOTAL DEBTS			$		$

Complete the following information about both the Applicant and Joint Applicant or Other Person (if applicable):

Are you obligated to make Alimony, Support or Maintenance Payments? ☐ No ☐ Yes

If yes, to (Name & Address) _____ Amt. per month $ _____

Are you a co-maker, endorser, or guarantor on any loan or contract? ☐ No ☐ Yes If yes, for whom? _____ To whom? _____

Are there any unsatisfied judgments against you? ☐ No ☐ Yes If yes, to whom owed? _____ Amount $ _____

Have you been declared bankrupt in the last 10 years? ☐ No ☐ Yes If yes, where? _____ Year? _____

SECTION E - SECURED CREDIT Complete only if credit is to be secured. Briefly describe the property to be given as security:

PROPERTY DESCRIPTION

NAMES & ADDRESSES OF ALL CO-OWNERS OF THE PROPERTY

IF THE SECURITY IS REAL ESTATE, GIVE THE FULL NAME OF YOUR SPOUSE (if any).

SIGNATURES I/We hereby certify that all the statements on both sides are true and complete and are made for the purpose of obtaining credit from the above creditor for the amount and purpose as stated. I/We authorize verification or re-verification of any information contained in the application which may be made at any time by the creditor, its agents, successors and assigns, either directly or through a credit reporting agency from any source named in this application. The original copy of this application will be retained by the creditor, even if the loan is not approved. I/We fully understand that it is a federal crime punishable by fine or imprisonment, or both, to knowingly make any false statements concerning any of the above facts on the application as applicable under the provisions of Title 18, United States Code, Section 1014. I/We understand that if the bank approves my/our request that I/we shall be furnished a copy of all agreements signed with the bank stating all terms and conditions.

_____ _____ _____ _____
Applicant's Signature   Date   Other Signature (Where Applicable)   Date

© 1986 Bankers Systems, Inc., St. Cloud, MN Form UCA 5/28/92 CUSTOMIZED

(page 2 of 2)

How to Read Your Credit File

This section includes your name, current and previous addresses and other identifying information reported by creditors.

This section includes public record items obtained from local, state and federal courts.

This section includes accounts that creditors have turned over to a collection agency.

This section contains both open and closed accounts.
1. The credit grantor reporting the information.
2. The account number reported by the credit grantor.
3. See explanation below.
4. The month and year the credit grantor opened the account.
5. Number of months account payment history has been reported.
6. The date of last payment, change or occurrence.
7. Highest amount charged or the credit limit.
8. Number of installments or monthly payment.
9. The amount owed as of the date reported.
10. The amount past due as of the date reported.
11. See explanation below.
12. Date of last account update.

This section includes a list of businesses that have received your credit file in the last 24 months.

Please address all future correspondence to: Credit Reporting Agency
Business Address
City, State 00000

SAMPLE CREDIT FILE

Personal Identification Information

Your Name   Social Security #:   123-45-6789
123 Current Address   Date of Birth: April 10th, 1940
City, State 00000

Previous Address(es)
456 Former Rd. Atlanta, GA 30000
P.O. Box XXXX Savannah, GA 40000

Last Reported Employment: Engineer, Highway Planning

Public Record Information

Lien Filed 03/93; Fulton CTY; Case or Other ID Number-32114; Amount-$26667; Class-State; Released 07/93; Verified 07/93

Bankruptcy Filed 12/92; Northern District Ct; Case or Other ID Number-673HC12; Liabilities-$15787; Personal; Individual; Discharged; Assets-$780

Satisfied Judgment Filed 07/94; Fulton CTY; Case or Other ID Number-898872; Defendant-Consumer; Amount-$8984; Plaintiff-ABC Real Estate; Satisfied 03/95; Verified 05/95

Collection Agency Account Information

Pro Coll (800) xxx-xxxx

Collection Reported 05/96; Assigned 09/93 to Pro Coll (800) XXX-XXXX Client - ABC Hospital; Amount-$978; Unpaid; Balance $978; Date of Last Activity 09/93; Individual Account; Account Number 787652JC

Credit Account Information

Company Name	Account Number	Whose Acct	Date Opened	Months Reviewed	Date of Last Activity	High Credit	Terms	Balance	Past Due	Status	Date Reported
1	2	3	4	5	6	7	8	9	10	11	12
Department St.	32514	J	10/86	36	9/97	$950		$0		R1	10/97
Bank	1004735	A	11/86	24	5/97	$750		$0		I1	4/97
Oil Company	541125	A	6/86	12	3/97	$500		$0		O1	4/97
Auto Finance	529778	I	5/85	48	12/96	$1100	$50	$300	$200	I5	4/97

Previous Payment History: 3 Times 30 days late; 4 Times 60 days late; 2 Times 90+ days late
Previous Status: 01/97 - I2; 02/97 - I3; 03/97 - I4

Companies that Requested your Credit File

09/06/97	Equifax - Disclosure	08/27/97	Department Store
07/29/97	PRM Bankcard	07/03/97	AM Bankcard
04/10/97	AR Department Store	12/31/96	Equifax - Disclosure ACIS 123456789

Whose Account	Status	Type of Account	The following inquiries are NOT reported to businesses:
Indicates who is responsible for the account and the type of participation you have with the account. J = Joint I = Individual U = Undesignated A = Authorized User T = Terminated M = Maker C = Co-Maker/Co-Signer B = On behalf of another person S = Shared	O = Open (entire balance due each month) R = Revolving (payment amount variable) I = Installment (fixed number of payments) **Timeliness of Payment** 0 = Approved not used; too new to rate 1 = Paid as agreed 2 = 30+ days past due 3 = 60+ days past due 4 = 90+ days past due 5 = Pays or paid 120+ days past the due date; or collection account 6 = Making regular payments under wage earner plan or similar arrangement 7 = 8 = Repossession 9 = Charged off to bad debt		**PRM** - This type of inquiry means that only your name and address were given to a credit grantor so they could offer you an application for credit. (PRM inquiries remain on file for 12 months.) **AM or AR** - These inquiries indicate a periodic review of your credit history by one of your creditors. (AM and AR inquiries remain on file for 12 months.) **EQUIFAX, ACIS or UPDATE** - These inquiries indicate Equifax's activity in response to your request for either a copy of your credit file or a request for research. **PRM, AM, AR, Equifax, ACIS, Update and INQ** - These inquiries do not appear on credit files businesses receive, only on copies provided to you.

Form 102631-8-98 USA

Date

Your Name
Your Address
Your City, State, Zip Code
Social Security Number

Complaint Department
Name of Credit Reporting Agency
Address
City, State, Zip Code

Dear Sir or Madam:

I am writing to dispute the following information in my file. The items I dispute are also encircled on the attached copy of the report I received. (Identify item(s) disputed by name of source, such as creditors or tax court, and identify type of item, such as credit account, judgment, etc.).

This item is (inaccurate or incomplete) because (describe what is inaccurate or incomplete and why). I am requesting that the item be deleted (or request another specific change) to correct the information.

Enclosed are copies of (use this sentence if applicable and describe any enclosed documentation, such as payment records, court documents) supporting my position. Please reinvestigate this (these) matter(s), and (delete or correct) the disputed item(s) as soon as possible.

Sincerely,

(Your name)
Enclosures: (List what you are enclosing)

Or, you can use a generic credit dispute form:

Investigation request form.

INVESTIGATION REQUEST FORM
Please complete the following personal information.

NAME _____
FIRST   MIDDLE   LAST   JR/SR

ADDRESS _____
NUMBER & STREET   APARTMENT

_____
CITY   STATE   ZIP

SOCIAL SECURITY NUMBER _____

HOME PHONE _____

DATE OF BIRTH _____

EMPLOYMENT _____

SIGNATURE _____
DATE

FILE NUMBER _____

Spouse's information and signature are required only when both of you are disputing information.

SPOUSE'S INFORMATION:

NAME _____

SOCIAL SECURITY NUMBER _____

DATE OF BIRTH _____

EMPLOYMENT _____

SIGNATURE _____
DATE

IF YOUR REPORT CHANGES AFTER OUR INVESTIGATION, OR IF A CONSUMER STATEMENT IS ADDED, AN UPDATED REPORT WILL BE SENT TO THE COMPANIES YOU LIST BELOW WHO HAVE RECEIVED YOUR REPORT IN THE PAST 2 YEARS FOR EMPLOYMENT PURPOSES, OR IN THE PAST 1 YEAR FOR ANY OTHER REASON:

1. _____   3. _____

2. _____   4. _____

If you disagree with the accuracy or completeness of any other information, please note below,
Use the back of this form if necessary.

COMPANY NAME: _____

ACCOUNT #: _____

☐NOT MY ACCOUNT   ☐NEVER PAID LATE

☐IN BANKRUPTCY   ☐PAID IN FULL

☐PAID BEFORE COLLECTION/CHARGE OFF

☐OTHER: _____

COMPANY NAME: _____

ACCOUNT #: _____

☐NOT MY ACCOUNT   ☐NEVER PAID LATE

☐IN BANKRUPTCY   ☐PAID IN FULL

☐PAID BEFORE COLLECTION/CHARGE OFF

☐OTHER: _____

COMPANY NAME: _____

ACCOUNT #: _____

☐NOT MY ACCOUNT   ☐NEVER PAID LATE

☐IN BANKRUPTCY   ☐PAID IN FULL

☐PAID BEFORE COLLECTION/CHARGE OFF

☐OTHER: _____

COMPANY NAME: _____

ACCOUNT #: _____

☐NOT MY ACCOUNT   ☐NEVER PAID LATE

☐IN BANKRUPTCY   ☐PAID IN FULL

☐PAID BEFORE COLLECTION/CHARGE OFF

☐OTHER: _____

RETURN THIS FORM TO THE ADDRESS LISTED AT THE END OF YOUR CREDIT REPORT.
YOU WILL RECEIVE WRITTEN NOTICE OF THE RESULTS OF OUR INVESTIGATION.
WE RECOMMEND THAT YOU DO NOT APPLY FOR CREDIT WHILE YOUR DISPUTE IS PENDING.

Monthly Budget Worksheet.

MONTHLY BUDGET WORKSHEET

	Projected	Actual	(+/-)
Housing (rent, mortgage)	$	$	$
Utilities	$	$	$
Household	$	$	$
Food	$	$	$
Transportation	$	$	$
Taxes (property taxes)	$	$	$
Insurance	$	$	$
Children	$	$	$
Clothing	$	$	$
Medical/Health Care	$	$	$
Education	$	$	$
Personal	$	$	$
Recreation/ Entertainment	$	$	$
Savings	$	$	$
Charitable Donations	$	$	$
Miscellaneous	$	$	$
Total Monthly Expenses	$	$	$

FORM 1. VOLUNTARY PETITION

United States Bankruptcy Court	VOLUNTARY
_____ District of _____	PETITION

IN RE (Name of debtor—If individual, enter Last, First, Middle) | NAME OF JOINT DEBTOR (Spouse) (Last, First, Middle)

ALL OTHER NAMES used by the debtor in the last 6 years (include married, maiden, and trade names) | ALL OTHER NAMES used by the debtor in the last 6 years (include married, maiden, and trade names)

SOC. SEC./TAX I.D. NO. (If more than one, state all) | SOC. SEC./TAX I.D. NO. (If more than one, state all)

STREET ADDRESS OF DEBTOR (No. and street, city, state, and zip code) | STREET ADDRESS OF JOINT DEBTOR (No. and street, city, state, and zip code)

| COUNTY OF RESIDENCE OR PRINCIPAL PLACE OF BUSINESS | | COUNTY OF RESIDENCE OR PRINCIPAL PLACE OF BUSINESS |

MAILING ADDRESS OF DEBTOR (If different from street address) | MAILING ADDRESS OF JOINT DEBTOR (If different from street address)

LOCATION OF PRINCIPAL ASSETS OF BUSINESS DEBTOR (if different from addresses listed above)

VENUE (Check one box)
- ☐ Debtor has been domiciled or has had a residence, principal place of business, or principal assets in this District for 180 days immediately preceding the date of this petition or a longer part of such 180 days than in any other District.
- ☐ There is a bankruptcy case concerning debtor's affiliate, general partner, or partnership pending in this District.

INFORMATION REGARDING DEBTOR (Check applicable boxes)

TYPE OF DEBTOR
- ☐ Individual
- ☐ Joint (Husband & Wife)
- ☐ Partnership
- ☐ Other: _____
- ☐ Corporation Publicly Held
- ☐ Corporation Not Publicly Held
- ☐ Municipality

NATURE OF DEBT
- ☐ Non-Business/Consumer
- ☐ Business — Complete A & B below

A. TYPE OF BUSINESS (Check one box)
- ☐ Farming
- ☐ Professional
- ☐ Retail/Wholesale
- ☐ Railroad
- ☐ Transportation
- ☐ Manufacturing/Mining
- ☐ Stockbroker
- ☐ Commodity Broker
- ☐ Construction
- ☐ Real Estate
- ☐ Other Business

B. BRIEFLY DESCRIBE NATURE OF BUSINESS

CHAPTER OR SECTION OF BANKRUPTCY CODE UNDER WHICH THE PETITION IS FILED (Check one box)
- ☐ Chapter 7
- ☐ Chapter 9
- ☐ Chapter 11
- ☐ Chapter 12
- ☐ Chapter 13
- ☐ Sec. 304—Case Ancillary to Foreign Proceeding

SMALL BUSINESS (Chapter 11 only)
- ☐ Debtor is a small business as defined in 11 U.S.C. § 101.
- ☐ Debtor is and elects to be considered as a small business under 11 USC § 1121(e) (Optional)

FILING FEE (Check one box)
- ☐ Filing fee attached
- ☐ Filing fee to be paid in installments. (Applicable to individuals only). Must attach signed application for the court's consideration certifying that the debtor is unable to pay fee except in installments. Rule 1006(b). See Official Form No. 3.

NAME AND ADDRESS OF LAW FIRM OR ATTORNEY

Telephone No.

NAME(S) OF ATTORNEY(S) DESIGNATED TO REPRESENT THE DEBTOR (Print or Type Names)

- ☐ Debtor is not represented by an attorney. Telephone No. of Debtor not represented by an attorney: ( )

STATISTICAL/ADMINISTRATIVE INFORMATION (28 U.S.C. § 604) (Estimates only) (Check applicable boxes)
- ☐ Debtor estimates that funds will be available for distribution to unsecured creditors.
- ☐ Debtor estimates that after any exempt property is excluded and administrative expenses paid, there will be no funds available for distribution to unsecured creditors.

THIS SPACE FOR COURT USE ONLY

ESTIMATED NUMBER OF CREDITORS

1-15	16-49	50-99	100-199	200-999	1,000-over
☐	☐	☐	☐	☐	☐

ESTIMATED ASSETS (In thousands of dollars)

Under 50	50-99	100-499	500-999	1,000-9,999	10,000-99,999	100,000-over
☐	☐	☐	☐	☐	☐	☐

ESTIMATED LIABILITIES (In thousands of dollars)

Under 50	50-99	100-499	500-999	1,000-9,999	10,000-99,999	100,000-over
☐	☐	☐	☐	☐	☐	☐

EST. NO. of Employees—CH. 11 & 12 ONLY

0	1-19	20-99	100-999	1,000-over
☐	☐	☐	☐	☐

EST. NO. OF EQUITY SECURITY HOLDERS—CH. 11 & 12 ONLY

0	1-19	20-99	100-999	1,000-over
☐	☐	☐	☐	☐

Voluntary Petition for Bankruptcy, front side. Source: *How to File for Bankruptcy*. Nolo Press.

Voluntary Petition for Bankruptcy, back side. Source: *How to File for Bankruptcy.* Nolo Press.

Name of Debtor _____

Case No. _____
(Court use only)

FILING OF PLAN

For Chapter 9, 11, 12 and 13 cases only. Check appropriate box.

☐ A copy of debtor's proposed plan dated _____ is attached. ☐ Debtor intends to file a plan within the time allowed by statute, rule, or order of the court.

PRIOR BANKRUPTCY CASE FILED WITHIN LAST 6 YEARS (If more than one, attach additional sheet)

Location Where Filed	Case Number	Dated Filed

PENDING BANKRUPTCY CASE FILED BY ANY SPOUSE, PARTNER, OR AFFILIATE OF THIS DEBTOR (If more than one, attach additional sheet)

Name of Debtor	Case Number	Date
Relationship	District	Judge

REQUEST FOR RELIEF

Debtor requests relief in accordance with the chapter of title 11, United States Code, specified in this petition.

SIGNATURES

ATTORNEY

X _____
Signature   Date

INDIVIDUAL/JOINT DEBTOR(S)	CORPORATE OR PARTNERSHIP DEBTOR
I declare under penalty of perjury that the information provided in this petition is true and correct.	I declare under penalty of perjury that the information provided in this petition is true and correct, and that the filing of this petition on behalf of the debtor has been authorized.
X _____ Signature of Debtor	X _____ Signature of Authorized Individual
Date _____	Print or Type Name of Authorized Individual
X _____ Signature of Joint Debtor	Title of Individual Authorized by Debtor to File This Petition
Date _____	Date _____ If debtor is a corporation filing under chapter 11, Exhibit "A" is attached and made part of this petition.

TO BE COMPLETED BY INDIVIDUAL CHAPTER 7 DEBTOR WITH PRIMARILY CONSUMER DEBTS (See P.L. 96-353 § 322)	CERTIFICATION AND SIGNATURE OF NON-ATTORNEY BANKRUPTCY PETITION PREPARER (See 11 U.S.C. § 110)
I am aware that I may proceed under Chapter 7, 11, or 12, or 13 of title 11, United States Code, understand the relief available under each such chapter, and choose to proceed under Chapter 7 of such title. If I am represented by an attorney, Exhibit "B" has been completed.	I certify that I am a bankruptcy petition preparer as defined in 11 U.S.C. § 110, that I prepared this document for compensation, and that I have provided the debtor with a copy of this document.
	Printed or Typed Name of Bankruptcy Petition Preparer
X _____ Signature of Debtor Date	Social Security Number
X _____ Signature of Joint Debtor Date	Address Tel. No.
EXHIBIT "B" (To be completed by attorney for individual Chapter 7 debtor(s) with primarily consumer debts.)	Names and Social Security numbers of all other individuals who prepared or assisted in preparing this document:
I, the attorney for the debtor(s) named in the foregoing petition, declare that I have informed the debtor(s) that (he, she, or they) may proceed under Chapter 7, 11, 12, or 13 of title 11, United States Code, and have explained the relief available under each such chapter.	If more than one person prepared this document, attach additional signed sheets conforming to the appropriate Official Form for each person. X _____ Signature of Bankruptcy Petition Preparer
X _____ Signature of Attorney Date	A bankruptcy petition preparer's failure to comply with the provisions of title 11 and the Federal Rules of Bankruptcy Procedure may result in fines or imprisonment or both. 11 U.S.C. § 110; 18 U.S.C. § 156.

PD F 5381 (I)
Department of the Treasury
Bureau of the Public Debt
(Revised October 1998)

www.treasurydirect.gov

TREASURY DIRECT®

TREASURY BILL, NOTE & BOND TENDER

OMB No. 1535-0069

For Tender Instructions, See PD F 5382

TYPE OR PRINT IN INK ONLY – TENDERS WILL NOT BE ACCEPTED WITH ALTERATIONS OR CORRECTIONS

1. BID INFORMATION (Must Be Completed)

Par Amount:

$_____
(Sold in units of $1,000)

Bid Type:
(Fill in One)

○ Noncompetitive

○ Competitive at ____.____ %
(Bid bids must end in 0 or 5.)

DEPARTMENT USE
HEADER NO.
RECEIVED POSTDATE

2. TreasuryDirect ACCOUNT NUMBER (If NOT furnished, a new account will be opened.)

_____-_____-_____

3. TAXPAYER ID NUMBER (Must Be Completed)

___-__-____ OR __-_____
Social Security Number (First-Named Owner)   Employer ID Number

ENTERED BY
APPROVED BY

4. TERM SELECTION (Fill in One)
(Must Be Completed)

Treasury Bill   Circle the Number of
$1,000 Minimum   Reinvestments

○ 13-Week......... 0 1 2 3 4
                   5 6 7 8

○ 26-Week......... 0 1 2 3 4

○ 52-Week......... 0 1 2

Treasury Note/Bond
$1,000 Minimum

○ 2-Year Note
○ 5-Year Note
○ 10-Year Note
○ 30-Year Bond
○ Inflation-Indexed
                   Term

5. ACCOUNT NAME Please Type or Print! (Must Be Completed)

6. ADDRESS (For new account or if changed.)   ○ New Address?

_____
City   State   ZIP Code

ISSUE DATE
CUSIP BILLING
CUSIP SECURITY
CUSIP STRIP
FOREIGN ☐
BACKUP ☐
PENALTY ☐

7. TELEPHONE NUMBERS (For new account or if changed.)   ○ New Phone Number?

Work ( )   -   Home ( )   -

8. PAYMENT INFORMATION (For new account only.)   Changes? Submit PD F 5179.

Routing Number |__|__|__|__|__|__|__|__|__|

Financial Institution Name _____

Account Number |__|__|__|__|__|__|__|__|__|__|__|__|__|__|__|__|__|

Name on Account _____

Account Type: (Fill in One)   ○ Checking   ○ Savings

9. PURCHASE METHOD
(Must Be Completed)

○ Pay Direct
(Existing TreasuryDirect Account Only)

○ Checks: $_____

○ Securities: $_____

○ Other $_____

Total Payment
Attached: $_____
CHECKS ARE DEPOSITED IMMEDIATELY

CHECK #

10. AUTHORIZATION (Must Be Completed – Original Signature Required)
Tender Submission: I submit this tender pursuant to the provisions of Department of the Treasury Circulars, Public Debt Series Nos. 2-86 (31 CFR Part 357) and 1-93 (31 CFR Part 356), and the applicable offering announcement. As the first-named owner and under penalties of perjury, I certify that: 1) The number shown on this form is my correct taxpayer identification number (or I am waiting for a number to be issued to me), and 2) I am not subject to backup withholding because: (a) I am exempt from backup withholding, or (b) I have not been notified by the Internal Revenue Service (IRS) that I am subject to backup withholding as a result of a failure to report all interest or dividends, or (c) the IRS has notified me that I am no longer subject to backup withholding. I further certify that all other information provided on this form is true, correct and complete.

Pay Direct. (If using this purchase method.) I authorize a debit to my account at the financial institution I designated in TreasuryDirect to pay for this security. I understand that the purchase price will be charged to my account on or after the settlement date. I also understand that if this transaction cannot be successfully completed, my tender can be rejected and the transaction canceled. If there is a dispute, a copy of this authorization may be provided to my financial institution.

_____   _____
Signature(s)   Date

SEE BACK FOR PRIVACY ACT AND PAPERWORK REDUCTION ACT NOTICE

Form for buying Treasury securities direct. You can also purchase Treasury securities online at www.publicdebt.treas.gov.

A sample consumer complaint letter. Source: Federal Reserve Board

If you are unable to resolve a problem with a financial institution, you may file a written complaint with the Federal Reserve following these guidelines:

Date

Your Name
Your Address
Your City, State, Zip Code
Daytime Telephone Number (including area code)

Board of Governors of the Federal Reserve System
Division of Consumer and Community Affairs
20th and C Streets, NW, Stop 198
Washington, D.C. 20551

Dear Sir or Madam:

I am writing to complain about problems that I have been having with (list the name and address of the bank involved in your complaint or inquiry, as well as your bank or credit card account number).

Although I have written to (list the name of the person you contacted at the bank, along with the date, if applicable), I have been unable to resolve this problem (describe the problem or complaint in as much detail as possible. State what happened, giving the dates involved and the names of those you dealt with at the bank).

Enclosed are copies of (use this sentence if applicable and describe any enclosed letters or other documentation that might help to investigate the complaint. Do not send originals).

Sincerely,

Your name

Enclosures: (List what you are enclosing)

Consumer complaints filed against state member banks are investigated by the 12 regional Federal Reserve Banks. See "Federal Agencies" in the Resource Guide, Appendix B, for a complete listing of regional banks and for the agency to contact for unresolved problems with other types of banks, savings and loan associations, credit unions, and other lenders. Use the same general format for your complaint letter, but substitute the appropriate agency in the address section.

Date

Your Name
Your Address
Your City, State, Zip Code

Name of Credit Card Issuer
Customer Service Department
Address
City, State, Zip Code

RE: (account number)

Dear Sir or Madam:

In accordance with the provisions of the Fair Credit Billing Act, I am writing to call your attention to a billing error on my recent statement of (date). In regard to reference number (number for the transaction in question on your bill), this item for (list the amount of the charge) is incorrect because (explain why you believe it is incorrect).

Enclosed are copies of (use this sentence if applicable and describe any enclosed documentation, such as payment records, cancellations, etc.) supporting my position. Please investigate this matter and correct the error as soon as possible. Thank you for your assistance.

Sincerely,
Your name

Enclosures: (List what you are enclosing—copies, never originals)

A sample billing error letter.

The *Unofficial Guide*™ Reader Questionnaire

If you would like to express your opinion about beating debt or this guide, please complete this questionnaire and mail it to:

The *Unofficial Guide*™ Reader Questionnaire
IDG Lifestyle Group
1633 Broadway, floor 7
New York, NY 10019-6785

Gender: ___ M ___ F

Age: ___ Under 30 ___ 31–40 ___ 41–50
___ Over 50

Education: ___ High school ___ College
___ Graduate/Professional

What is your occupation?

_____

How did you hear about this guide?
___ Friend or relative
___ Newspaper, magazine, or Internet
___ Radio or TV
___ Recommended at bookstore
___ Recommended by librarian
___ Picked it up on my own
___ Familiar with the *Unofficial Guide*™ travel series

Did you go to the bookstore specifically for a book on beating debt? Yes ___ No ___

Have you used any other Unofficial Guides™?
Yes ___ No ___

If Yes, which ones?

_____
_____
_____

What other book(s) on beating debt have you
purchased? _____
_____
_____

Was this book:
___ more helpful than other(s)
___ less helpful than other(s)

Do you think this book was worth its price?
Yes ___   No ___

Did this book cover all topics related to beating
debt adequately?
Yes ___   No ___

Please explain your answer:
_____
_____
_____

Were there any specific sections in this book that
were of particular help to you?   Yes ___   No ___

Please explain your answer:
_____
_____
_____

On a scale of 1 to 10, with 10 being the best rating,
how would you rate this guide? ___

What other titles would you like to see published in
the *Unofficial Guide*™ series?
_____
_____

Are Unofficial Guides™ readily available in your
area?   Yes ___   No ___

Other comments:
_____
_____
_____
_____

Get the inside scoop...with the *Unofficial Guides*™!

Health and Fitness

The Unofficial Guide to Alternative Medicine
ISBN: 0-02-862526-9 Price: $15.95

The Unofficial Guide to Conquering Impotence
ISBN: 0-02-862870-5 Price: $15.95

The Unofficial Guide to Coping with Menopause
ISBN: 0-02-862694-x Price: $15.95

The Unofficial Guide to Cosmetic Surgery
ISBN: 0-02-862522-6 Price: $15.95

The Unofficial Guide to Dieting Safely
ISBN: 0-02-862521-8 Price: $15.95

The Unofficial Guide to Having a Baby
ISBN: 0-02-862695-8 Price: $15.95

The Unofficial Guide to Living with Diabetes
ISBN: 0-02-862919-1 Price: $15.95

The Unofficial Guide to Overcoming Arthritis
ISBN: 0-02-862714-8 Price: $15.95

The Unofficial Guide to Overcoming Infertility
ISBN: 0-02-862916-7 Price: $15.95

Career Planning

The Unofficial Guide to Acing the Interview
ISBN: 0-02-862924-8 Price: $15.95

The Unofficial Guide to Earning What You Deserve
ISBN: 0-02-862523-4 Price: $15.95

The Unofficial Guide to Hiring and Firing People
ISBN: 0-02-862523-4 Price: $15.95

Business and Personal Finance

The Unofficial Guide to Investing
ISBN: 0-02-862458-0 Price: $15.95

The Unofficial Guide to Investing in Mutual Funds
ISBN: 0-02-862920-5 Price: $15.95

The Unofficial Guide to Managing Your Personal Finances
ISBN: 0-02-862921-3 Price: $15.95

The Unofficial Guide to Starting a Small Business
ISBN: 0-02-862525-0 Price: $15.95

Home and Automotive

The Unofficial Guide to Buying a Home
ISBN: 0-02-862461-0 Price: $15.95

The Unofficial Guide to Buying or Leasing a Car
ISBN: 0-02-862524-2 Price: $15.95

The Unofficial Guide to Hiring Contractors
ISBN: 0-02-862460-2 Price: $15.95

Family and Relationships

The Unofficial Guide to Childcare
ISBN: 0-02-862457-2 Price: $15.95

The Unofficial Guide to Dating Again
ISBN: 0-02-862454-8 Price: $15.95

The Unofficial Guide to Divorce
ISBN: 0-02-862455-6 Price: $15.95

The Unofficial Guide to Eldercare
ISBN: 0-02-862456-4 Price: $15.95

The Unofficial Guide to Planning Your Wedding
ISBN: 0-02-862459-9 Price: $15.95

Hobbies and Recreation

The Unofficial Guide to Finding Rare Antiques
ISBN: 0-02-862922-1 Price: $15.95

The Unofficial Guide to Casino Gambling
ISBN: 0-02-862917-5 Price: $15.95

All books in the *Unofficial Guide* series are available at your local bookseller, or by calling 1-800-428-5331.